Finish

Line

Feeling

D1377726

Finish

Line

Feeling

LIZ FERRO

Unlimited Publishing LLC

First Edition
ISBN:
978-1-58832-191-6

This fine book and many others are available at:
http://www.unlimitedpublishing.com

Unlimited Publishing LLC is a proud member of the Independent Book Publishers Association (http://www.IBPA-online.org), serving thousands of publishers across North America and around the world since 1983.

Where to Find this Book:

Also from Unlimited Publishing LLC:

Contents

No one can go back and make a brand new start. Anyone can start from now and make a brand new ending.

—Unknown

Foreword

By Susan M. Brown, L.P.C.
Residential Treatment Center, C-Wing Counselor
Multi-County Juvenile Attention System, Canton, Ohio

I am a mental health counselor with the Residential Treatment Center of Multi-County Juvenile Attention System in Stark County, Ohio. We work with 13- to 18-year-old girls who have been placed with us from six months to one year by the courts and/or Children's Services. All of the girls we work with have been abused, suffered neglect, and have lived through multiple traumas and losses. Our girls feel that they have lost, or have had taken from them, any power and control in their lives. Being placed with us often identifies them as the problem. Our work is to provide counseling, life skills, schooling, and the tools needed to send them back into their communities and to succeed, often on their own. This is no easy task.

The majority of our girls are runners by nature. They have run from abusive homes, the police, and any and all problems. They have run to substances, other abusive relationships, and prostitution.

When Liz came to us, not only did she bring fitness, liveliness, self-esteem, and encouragement to our girls, she also brought a purpose to their lives. Now they have a reason to run for themselves in a healthy way. They have been shown a way in which to reclaim the power and control they have been led to believe they don't possess.

Girls With Sole comes to our facility several times a month and offers our girls a chance to dance, to run, to come together as a group, to support one another, and above all, see firsthand that they can overcome what has been done to them.

Our girls typically come to us with very little. Making sure they have life's essentials is a battle of its own.

Thanks to Liz's efforts, they all now have brand-new running shoes, sports bras, water bottles, and treasures they have acquired from attending 5K races that Liz has sponsored them to run in. We have been privileged to attend several 5Ks to date with Liz and *Girls With Sole*. All of our girls who have attended the 5Ks proudly wear their race shirts.

Not only have these activities outside of the facility provided our girls with "stuff," they have provided the girls with new experiences. They have been able to see a world outside of their own, where people are healthy, motivated, successful, friendly, and encouraging. They experience support and a sense of belonging to something. When we attended the first 5K with Liz, many of the girls were simply giddy with excitement. They were amazed at all the activity surrounding them, the welcoming atmosphere, and the feeling of achievement when they completed a race. When we left that race, one girl commented that she couldn't believe she'd had so much fun so early in the morning and that she didn't have to be stoned or drunk to have a blast.

So, to Liz, I say thank you on behalf of our girls, Multi-County, and myself. We are proud and privileged to have you as part of all of our lives, and are thankful for the hope and joy you continue to bring. *Girls With Sole* is truly a blessing to our girls.

Just when the caterpillar thought the world was over, it became a butterfly.

—Proverb

Prologue

I REMEMBER THE SUITCASE so vividly and clearly, as if I had packed it yesterday. It had an ice blue and electric pink '70s paisley pattern on its soft cardboard casing. The zipper always got stuck and the plastic edges in the front that helped to guide the zipper were breaking down, but I loved that suitcase. Although it was very small, it seemed big enough to fit all the necessities of a young world traveler such as myself. I don't remember the exact reason I had decided to leave that night, but I do recall feeling as if it was what I needed to do and that there was no sense in putting off the inevitable.

I was determined to pack it up, pack it in, and get going before someone could tell me that I had to leave. Rejection is never a good feeling, but the sting is lessened when it is experienced on your own terms. I didn't know it at the time, but that was the beginning of a cycle that would continue in my life for many years to come. This would be my approach and "M.O." for the majority of my future relationships: Leave them – before they leave me.

In many different ways, and on many different levels, my life has revolved around running. For a time all I could do was try to run away. Then I ran into trouble. As time passed, with endurance and tenacity, I ran with the idea of helping girls in need and haven't stopped since.

In August of 2009 I founded the nonprofit organization, *Girls With Sole*, which uses free fitness and wellness programs to empower at-risk girls and those who have experienced any type of abuse. Turning a negative into a positive, I have made it my life's mission to instill strength, self-confidence, and pride in girls, and to help them embrace running (and other sports) – for all the right reasons.

My greatest satisfaction is seeing our girls reach a goal, cross that finish line, and begin to believe in themselves because of *Girls With Sole*. There is nothing like it. The smiles on their faces are priceless, and not something they give out easily. But the finish line draws golden sunshine from within their hearts that they didn't know existed.

The finish line feeling is truly life-changing.

What has surprised me the most about *Girls With Sole* is how truly needed it is and how quickly the girls respond to it in a positive manner – even those who walk into the room in the worst moods, proclaiming they will not participate.

Within 20 to 30 minutes these same girls are running, dancing, or playing basketball or volleyball. They are laughing, smiling, and having a great time being kids – and that is what it is really all about.

Saints are sinners who kept on going.

—Robert Louis Stevenson

I

I WAS 4 YEARS OLD, and in the two years that I had come to live with them as their child, I still had never told my parents that I loved them. Although I was adopted when I was around 2, I never expressed love to anyone until sometime after I turned 6. I hated saying "I love you" more than I hated peas, which was saying a lot. It's strange to think about that, now that I have my own children, because they expressed their love to me nonverbally before they could speak by showing trust and by squeezing me around my neck like baby monkeys. When they learned to talk, I heard "I love you Mommy" as often as I heard "Why?" or "I want juice." It was second nature to them and not something that they guarded and jadedly kept to themselves, the way I did at their age.

No matter how many times my parents tried to reassure me and tell me that they loved me, my answer to them was always, "Okay."

I didn't know she was on to me until the day my mom tried to explain that I didn't need to take things out of my brothers' rooms and stash them in my pillowcase. She said that I would be staying and that I didn't need to take souvenirs or prepare to leave. Again, I answered with "Okay," but I didn't believe her.

In my mind I knew that I would be left behind or sent away, just as it had been in the four foster homes I lived in before I was adopted (the different places I lived between birth and 2 years old that left me petrified of men and afraid to be left alone). I was told later in life that my time in foster care was somewhat traumatic and was said to be the root of my fear of loud and sudden noises and fear of the dark, as well as the continuous crying and nervous rash that was always on my face when I first came to my parents. The trauma I experienced in the foster homes may also be the reason that I sucked my thumb until college, wet my bed for much too long, and had "outbursts" that could scare a Marine drill sergeant.

The pint-sized paisley suitcase filled quickly, requiring last-minute judgment calls regarding important, yet difficult, decisions such as which stuffed animals to bring and which to leave behind. There was only room for one nightgown and one set of Garanimals. The monkey Garanimals were my favorite, so I crammed the matching top and bottom set in next to the items I had stolen from the rooms of my brothers. There weren't many things I liked better than rummaging through their stuff when they weren't around and pocketing the particularly choice items. There was also a certain thrill that went along with the feeling that I could be caught in a stranger's room looking through and possibly pilfering their personal treasures – but I lived there, so technically they were not strangers at all.

I studied each item very closely, and those that were up to snuff went back with me to my bedroom so I could stash them in my pillowcase until it was time for me to pack them up and take them to wherever I would end up next. I looked at the winning trinkets that had been transferred from pillowcase to suitcase, and decided they were worth the extra weight. I left them nestled next to my yellow polyester nightgown and purple monkey corduroys, closed the lid, wrestled with the zipper, and made my way down the hallway to the top of the stairs.

I stopped to listen for my parents' voices downstairs, which I determined to be coming from the living room. This wasn't ideal, because the front door of our house was just off to the right of the living room, so they would definitely see me walking past them wearing a jacket and carrying a suitcase. The plan was to keep my head down and keep moving. I lugged the heavy little suitcase down each stair one at a time, and when I reached the bottom of the stairs I looked down at the floor and made a beeline for the front door. Right away I heard my mother running toward me and yelling to my dad in a panicky voice:

"Dad! Stop her! She's *leaving!*"

(Even as a young kid I found it odd that my parents referred to each other as "Mom" and "Dad." When they spoke to each other or about each other, they never used their given names.) My father, ever the calming voice of reason, responded with:

"Take it easy. It's dark outside. It's nighttime. She won't even make it down the driveway."

I walked out the front door and past the lamppost. I passed the plum trees that flanked the driveway of my childhood home in Upstate New York, made a right turn onto the sidewalk, and kept on walking. I made it all the way to the end of our street before my father picked me up in his car to take me back home, and that was the last time reverse psychology was ever used on me by my parents.

My dad was born and raised in Cleveland, Ohio, and my mom was from Furth, Germany, and grew up during World War II. When she came to the United States she was sponsored by a family in New Jersey and worked as a secretary for the American Army. In an attempt to get her out to meet people, my mom had been talked into going to a party by an American friend. Living in New Jersey at the time as well, my dad was an engineer for DuPont and turned out to be the person my mother was destined to meet at that party.

My father was a very loyal and loving husband, and my parents would still be together today, except that my father passed away in July of 2000. My parents moved around a bit after getting married, but ended up back in Cleveland where my dad worked as an engineer during the day and went to Case University at night in his pursuit to become a patent attorney. By this time my mom had given birth to my oldest brother, David, their only biological child. My parents loved children and wanted a bigger family, but my mom endured many complications during subsequent pregnancies and ended up getting a full hysterectomy. In the meantime, my father was able to complete law school while working full time during the day, and studying late at night while also giving their new son his 3:00 a.m. bottle. The first job my father had as a patent attorney was with the United States Patent and Trademark Office in Washington, D.C. It was in Washington that my parents adopted their second child, and named their new infant Paul. My parents now had two little boys and my dad had a brand-new career. He was in his 40s – I think they were ahead of their time in this regard.

People back then didn't adopt kids or completely change careers in their 40s, but my dad did. After working for the U.S. Patent and Trademark Office my dad decided he would be happier working for a corporation, so he took a job as an international patent attorney at the Eastman Kodak Company, which brought them all to Rochester, New York, and unknowingly, to me. I was a Catholic

Charities baby who was moved between four different foster homes before being adopted for good by my mom and dad. I have never met my biological parents, nor have I ever looked for them. I don't have any desire to find my real mom (or dad) and to be honest, I don't think I want to know what I might find by bringing them into my life. I don't feel the need to rock the boat by bringing a new person into the equation or by trying to locate someone who might not want anything to do with me anyway. I'm satisfied with the family I have created with my husband and two children. They are my real family.

My parents had been talking about adopting another child after my brother Paul, but the timing didn't seem to be right. They got all the necessary paperwork together, but they were busy and happy, so adopting another child went on the back burner and the paperwork was temporarily forgotten.

The words "paperwork" and "the bookshelf" were very prominent and often-used terms in our family. My parents loved the term "paperwork" and used it all the time to describe things of great importance that needed to be filled out by hand, such as forms for school, permission slips, and fliers brought home in our school bags, as well as any registration forms or official documentation. Items such as car keys, reading glasses, passports, driver's licenses, or anything else someone in the family might be desperately searching for could also usually be located on the bookshelf.

It was my father's love of books that resulted in an unusually enormous amount of them in our house as well as the need for bookshelves in literally every room. Most of them were hard-cover books from the Book of the Month Club that were never read due to lack of time. But like his other unfinished chores, he was going to get around to them. He was also going to get around to the giant stack of newspapers that were placed not so neatly next to his Lazy Boy. My mother begged him to throw the pile of eyesores away, but my father wouldn't do it because he had every intention of getting around to reading each and every paper. Eventually my mom bought him a poster that had an illustration of a big circle with the word "roundtoit" written in the middle of it. The caption underneath said: "Everything I have been meaning to do will get done – now that I've finally gotten a roundtoit!" The poster wasn't enough to do the trick, and also wasn't that clever or funny. It was actually rather ugly and I hated that my mom hung it in the kitchen next to our fridge.

The piles of papers continued to be a constant in our house, as were the books which seemed to multiply like rabbits. Needless to say, the bookshelves were super important in our home and as a child I was fascinated and proud of all the books my dad had. To me, the plethora of books told the world how intelligent my dad was. They made me feel proud of my dad, and evoked a sense of pride and comfort from the statement I felt they made about my home and the people who lived there. The biggest and most prominent bookshelf in the house was a built-in that took up an entire wall of our living room. It was painted white, and with all the different colors and cover designs of the books, in my eyes, it looked like art on canvas. I liked it much better than the actual art my parents hung on the walls, which was a combination of mountains in Germany, Bavarian knickknacks, or souvenirs from my dad's trips to Japan (not a good eclectic mix, in my opinion). That this shelf was a catch-all for anything that my parents didn't want to look at right away, but that they also didn't want to misplace, did not make it look like a work of art. It was not uncommon to hear someone in our house yell, "Dad! I can't find my report card that you were supposed to sign. Where is it?"

The answer was always, "It's on the bookshelf."

The Bookshelf.

Of course there was more than one bookshelf in our house but when someone referred to "the bookshelf," everyone knew to go to the one in the living room. It was the one we posed in front of for each of our First Communion photos, Christmas pictures, prom pictures, in our Halloween costumes, and all other important occasions. It was the one where all the extremely important paperwork eventually laid to rest. So it made perfect sense that the adoption paperwork sat patiently for months and months on the white bookshelf, gathering dust amongst the books my dad intended to get around to reading.

The way my dad told the story, God spoke to him one day in church and told him to adopt me. I am not a religious person, but my parents both had/have a very deep faith. My dad told me, as he told anyone who wanted to know why they had adopted me, that he knew it was time because God said there was a little girl who needed him. After church that day he went home and headed straight to the bookshelf to get the paperwork. He got it all in order and submitted it, which inevitably led my parents to me. When they knew for sure that I would be coming to them, they told my brothers they would be getting a baby sister. My brother Paul was thoroughly disappointed when I showed up and could walk and talk (although I didn't say much), since these were not things that a "baby" should be able to do. The social worker brought me to the house and my mom said that I had the saddest, most questioning eyes she had ever seen. That speaks volumes, coming from a woman who grew up during World War II in Germany.

I was brought over to the house without any clothes or belongings aside from what I was wearing. The way my mom tells it, she asked the social worker where my things were, and the woman told my mom she didn't bring anything with me in case they wanted to give me back. What my mom said next, I probably could have done without being told. She told the social worker that I was not a dog, and that they weren't going to send me back – so she should go and get my things because I would be staying. I guess in my mom's mind she thought I should know about this exchange with the social worker because she felt that it was some type of compliment, but I never felt as if it was.

Each one of my parents' children come from different biological parents, and were born and "collected" in a different city. Most people collect snow globes from various cities or those little metal spoons, but my parents picked up a kid in each prominent place in which they resided. I guess it's no different from people being conceived on a family vacation in different destinations, but it still strikes me as being rather cool and progressive, yet also a bit odd. I was 2, Paul was 7, and Dave was 11 years old when we became siblings.

It seemed to me that a lot of time (too much time) was spent trying to figure me out – everything from the way I looked to the way I behaved – and in every way I felt I was a huge disappointment. I guess because I was adopted and looked nothing like my mom, dad, or brothers (and because I was a girl), there was always scrutiny and speculation among my mother and her friends about how I would "turn out." Big feet, long legs, and long, thick eyelashes with good bone structure were constantly mentioned – leading them to surmise I was a budding model.

I never cared that I didn't look like the rest of my family, but the importance of my looks and the focus on them seemed to magnify as I got older, and I wished that they didn't make such a big deal out of it when I was around to hear it. This was a growing point of contention that festered within me as a teenager. I stared at myself for hours in the mirror, mentally tearing apart each feature. I started scrutinizing every centimeter of my face, trying to see if I could figure myself out by picking apart my features and predicting what they would turn into when I got older.

Over time I began to grow into my big feet, my legs were no longer considered long by any means and were nothing close to "model-like," and my nose would never look like Cheryl Ladd's. The only thing that made me feel better was that I knew my legs were athletic and strong and they allowed me to do gymnastics and to run fast. I would never be one of *Charlie's Angels*, but I could pretend to be the *Bionic Woman*, which I thought was cooler anyway.

It was hard for me to sit still, to stay quiet, and to contain myself. My mother's friends suggested she put me on Ritalin, but she told them that she didn't want to crush my spirit. It was much later that I discovered these to be normal traits for a person who has suffered abuse or trauma, but at the time I just thought that I was defective somehow. I wished I could shed my own skin and be someone else. I looked at models in magazines and agonized that I would never look like them. In my frustration and anger I rebelled against authority and acted out in inappropriate and self-destructive ways. I hated having people looking at me and scrutinizing me and felt that everyone I came in contact with was doing it, although that probably wasn't so. If someone looked at me, I assumed they were thinking negative things about me and I would flip out. There was a dark and angry storm that could visibly shake the most stable foundations, brewing deep beneath my outer layer of sunshine and blue skies. Those who set me off, or simply looked for a little too long, ended up caught in the tempest with no umbrella or shelter to be found.

A pearl is a beautiful thing that is produced by an injured life. It is the tear that results from the injury of the oyster. The treasure of our being in this world is also produced by an injured life. If we had not been wounded, if we had not been injured, then we will not produce the pearl.

—Stephan Hoeller

II

DURING THE '70S I grew up watching TV and was completely sucked in by various TV families and even by the commercials, such as those for Country Time Lemonade.

I adored those commercials and really believed that we were getting a glimpse into the lives of the people in them. They were people who lived in the country and spent hot and hazy afternoons on a great big front porch or in a hammock or tire swing sipping lemonade. It's funny to think about now, but I was actually rather jealous of the kids who lived in this alternate universe as they ran down the long wooden dock and jumped into the blue lake water while their dog cheered them on and then jumped in right behind them. Part of me was even jealous that the kids in the commercial were always hanging out with their grandpa. There was a brother and a sister who seemed to do everything together with their grandpa. Whenever they were "hot and thirsty" all they had to do was whine to their grandpa and before they knew it they were refreshing themselves with the wonderful "not too tart and not too sweet" goodness of Country Time Lemonade in a big glass pitcher. They were so lucky.

My summers as a child were actually, for the most part, incredible, as were a lot of things about my childhood. I really can't complain about how I was raised or about the things we did as a family. I was lucky too – just like those two kids in the commercials. Every year we went to Ocean City, New Jersey, and stayed in the same beach house during the same week in June. (I was a whole different type of "situation" on the Jersey Shore.) My dad was all about tradition and he did not like change. One of his favorite lines was, "If it's not broke, don't fix it." He lived by this motto and used it as a mantra of sorts. At Baskin-Robbins 31 Flavors it seemed to me that half the excitement was to see the vast array of colorful tubs neatly packed in their coolers, and to be able to pick a different one every time. Not for my dad. No matter what enticing new flavor was being featured or how many you could pick from, he would get cherry ice cream every single solitary time.

The house my parents rented was right on the beach and it was always a full week of good old-fashioned family vacation fun. We shared the house with the family that my mom was sponsored by and lived with when she first came to the United States from Germany. They were close friends of the family and we called them Aunt Rosemary and Uncle Reed. Aunt Rosemary made a special, syrupy-moist orange and lemon cake that was everyone's favorite, so she brought it every year. It was quickly christened (and always referred to as) "Beach Cake." There was also a "Taco Salad" that she made, which I loved because it had broken-up Doritos in it and it tasted awesome, but it looked like puke. It was tradition as well as expected to have both of these beach delicacies every single year, and I think we would have all shit ourselves if Aunt Rosemary had shown up one year and said she decided to make brownies and chicken salad.

Uncle Reed was really funny and loved flying kites. So on windy days, we would all go to the beach with his many kites, and would fly them high over the sand and the ocean. The kites he brought to the beach were awesome and came in the form of airplanes and eagles. I was enthralled by them and getting them to go higher and higher brought a special childhood thrill.

When we had scraps of ham or other food left over from dinner we would go to the beach with Uncle Reed and throw them up in the air to feed the gulls. It would only take one or two tosses of a piece of fat or gristle before a cloud of gray and white hovered above our heads screaming in unison for the morsels.

During the day we played in the ocean and rode the waves on rafts. We usually used whatever rough rubber rafts were left behind in the storage closet, but sometimes I got to pick out a cool new raft at one of the shops on the Boardwalk where they sold hermit crabs and other must-haves. I begged my parents every year for a hermit crab, but they never gave in. My woes of leaving the shop without a crab with a shell painted to look like *Herbie The Love Bug* quickly evaporated after I had picked out a Hawaiian Punch or shark-themed raft. We rarely left the Boardwalk without a visit to the Kohr Bros frozen custard stand for a chocolate/vanilla twist covered in chocolate sprinkles, which everyone there called "Jimmies."

On the beach I dug for sand crabs and built sand castles for hours. When my brothers were still living at home and went with us on our vacations, David combed the beach for girls, while Paul stayed inside for the most part and read a book or watched TV. He hated the sun and acted like a vampire whenever my parents made him come outside. He didn't wear a bathing suit in his adolescent years – ever.

You couldn't get me out of my suit or out of the water. I loved riding the waves on my raft and diving into them just before they broke. There were many times that the waves would get as big as 8 or 10 feet high. They would come crashing down on me and toss me around under the water for what always seemed like just the tiniest bit too long. The giant waves turned me around and upside down as if I was in a giant washing machine – making me dizzy, scared, and excited all at once. At night when I finally took my bathing suit off, enough sand to create a beach fell out of my suit and covered the floor. The sand was everywhere, and sometimes even long after I ate dinner, showered, and brushed my teeth, I could be in bed and closing my mouth after a big yawn, only to crunch down on a grain that got away.

At night we went to the Boardwalk and got ice cream or frozen custard, shopped for souvenirs, played mini-golf, and went to the movies. The year that *Jaws* came out it was a really big deal to see it on the Boardwalk. I begged my parents to let me go, but they wouldn't let me. My parents said it would be too scary for me and they didn't give in even though simply *everyone* was going. The next day I was the only one swimming in the ocean.

When we got older, and I was in middle school and high school, my brothers were no longer joining us on the yearly vacations to the beach. My parents would let me bring a friend with us as a way to keep me occupied and placated. On more than one occasion I brought my friend Lisa, and we would have a blast laying in the sun and sneaking off at night to meet boys and go to parties. Ocean City holds many fond childhood memories for me, and much like "the bookshelf" in our house, when anyone said "the beach," there was only one, and it was in Ocean City, New Jersey.

Even when we weren't on vacation, my summers were full of getting ice cream cones with my dad in the evenings after dinner, eating watermelon or popsicles on the front steps with my friends, riding my bike, Day Camp at Brookview School with Kristen, Mick, and the Cromley brothers, and playing Kick The Can, or Ghost In The Graveyard every night in our neighborhood until I was forced to come inside.

Mosquito bites, scraped knees with scaly scabs, and sparklers on the Fourth of July were the things that filled my childhood summers, along with swimming, running through sprinklers, and a horrible lack of air conditioning. During the day it wasn't a big deal, but I can remember how hot it was in my room at night. I would lie on top of the sheet with nothing on but underwear, both windows as wide open as they would go, while a fan blew directly on me so that I could try to fall asleep. A lot of time was spent before going to bed setting the fan up just so, making sure it was blowing on me in the most efficient manner. I would place the big hulking plastic monstrosity precariously on my nightstand and then leap onto the bed in an attempt to lie down really fast and see where the air was hitting me, only to jump back up and readjust the plastic knob in the back after carefully testing and retesting the exact direction of its vacillation.

This is an exercise that kids today should still be forced to experience. Not only did it impart a practical use to the scientific method we learned about in school, but it also created a mission and purpose on those long hot summer nights that awakened the competitive spirit inside of me. I couldn't let the heat beat me. I was the Coyote and the heat was the Road Runner, and my new fan had just been delivered by the Acme Company. After the elaborate testing phase was complete, I would lie on the sheets and try to be as still as possible, for even the slightest movement would invite the heat back in, and I would be forced to lie in sweaty defeat until I drifted off to sleep to the rhythmic whirring of the fan.

During the day I spent a lot of time outside. I often complained to my mom about being bored – much as my own children do to me today. I guess the big difference between my own kids and me is that I actually went outside when I was bored. With my kids I have to tell them over and over to go outside and be kids. I rode my bike around for hours and hours on the days that none of my friends could play, and I spent a lot of time out in our yard, sometimes so parched that you could light a match on my tongue, but I still didn't go inside.

My dad planted a vegetable garden in our back yard every year and I loved digging for worms in it. Finding a squirming worm in the rich, dark soil was like uncovering buried treasure. There was always a surge of excitement and a big thrill with each new discovery. I loved when it started to get dark outside, but the earth still held a heavy, rich aroma from its long day in the sun. My dad always watered the plants when it began to get dark – the fresh splashes of water bringing new hope to the tired and parched back yard life.

He also planted tomato, raspberry, and strawberry plants. I guess being in the garden and feeling the soil was relaxing for him after being in an office all day doing whatever it was that a patent attorney did. "Intellectual Property" is not easily understood by an 8-year-old, but I knew it meant my dad was important and smart and that's all that mattered to me. It also meant that he had to go to Germany or Japan occasionally to try cases for his work. We would go with him sometimes, when he went to Germany, because my mom had relatives there that we would visit while my dad was working. When my dad went to Japan he didn't take us with him, and I remember being very proud to tell my friends that my dad was in Japan. Most of the kids at school didn't believe me, because to them I might as well have said that my dad went to Mars. Nobody actually *went* to Japan!

The back yard always felt ominously heavy with heat and humidity. Wafts of dill seemed to linger and hang in the air along with a mixture of fresh-cut grass and a tinge of motor oil from our lawn mower. Right smack in the middle of everything my dad decided it would be a great idea to plant a couple of pear trees and one or two peach trees, which made it really difficult to run around in the grass, and virtually impossible to play baseball, kickball, or football with all the trees in the middle of the field. The peaches got heavy, fell off, and ripened so sticky sweet that the bees seemed to come for miles to visit our back yard. My brother Paul always scared me with the urban legend that the killer bees were on their way from Africa and would soon kill us all.

On one side of our house there was a metal chain-link fence that separated our house from the Rosenbergs'. They had an above-ground pool and kids who were grown up. I often saw Mrs. Rosenberg sunning herself by the pool, drinking tall glasses of ice coffee and smoking. Her skin looked dark and leathery in her strapless bikini top, and her voice was deep and raspy from her chain-smoking. She was friendly towards me when I would say hello to her through the fence, but for the most part she only paid attention to me when one of my balls flew over the fence and into her yard or her pool. It was along that fence where my dad planted the raspberries and laid down beds of straw that baked so hot in the sun around the strawberries I thought they would catch fire.

One day when I was around 9 or 10 years old, my friend Tommy and I were playing "fort" and we came up with a grand idea that sent me inside on a secret mission to my mom's closet. I stole one of my mom's hat boxes, came back outside with it, and together we found a stick to poke a hole in the bottom of it. We built a little fort over by some of the bushes near the Rosenbergs' fence and the hat box was our toilet. My parents were pissed (pardon the pun) when they found out that Tommy and I were peeing in front of each other into the hat box. I tried to explain to my dad that it wasn't a hat box – it was a toilet! What else were we supposed to do? (Sheesh, parents don't understand anything.)

The back left-hand corner of the yard was where an old swing set sat alone and rusty. I never used it anymore because I was too big for it, but my father never took it down. He was the type of guy who also left the Christmas lights on the big pine tree in the back yard all year round. Next to the swing set was what my dad called "the shed." It was like a tiny little house that was made of flimsy metal, the door sticky with rust. When we first got it I immediately wanted to use it as a fort or club house, but it was soon overcrowded with garden tools, buckets, and gross cobwebs. The few times I went in there to hide, I hated how hot it was, and the smell of chemical fertilizer and gasoline was overpowering.

Along the back of our back yard, there was a white painted wooden fence, put in by our neighbors who lived directly behind us. They had an in-ground pool that I never used but always wanted to try. On our side of the fence was a huge mound of pachysandra, mint plants, and my dad's compost pile for his garden. I always wanted to be on the other side of the fence, and wondered about the people who lived there and their lives. I liked watching them during their cocktail parties and back yard barbeques. I felt that they had it made in the shade with their beautiful lawn and in-ground pool. If you stood by that fence and turned around, you would be facing the back of our house and the place where my dad planted all the tomato plants. It was next to the string of tomato plants, floating in the back yard limbo, that my dad's vegetable garden was located. Beside the garden grew a large blue spruce tree that my brother Paul had planted as a sapling. Both the garden and the tree served as a natural fence, separating our house from the other next-door neighbors, the Robertsons.

I never liked the color of our house. It was a dark charcoal gray for a good portion of my childhood. The back of the house had cow spots of white primer where my father had started to paint the house but never finished it. He seemed to spend a long time scraping and priming and then never completed the project. I stood outside with him as the summer sun roasted our backs and watched him work, wanting so badly to help him paint, but I wasn't allowed. The back of our house sported that spotted white and gray look until I was in high school and my dad finally decided we should get aluminum siding. He and my mom picked out a shade of light green that, to me, resembled a Shamrock Shake. I began to think the charcoal gray wasn't as bad as I had thought it was.

I remember standing next to our house long before the green siding, with the heat billowing off of it, and looking just beyond my dad's garden into the Robertsons' yard. Compared with our yard, with the incomplete projects and the ugly shed and patchy brown grass, the Robertsons' yard looked like a Royal Botanical Garden. Even if our yard had looked like a photograph in *Better Homes and Gardens Magazine*, their yard would still have put it to shame. It was pristine and beautiful. The flower and vegetable beds in the back were perfectly shaped rectangles with just the right amount of green grass in between to walk through. There were flowers and vegetables of all types and although we lived in the suburbs they yielded an overflow of squash and cucumbers that the Robertsons often brought over and gave to my parents. There was only the two of them, and they couldn't eat it all before it went bad. They were an older couple, in their 60s, I guess, who never had children. They worked very hard in their gardens and on the lawn, which could rival any golf course. Mr. Robertson used some type of sharp object to carefully create a narrow moat between the grass and the sidewalk. I hated those moats with a passion, since my bicycle tire always got caught in them, causing a crash or a near-fatal wipeout.

Mrs. Robertson wore floral dresses and pearls. Even when she was out working in the yard she looked as if she was going to church. She would often come outside in a wide-brimmed hat, clapping her hands at our cats in order to shoo them away from her bushes and flowers. She reminded me a lot of Aunt Bee from *The Andy Griffith Show*, although Aunt Bee had a warmer disposition. No matter how hot and dry the summer was, their lawn was always lush, green, and perfect. I used to like to hang around with them and chat while they worked outside. They seemed to really enjoy having me around, and I loved feeling as though I had a grandma and a grandpa to hang out with when I was alone and bored during summer vacation. I would spend hours at a time on the weekends with Mr. and Mrs. Robertson, and often played cards with them at their little kitchen table. They gave me cookies and milk and let me win at Go Fish. Since I had never met either of my grandfathers (because they were both dead long before I was adopted) and my grandmas both lived far away (one in Germany and one in Cleveland), I reveled in the relationship I had with Mr. and Mrs. Robertson.

It was cool having your grandparents right next door, willing to play cards and dole out cookies and lemonade at any time. Strangely enough it was often Country Time Lemonade and I loved drinking it with them because it was just like the commercial! Mr. Robertson even resembled the grandpa in the lemonade ads. He was tall with white hair and glasses – much like the TV grandpa. He always wore those cargo-type work pants or khakis, with a white short-sleeve shirt that had a collar and buttons down the front. It was like having Mr. Green Jeans living right next door to me, minus the moose and the ping pong balls. The shirts he wore were like the kind that my dad wore to work, except my dad wore a tie and a suit. Mr. Robertson wore those short-sleeve dress shirts every day even though he was retired and was constantly out working in his yard. The only time he wasn't dressed like that was when he and Mrs. Robertson got really dressed up for church on Sundays.

I basically only saw Mrs. Robertson on the weekends and in the evenings because she still worked at an office during the day. When she wasn't dressed up in suits and pearls for church, she wore her print dresses and nude-colored stockings that came in an egg. She was short and stout and she too had white hair and glasses. I wouldn't describe her as mean, exactly, but she had a curt way about her, and she wouldn't tolerate any bad manners. I always made sure to say "please" and "thank you" and to put my plate or glass in the sink. I didn't want them to stop playing cards with me when I was at their house for a visit. I liked hanging out at their house and spending time with them, so I tried to be on my best behavior to make sure I was always invited back.

During the long afternoons of summer it was a challenge to find ways to fill the time. I often chose to hang out in the front yard instead of in the back because it felt less claustrophobic, and in the front yard there was the promise of action. Nothing interesting was ever going to happen in the back yard. In the front there was more excitement. Maybe a car would drive by or a potential playmate might ride past on his or her bike. One of the neighbors might come out into his or her yard or driveway, which to me was an open invitation to go over and talk. I would hang out in the front yard playing in the sprinkler or picking dandelions (and popping their heads off) until someone I could wander over to and chat with would come out to work on his or her lawn. That someone was always Mr. Robertson. He seemed to live outside and constantly worked on his meticulously perfect lawn. I don't know what on Earth he even had left to do to it, and apparently he agreed, because just when it seemed it couldn't be any more picture perfect, he would dig it up by the roots and start all over again, unrolling beautiful strips of real grass that looked like plush green carpet.

If he saw me riding my bike around, he always stopped what he was doing and waved me over. I loved talking to him because he was charming and funny. He took a great interest in me and everything that I did. He made funny jokes and came up with clever ways to say my name. By way of greeting he would say, "How is, Liz?" Or "Hey Liz! How is?"

It didn't take much to make me laugh at 8 years old, and I got a real kick out of the things that he said and how he said them. We talked, and he made me laugh, and would even let me help him with whatever he was working on. My dad never let me help him in the yard because he knew I would mess it up which would cause even more work for him in the end. Mr. Robertson didn't seem to mind what I did or if I messed it up and he let me use the shovel or the rake or whatever tool was needed at the time to get the job done.

Each betrayal begins with trust.

—Phish

III

SOMETIMES MR. ROBERTSON would go inside and get a jar of Planters Peanuts and we would have a snack together. All this hard work in the sun and eating salty nuts made a person thirsty, so he would suggest we go inside for something to drink. I agreed with him, and would readily bound into the house that I was already quite accustomed to spending time in.

On that first occasion when we were alone together and something had happened, I felt something come over me that I didn't recognize at all. It was an uneasy, queasy feeling that was trying to tell me something wasn't quite right, but as an 8-year-old who was outgoing, high energy, and fearless...I had no idea what the voice was trying to say.

The house seemed so different when Mrs. Robertson wasn't there. It was always immaculately clean and neat, with a traditional and rather stuffy-looking décor that only people without kids could pull off. It smelled of pipe tobacco, which I still hate getting a whiff of today on the rare occasion that I might come across a person smoking a pipe. It freaks me out when I'm out on a run or walking outside with the dog, and a car passes with the window cracked, releasing a tiny bit of that very distinct pipe tobacco smell. When it reaches my nose it feels like a smack in the face, just like in the old cartoons when you could see the white wafting scent of delicious food twisting in the air and when it reaches the hungry, sleeping dog lying next to his doghouse and the big empty food bowl, it clenches itself into a fist and...*pow!*

The house was a ranch style, painted in a pristine white with prim black shutters. It seemed much bigger on the inside when Mrs. Robertson wasn't home and Mr. Robertson and I were standing alone in the kitchen. The rest of the house had oriental carpets on hardwood floors and all the furniture was antique and made of dark woods, giving the rooms a haunting and ominous appearance. The impressively large and beautiful grandfather clock could always be heard in the background. Its pendulum swung back and forth ticking away the time in between beautiful chimes that indicated the hour and the half hour. At the very top of the clock, behind the glass door, was the serious face of a golden yellow moon that was always watching. From where he stood in the hallway the Man in the Moon could see Mr. Robertson put down his lemonade glass. He knew before I did that Mr. Robertson was coming up behind me to wrap his arms around me.

I stood frozen, still holding my lemonade and trying to look at him standing behind me without turning my head, my eyes pressed hard in their corners. He turned me around, took the glass from my hand, and placed it on the kitchen table where we usually played cards and ate cookies with his wife. He pulled me into his body and slid both of his hands into the back of my pants and down into my underwear. I didn't like what was happening but I didn't make a move or say a word. I stood there with my arms stiff as boards down by my sides. I didn't hug him back but I didn't push him away.

I was suddenly the Tin Man from *The Wizard of Oz* and there wasn't a can of oil in sight. The way he was breathing both scared and appalled me. It was choppy and heavy, as if he couldn't catch his breath, yet we were standing still. It was a raw type of panting that made me feel weird and sick to my stomach; the heavy and erratic breathing usually associated with fumbling teens making out and getting busy – not with a grandfatherly type and a little girl in pigtails and culottes snacking on Bugles and Planters Peanuts. (No offense, Mr. Peanut, but the sight of you in your monocle and top hat still creeps me out to this day. I do realize this is a serious case of guilt by association. I am quite sure that you are an extremely kind and dignified man-legume who also, by the way, possesses a refined sense of style and taste. Please accept my apologies.)

I vividly remember that first time because my head was turned to the side, facing the door that we had just walked through only minutes before. I just stared at the screen door that led outside and back into the bright afternoon sunshine as he whispered breathlessly into my ear, "Do you like to have your bottom rubbed?"

I knew what he was doing was wrong but I couldn't stand up to him and tell him to stop. This type of inner conflict was not something I was equipped to handle as a kid.

In first grade Adam Fishbein thought he would impress me when he took me out to the front of the church one day at recess and proceeded to pee my name in cursive onto the building. The wet letters of my name dripped down the brick and mortar that made up the church, which also doubled as my grade school. I have to admit that his "penmanship" was quite impressive; but nevertheless, I was horrified and I promptly ran inside to tell on him right away.

But this was different. This was an adult, which meant that he must be the one who was right and I must be the one who was doing something wrong. I was scared but I felt that saying no to him would only lead to enormous trouble as well as embarrassment for me.

I grew up in a home that most people would consider very prudish. My mom and dad made an extremely uncomfortable and huge deal out of it whenever anyone even made out on TV. Nobody in our house mentioned the word "sex," or explained the facts of life. There were some books I found on the shelf in our den one day that explained it and had diagrams of a penis and a vagina – but the books weren't even given to me with an explanation. They were just tucked in with the rest of the books, baiting me to look at them on my own time someday when no one was around to be embarrassed by the subject matter. It was like throwing chum in the water and waiting for the sharks to come and feed. Of course if you put it out there a curious shark, or kid, will easily sniff it out and take the bait. Once I found the books, I enjoyed the pictures in the same way that I liked looking at the naked Pygmy tribes in my dad's *National Geographic Magazines*. Neither of the aforementioned reading materials was used by me for educational purposes.

I wasn't even allowed to watch *The Dukes of Hazzard* because, in my mom's opinion, Daisy Duke was "too sexy."

When every single one of my friends saw the movie *Grease*, and every birthday party I was invited to was a

Grease-themed costume party, I wasn't allowed to see that either. I saw the album at my friends' houses and got the idea of what the movie was about from listening to the songs, but when my friends talked about the parts they liked the best I had to play along as if I actually saw the movie when in actuality I knew nothing about what everyone was talking about.

My mom had a weird German word she used in place of the word "vagina" and in our house I don't think any word for "penis" even existed – not even the actual word "penis." Maybe my parents figured if I never heard the word, I wouldn't think it actually existed either, and it would save me from getting into trouble with one down the road.

There was even a word that my parents used instead of "butt," or "ass," or "bottom." I hated *that* word more than anything in the world and I still do. It creeps me out and bothers me to my core. I don't even want to type the word; it is just one of those things that I can't even stand to think about. I have a friend who hates the word "moist" and if you say it around her, she just might slap you. She hates it that much. Everyone has a word that turns his or her stomach. Mine was said in my house all the time because my parents refused to say "ass." The word is "bubbus." I also hate the word "bottom" (for obvious reasons) when one is referring to someone's ass.

At 8 years old I knew that certain body parts and sexy things like kissing and putting your hands into someone's pants were really bad things that no one was to speak of or do. If I was doing these things it meant that I was a horrible person, and I was afraid that somehow my parents or Mrs. Robertson would find out and I would be in the worst trouble imaginable. For surely a person who can't stand to see kissing on TV or even say the word "ass" would never forgive me for what the Man in the Moon was witnessing.

Just as it was my fault that the person who gave birth to me didn't want to keep me, that I was in four different foster homes with no real belongings of my own to speak of, that I was a troublemaker in school with too much energy and nowhere good to put it – and was kicked out of the Girl Scouts for the very same reason – I was sure that this too was my fault. In my mind I was sure that just going along with whatever Mr. Robertson said or did was the best course of action. I was going to do what he said to do or else really bad things would probably happen, and I would be to blame for them all. For the rest of that summer and on into the fall, as well as the following school year, I was brought into various scenarios with Mr. Robertson while his wife was at work and his grandfather clock disapprovingly clucked its long golden tongue at me.

When I stepped out of the bright sunlight and into his kitchen, it always looked so dark and gray until my eyes adjusted. We never stayed in the kitchen very long. There was always something that he had to get ready for and he would ask me to keep him company in the bathroom while he went about showering and shaving or brushing his teeth. I would sit on the toilet, with the lid down, next to the sink, and nervously watch him shave. I didn't know where to look, so I studied the healing progression of the various scabs on my knees. Much like my heart, the scabs on my knees would begin to heal and then something would happen that reopened the wounds.

The sink was full of water that he used to rinse the razor in between strokes. He would be in his boxer shorts and somehow the opening in the front would end up revealing his penis. He told me what to do with it, and whether to use my hand or my mouth, while he looked in the mirror to complete his perfectly smooth shave. I guess he must have figured that if he stayed busy while I was doing things to him, then it was as if he wasn't really a part of what was happening. In a strange way I was left with the impression that it was *my* idea to do this to him while he wasn't looking. When I went home and thought about it I actually wondered if I had done it because I wanted to, and tried to get the job done before he noticed what I was doing. He didn't acknowledge it and went right on shaving his face and neck, and acted as if he had no idea that it was even happening; so it *must* have been my idea.

I decided that I was a disgusting person for taking advantage of him like that. Why would I want to do something like that to him when he wasn't looking? Other days he did look. When he was done brushing his teeth he would put me in the tub and wash me with green Irish Spring soap. The soapy smell and the sting between my legs made me want to cry but I never did. My maiden name is Vidmar and my dad always told me that Vidmars don't cry. He told me that I am strong and I am a Vidmar. My father was a Marine, and although he was never "militant" with me, strength was very important to him. I took this to heart and knew that names and strength were very important to my dad.

For the first two years of my life my name was Tammy Ann, but when I was adopted, my parents changed my name. My dad told me that they picked my name from the Bible because in their opinion "Tammy Ann" was not a strong Biblical name but "Elizabeth Sarah" was. Most of the time it is weird to think of myself as someone else with a different name, but when I was in the tub and fingers found their way inside of me, it became necessary to be someone else in some other place with some other name. A bar of Irish Spring with its clean fresh smell and two stripes of deodorants will never wash away this type of dirt, no matter how you slice it with a pocket knife, or how well you can whistle. Yes, I grew up watching a lot of TV. And yes, the smells of Irish Spring soap and Scope mouthwash still stir up sick feelings in my stomach when I smell them today. I wonder if Mrs. Robertson could smell the Irish Spring too, or if she wondered why towels and tub liners were still wet so late into the day.

There were times that we didn't go inside at all. There were days that we would step into his garage to get a much-needed tool or the watering can. Maybe he would offer me some cookies or a snack. As far as garages go, his was fairly clean with all the nails and bolts and screws neatly placed in little jars, each tool in its proper place on hooks hanging from the walls. It was nothing like the chaos in our garage with stacks of newspapers and kids' bicycles and crap everywhere. I liked our garage better.

The floor of Mr. Robertson's garage was concrete and smooth, but he would often lay an old chaise lounge cushion down on the floor and have me lie down on top of it. His shaky heavy breathing while he touched me bothered me deep into my core. He was grossly excited and his breath kept catching in the back of his throat. His hands felt rough from all the yard work and he didn't act or feel like a grandpa although he told me that he loved me. I wasn't allowed to watch on television what my neighbor was doing to me in real life. During these times I was uncharacteristically quiet. I never spoke to him when he was like that. I was afraid to disturb him or to anger or excite him, and decided it would be best to let it happen as quickly as possible. The rubbing and the noises and having things in my mouth that didn't belong there would come to an end and we could go about the rest of the day as if nothing had happened. I just had to get through it and get it over with. He always wanted me to go home when he was done. I wanted to go home…but I didn't want him to act as though he wanted me to leave because I had done something wrong. It was all so confusing and made me angry and sad. I always had to ruin everything.

It was more than fortunate for me that I had swim practice every night of the week, except for Sunday. I think my head would have exploded if I didn't have the cool water to sink into and the sound of it washing over my ears as I swam back and forth in the strongly chlorinated water of the high school pool. I had fun with the other kids on the team and loved being a part of something that made me feel good. A long practice made me feel less anxious and the chlorine smell was clean and soothing to me. Swimming was my therapy, but at the time all that mattered was that it made me feel better and when I was in the water I was happy. Being with my friends and acting silly after practice in the locker room helped to take my mind off of things and to feel as though I was actually a normal person.

Now that I am a mother myself, I often wonder what on Earth my mom was thinking by letting me stay at the neighbor's house alone so often and for such long periods of time. I was gone for hours and she had to know that most of the time I was inside his house. Maybe she didn't. I know that she was aware that his wife was at work. I can't even imagine allowing my daughter to play with a man in his house alone for hours on end.

I never told anyone what was happening, but the need to get it out was too great not to at least write it down. Long before I knew what therapy was, or journals, I was trying to get the bad stuff out by writing it down as a manner of purging my soul. My soul-purging was done at night before I went to sleep in an extra assignment pad I had but didn't use for school. It had Garfield on the front of it, sitting cozily in a box with a blanket and his bear, Pooky. I wrote all kinds of witty quips in that assignment pad (or at least I thought they were witty) and used it to make fun of a lot of my parents' friends. Usually my entries were about a sentence in length and got straight to the point. I remember trying to rip on a guy who wore a toupee by writing that my parents had a guy over for dinner who clearly stored his hair in a box every night when he went to sleep. This was my idea of sarcastic wit at the age of 9. I also wrote bits and pieces about the "dirty old man next door" and how he put his hands in my pants and panted like a dog. Some of the things I wrote were specific, but most of it was basically me making fun of him.

One day I came home from school and my mom was waiting for me. I could tell that I was in trouble for something, but that was the norm for me so I wasn't too worried about it. My mom held the assignment pad out to me to show me why she was mad. She didn't have to tell me what we would be discussing; I knew it wasn't the guy with the bad rug. My mother was angry with me, just as I had predicted all along, and demanded to know why I wrote the things that I did. She asked me if I wrote them down because they were important to me, which made me feel as if she actually believed I was proud and happy to have such "wonderful" things to write about – as if I liked it, or wanted it to happen.

Like any kid I answered my mom's question with, "I don't know."

Then she asked me if it was even true. I told her that it was. The decision was made quickly and without discussion of any kind. My mother never made any decisions without my father's input and if this one isn't proof positive that that was a good thing, I don't know what would be. It was decided right then and there in my pink and gray animal print wallpapered room that we would never tell anyone.

She said we could never tell my father because if he found out he would kill Mr. Robertson and then would go to jail, and it would be my fault my father was in jail. This all seemed very plausible to me. I knew shit was going to hit the fan if anyone found out what I had done. I didn't want my dad to go to jail and I didn't want to face the embarrassment of anyone else yelling at me about what had happened next door. The babyish pink and gray jungle animals on my walls looked even dopier and sadder that day. Their big round eyes looked down at me, ashamed. My mom left me in my room and that was it. We went on living our lives "like normal" which for my mom meant in denial and for me meant a silent hell.

During the winter it was easy to avoid seeing Mr. Robertson and I stopped going over there to hang out and play cards. When the weather started getting nicer I became an expert at never having to see him at all. I always made sure to check outside through the windows before leaving the house, and would run out the front door and in the direction of the Rosenbergs' house, even if it meant taking a longer route to where I was going. I would not walk or ride my bike past his house no matter what. I stopped playing in our yard, and if I wanted to lie out in the sun, I had to do it when it was shining on the "good" side of the house. Once the time of day arrived when the sun moved and was tucked in behind the split-level roof...it was time to pack up the baby oil and blanket and go back inside. I couldn't go into the front or the back yard to lie out in my bathing suit with him around.

As I got older I barely ever saw him at all and everyone went about his or her business as if nothing had happened. I thought I was okay, but I really wasn't. When I graduated from high school and received a card from the Robertsons with some money in it, my mother actually yelled at me for not going next door to say "thank you" to them, and said I was selfish for not saying goodbye to them when I left for college.

It never occurred to me (back then) that my mom did me such a disservice by not helping me. She was the only one who knew what the neighbor was doing and she chose to ignore it. Subconsciously, the message I received from that was: it was my fault and I must have done something wrong; I was a bad person, unlovable and disgusting, and we would all be best served by going about our lives as if nothing had happened because that was all that could be done with a wretch like me; I was lucky to be taken in and put up with; I was horrible, ugly, and worthless and always would be.

Strength does not come from physical capacity. It comes from indomitable will.

—Mahatma Gandhi

IV

IN 1980 THE WINTER OLYMPICS were held in Lake Placid, New York, and the event seemed to captivate my parents both for the love of watching the talented athletes as well as because of a new-found love of Lake Placid itself. Since my mother is from Germany, she was very drawn to the beauty and European feel that the mountains and village of Lake Placid possess. We visited Lake Placid, my parents fell in love with it, and the next thing I knew they bought a completely furnished Swiss chalet-style house on the Ausable River.

I was only 11 years old and appreciated a new pair of jeans much more than a second home, but even I recognized that it was an incredible house. It was very secluded because it was located far in the back of the Ausable Acres, nestled on the edge of government-owned land that no one could build on, with the Ausable River running in the front and a perfect view of Whiteface Mountain. To complete the Alpine-like picture there was a little farm with a few cows just beyond the river that we could also see from the picture window. This was to be our weekend house. A six-hour drive to a weekend house sounds like a nightmare to any kid – and I was no different – but I loved to be there once the car ride was over. (You can't run or do cartwheels in the car, so long car trips were never my thing.) I loved the balcony outside the master bedroom; the wrap-around deck on the first floor; and the pine-beamed ceilings and walls throughout the whole place. It was both scary and cool that we often had bears in our driveway when we pulled in, and the silence at night could actually keep you awake.

During the winter it got so cold there that we had to plug the car in overnight to keep it from freezing, and Whiteface Mountain took on the nickname "Iceface" Mountain. That house was really special. Mr. Robertson was six hours away and I was surrounded by peaceful wooded trails, mountains, and beauty. It was the perfect place to test how far I could run or cross-country ski. There were times that my dad would follow me in the car when I ran long distances in the Acres to help me track my mileage and to keep me safe from bears or getting lost.

One year I brought my friend Joyce with me and we got lost for hours on our cross-country skis. We were in high school and I remember laughing about it the whole time...but inside I really was worried that we would never be found. What was meant to be a little jaunt on the cross-country skis turned into about a five-hour excursion. But we were okay. We were athletes, young and fearless.

I also remember the summer that I brought my friend Lisa to Lake Placid for a weekend. We had a blast riding horseback and playing in the river, and we'd stay up all night talking about parties and boys, and playing Atari. (Yes, my parents let me bring the Atari with me because we didn't get any TV stations at the house because of the mountains.) There was a medium-sized man-made lake near our house that Lisa and I also liked to visit, to swim and get away from my parents. On the bank of the lake sat a small rowboat. I didn't know who owned the boat, but I did know that it wasn't ours. Lisa and I convinced ourselves that the owners of the boat surely wouldn't mind letting two nice girls borrow it for a little summertime enjoyment. There were no paddles to be found – but who needed those? We were simply going to float around and sun ourselves and then put the boat back in its place when we were done.

We pushed the little boat into the water, hopped in, and stretched out on opposite ends of it while closing our eyes as we chatted and caught rays. Of course the boat drifted to the other side of the lake, which was probably a mile and a half or so from the side we were supposed to be on. When we opened our eyes we knew we were in big trouble. We didn't want my parents to know we *borrowed* someone's boat...and my dad would probably be there any minute to pick us up! Frantically we tried to paddle our way back to shore with our arms and hands! Both Lisa and I had been on the swim team together since we were 6 years old. Being on or in the water wasn't scary – but dealing with the prospect of my dad finding out what we did, was!

We decided that one of us needed to get in the water and look for a long stick to use as a paddle. We had been told that there were snakes in the water, so neither of us wanted to get in. I had more to lose if we got caught than Lisa did, however, so the incentive to get in was greater for me than for her. I got in the lake and pulled the boat with one hand, while sidestroking with the other. The boat was heavy and I could barely see the shore, but I rather enjoyed the physical effort and the excitement of the situation. In a short time I was able to make out a figure on the beach. It looked like a small, squared-off version of my dad. Oh crap...it *was* my dad – and he had his hands on his hips. (This was a very bad sign; I knew I was in for it if his hands were on his hips.) Luckily I also knew that my dad was a softy when it came to me and my shenanigans, so I would probably only have to endure getting yelled at and a lecture about other people's property – the lecture being the worse of the two.

It took a very long time to swim the boat to shore, and my dad was *very* mad. Lisa and I giggled through the lecture – making matters worse, but at least I had made it in to shore with the boat, and Lisa, and me, all unscathed. My poor dad looked like his head was going to blow off when we got there. Maybe it wasn't all the bologna sandwiches and beer that gave him a bad heart. Hmmm.

Anyway...that day sparked something in Lisa and me. That night in our room when it was time to try to sleep, instead we talked. We decided that we would both do that Ironman thing we had seen on TV and we would also swim across Lake Champlain. It was fun to plan how we would execute the grandiose open-water swim – never mind that the day's calamity was my first-ever open-water swim, and Lisa didn't even get in the water to help until the very end when she could see my dad's temple throbbing from where she sat in the rowboat. This would be great! We would get someone to follow us in a boat to keep us from getting hit by other boats, and he or she could give us food and water to keep us going as we made our way across Lake Champlain.

The Ironman Triathlon looked just crazy and untouchable enough to talk about doing as well because we knew that it was so hard that people actually pooped in their pants while attempting it. Anything that forces a person to dump a load in their own pants on national TV was exactly the type of crazy challenge we wanted the pride of accomplishing! (Maybe without the poop part, though.) The next day we were overcome with excitement about our new goals, and announced them in full animated detail to my dad. He listened and smiled. It wasn't a condescending smile, but one that parents display when their children rattle on about Santa Claus. It's a knowing smile that says:

"Hold onto your dreams, girls! They are quite farfetched and unrealistic – but I love that you want to believe."

I did my first Iron-distance triathlon in 1995 in Clermont, Florida, while my dad was in the intensive care unit in Ohio. He couldn't be there to watch me, but he was beyond proud when I told him that I had finished. He said that he didn't think he would ever know someone who actually did an Ironman, but now his own daughter had done one. It may seem silly, but hearing my dad say those words to me welled up such a sense of pride and accomplishment inside of me that I wish I could have bottled it and sold it for $19.95 a pop. It was almost as empowering as when I actually crossed the finish line. Nothing was impossible. I had done something that not many people could do, and I did it on my own, and no one could take it away from me. For me this was a very real source of strength and pride that I could carry over into other areas of my life when I needed to. After my father had passed away, I could at least take comfort that he knew I had achieved a goal I set all those years ago in Lake Placid.

If I'm too strong for some people, that's their problem.

—Glenda Jackson

V

ONE OF MY DAD'S favorite sayings (he had a few) that he reserved specifically for me when I was in high school was:

"You can't major in fun when you're in college."

Education meant everything to my father, and partying, boys, and playing sports meant everything to me. That combination was like fire and water, especially in a house like mine where differing opinions weren't just discussed – they were discussed *loudly*! My father and I often had screaming wars over everything from my "crazy" behavior to him chewing too loudly or looking at me at the dinner table. Most likely stemming from the scrutiny over my looks as a child, as well as the sexual abuse, I always had this weird issue with people looking at me, and I actually still do, to a much smaller extent, today. As a teen, I would go ballistic if people looked at me too long and would often yell accusingly at my dad at the dinner table, "*What* are you *looking* at? Don't *look* at me!"

He would always say he wasn't "*looking*" at me, but that because I was sitting at the same table and in the same room, I was in his "line of vision," and that if he looked up from his plate he had no choice but to look at me. This was not an acceptable explanation to me as an angry and hormonal teenager, so I would flip out and scream at him to stop looking at me. My poor dad was so tired and exasperated with me, and after a long day at work all he wanted to do was eat his food without being yelled at for setting his eyes on his own kid seated directly in front of him.

Many studies show that because of "Nature versus Nurture," and because yelling is a learned behavior, I can probably attribute my short temper to my father's even *shorter* fuse. Old cartoons often showed a thermometer in place of a character's head when that character was getting mad…and the mercury would rise up to the top until it blew up and all the steam would come out of the cartoon character's head, accompanied by the sound of a blaring steam engine. This is often what I saw when my father and I would fight. I can picture Elmer Fudd at his wits' end with Bugs Bunny's wise-ass shenanigans until he couldn't take it anymore and his head became an exploding thermometer. That was my dad and me. Unfortunately for him, he was always Elmer Fudd and I was always Bugs Bunny. He would often explode in anger at my ridiculous ranting regarding where he was looking while he ate his tuna casserole. My mom would usually get upset about the screaming, and because she worried that the neighbors would hear us (heaven forbid), she would often get up from the table to close the windows and then she would go into another room to cry.

To be honest, I don't know how my parents even put up with me sometimes – especially my dad, who had no idea why I was always so angry and emotional, yet he was the one who had the most patience in dealing with me. I was 15 years old and had been giving my mom a particularly hard time one day after school. I was so mouthy and disrespectful that she finally lost her cool and slapped my face. We were in my parents' bedroom and she was standing next to her bed when she did it. I think it shocked us both equally, because she had never laid a finger on me before then. This particular time the battery acid that I often spewed forth in the form of words was enough to make her cry. After I saw that she was crying I got even meaner and laid into her, taunting, "Oh, little baby is *crying*. Is the baby going to tell daddy on me when he gets home?"

I guess that's when she lost it and the slap went through me like lightning, igniting a fire that made me push her on the bed and hover over her proclaiming, "If you ever touch me again, I will *fucking goon you!*"

("Goon" was a term that we used in my high school – mostly to describe what the hockey players did to each other against the glass.)

Had the circumstances been different, it would have been a comical thing to say, looking back on it now. Back then, however, I can assure you that not one person found humor in it. By the time my dad got home from work he had already been briefed on what I had said and done, and he was pissed. We argued and I used every weapon I had in my arsenal from being aloof to calling my dad a "dick scratch" right up in his face. "Dick scratch" didn't go over very well and the look in my dad's eyes told me that I had better turn around and run. I ran up the stairs to my room, all the time holding onto my butt with both hands because my dad was chasing me and halfheartedly attempting to slap at it. When I reached my bedroom I did a gymnast-type twist in the air and landed on my bed, flat on my back so that my dad couldn't get to my ass. I knew that he would never hit me anywhere else, so I was sure to keep the only area he might spank me well out of reach.

He leaned over me and was screaming at me from a distance of about a centimeter, in the red-faced rage of a man on the edge. I think he may have been speaking in tongues as the spit flew from his infuriated lips. I can remember the way I leaned my head back, laughing, with my only response being, "Jesus, Dad! Twisted Sister video or what?"

(The *We're Not Going to Take It* video had just come out and was one of my favorites at the time. It was the one that opened with the dad screaming and spitting in a fit of rage in his son's face.) I thought I was pretty awesome in that I was able to reference it in the proper context and everything! My dad had no idea what I was talking about, so it also carried with it the added bonus of further infuriating my already frazzled father.

Character cannot be developed in ease and quiet. Only through experience of trial and suffering can the soul be strengthened, ambition inspired, and success achieved.

—Helen Keller

VI

ONCE I WAS KNEE-DEEP into one of my angry tirades it was really hard for me to reel myself back in, pull myself out, and put a stop to it. Somewhere deep inside I wanted to make it stop. In a helpless and childlike way, something deep inside my soul searched frantically for a lifeline that could pull me out, but outwardly I just couldn't find one. As the floodwaters rose higher and higher, the dam couldn't contain them, and eventually it cracked and broke and the water poured out, only to demolish everything in its path until there was nothing left but a trickle. When that happened I was able to get out what I needed to in order to feel better for the moment, and could then make a quick recovery back to "normal."

For the most part this was not so for anyone who had witnessed the floodgates breaking open. Looking back on it – and knowing how truly ugly and scary my anger could be for my family, store clerks, people in elevators, or someone who disturbed my run after I reached the 30-minute time limit on a treadmill that I wasn't ready to get off of yet – I am sure the experience was much like an unexpected hurricane. When I was done and over it, I just expected everyone else to be over it as well. For me the winds died down and blue sky and sun came back out with birds chirping and going about their normal routine, while people stood amongst the rubble and sticks that had been their homes and shelter. In my mind the waters were calm and the storm was over, but everyone around me was left floundering in the wake.

My parents had a name for these times. They called them "Liz's Outbursts." When explaining why we were late or why everyone was upset, or why I wasn't talking to anyone, all they had to say was:

"Liz had one of her outbursts."

This was all that needed to be said. Everyone who knew us had either witnessed one firsthand, or had heard the tales of them from my mother. I was often stared at by my own relatives at various holiday get-togethers in a way that seemed like a combination of fear, pity, and disgust. You could see by the look in their eyes, and the way they regarded me, that they felt sorry for my parents. My mom was often at wits' end with me because of my outbursts – outbursts which, today, would be labeled as "Post-Traumatic Stress Disorder." Who knew there was a name for them other than "Liz's Outbursts?"

Nobody knew about what my neighbor had done to me, so my behavior was a mystery to almost everyone. *My mom knew; I knew...and he knew.* It wasn't a mystery to any of us, but that didn't help me when seen through everyone else's blind eyes.

It was hard for me to contain myself and my anger, and even harder for the people around me to understand my "crazy" behavior. I felt that many adults looked at me as an ungrateful spoiled brat who should be happy that someone had adopted her. I had it all in some people's eyes – athleticism, looks, and a dad who gave me the credit card to go shopping. And what did I do with it? I got myself kicked out of the Girl Scouts, got in trouble in school and in the neighborhood, and had outbursts anywhere and everywhere, including the mall where I would yell at the store clerks for looking at me while I was trying on shoes. (I had issues with my feet, so I hated that the most.)

The anger welled up from deep down in the bowels of my soul and worked its way up and out of me in a hot tingly malevolent fervor. At those times, it was much like I would guess an out-of-body experience to be like. The "evil" Liz took over the "good" Liz and didn't care where we were, who was around to hear, or what anyone thought of me. The recipient of my verbal assault could be anyone from a boyfriend, a family member, or a perfect stranger. If they were experienced and seasoned veterans of these attacks, they would let me go until I fizzled myself out. This was not an easy task, and although it would be extremely uncomfortable and embarrassing, it was the quickest way to diffuse the situation and ensure an end to it.

The kiss of death was when someone decided to step into the mine field and tried to stop the carnage on his own. In his hasty attempts to get rid of the stares and the "scene" that was being created, Mistake Number One on his part was to "shush" me or tell me to "calm down." Oh God! *Never* feed a Gremlin after midnight, *don't* make The Hulk angry, and don't *ever* tell Liz to shut up, shush, or calm down when she is in freakout mode. Yikes! If you do that, you just earned yourself an additional, and even scarier, arsenal that will take even longer to burn through.

Mistake Number Two was to fight back. I realize how important standing up for oneself is, but that only holds true when you are having a discussion or even an argument with a rational human being. Back in those days of displaced anger and unwanted glassy-eyed outbursts, I was not a rational human being, and adding fuel to the flames was completely and irrevocably ill-advised.

I have no idea what my brothers did when my "evil twin" came out and ruined everything – besides take cover. David was away at college for most of that time in my life and Paul tried to avoid me at all costs anyway – and with good reason. I was beyond just being an annoying little sister, and could actually be quite abusive to him at times. Although David and I are nine years apart in age, our actual birthdays are only two days apart in the month of March. His is the 25th and mine is the 27th. When we were growing up we always had a family dinner and a cake that celebrated both of our birthdays together. Sometimes I would have a friend over for dinner and cake, and afterwards we would open a couple of gifts, and Paul would get a "half"-birthday gift so that he didn't feel left out. My parents were really into half-birthdays and making sure that no one ever felt left out when someone was getting attention or presents. The family celebrations were usually really nice unless something triggered an "outburst" and I ended up spitting on the cake (to ensure that no one would be able to eat it while I was sent to my room). Of course, my friend would be promptly sent home.

Many times over the years my mom would say to me, "I hope you have a daughter just like you someday."

And I would answer back, "Me too, because that would mean she would be fucking awesome!"

I believe that I was lucky to have suffered. Some people don't realize that in suffering there is great potential, because if you are deprived for any reason... politically, financially, socially or otherwise... and if you set your mind in the right direction, you will find that the only way to survive is for you to excel, by being better so you can be treated better.

—Talal Abu-Ghazaleh

VII

BEING THE YOUNGEST CHILD and the only girl were both good and bad, but I would have to say mostly good. After my brothers were both old enough to have moved out of the house it was much as if I was an only child. In fact, many of my friends thought that I was. By most people's standards I was extremely spoiled and was given not only everything that I needed, but plenty that I didn't need as well.

I shopped with my mom on the weekends, or without my mom but with my dad's credit card when I was old enough to hit the mall alone or with my friends. Oftentimes when my father had to try a case in Germany or attend a conference in Florida, he would take me out of school and my mother and I would go with him on the trip. He figured I would learn more by going to Europe than by sitting in the classroom for the two-week period that I would be gone, and who was I to argue? Almost everything was done for me by my parents, particularly my dad. My whole life I didn't have to problem-solve on my own, and that was a disservice to me later in life. Luckily sports and athletics taught me to overcome obstacles on my own, because without that lesson I probably would have been much worse off than I was, especially after my father passed away and couldn't take care of me anymore.

I swam for the high school varsity team when I was an 8th grader. Oftentimes my dad would help me with my homework, which is to say, he usually did it for me. I remember when my Social Studies teacher, Mrs. Marver (affectionately nicknamed "Mad Dog Marver") assigned the book report project for *The Red Badge of Courage*. Mad Dog was not a teacher you messed around with. She was a short, stout, and hard-shelled disciplinarian who most of the students feared. I'm not sure if the fear she invoked in students had more to do with her stern demeanor, or because even early morning during first period she already sported sweat-stained, yellow-pitted bologna slices under the armpits of her white Oxford shirts, and if you had the misfortune of being seated in the front row of her class, you could be sure to enjoy a coffee-infused saliva shower that could only be avoided if you had a plastic salad bar sneeze guard. If you want to know dead on what Mad Dog looked and sounded like on a daily basis when angered, simply picture a cross between Sam Kinison in mid-act, and the Heat Miser from *The Year Without a Santa Claus*. Clearly this was not a teacher whose shit-list you wanted to be on, but I usually was.

She loved both of my brothers who she had taught before me, and couldn't understand where on Earth I came from or how I could be related to them. Yeah, lady, get in line! The night before the big *Red Badge of Courage* report was due, I was sitting at dinner after swim practice reeking of chlorine and trying to keep my eyes open when it dawned on me that I was supposed to have read some book and then write something about what I read. It was somewhere around 7:00 at night when I told my parents that I was in a bit of a quandary, since I had done neither. My dad wasn't happy about it, but he immediately came to the rescue. I went to bed and my dad stayed up and read the book and then wrote the report for me. He handed the report off to my mom, who got up early in the morning to make my lunch, type the report, put it into a plastic binder, and then hand it all off to me as I bounced out the door to go to school. I got an A-minus on the book report with a little note that said: "Great job! Did you have help?"

There wasn't much that I did on my own, and I think it was assumed by many that I wasn't capable of doing anything by myself. I didn't argue with anyone who thought I needed help and couldn't handle anything on my own. I simply let people do things for me (encouraged it, really) but in my heart underneath the fear, anger, and laissez faire attitude, I knew if I had to, I could accomplish anything I wanted to without anyone's help. If someone else was willing to help me accomplish something when I was younger, I was always willing to let him or her because I liked feeling taken care of and I hated feeling alone and left to my own decisions, thoughts, and fears.

One of my biggest fears was being alone. I couldn't stand it. In grade school and high school I had a lot of really close friends, made even closer from all the years of being on the swim team together, but I still felt lonely, restless, and bored. I needed constant company and stimulation. My friends who had big families with lots of kids and constant action were my favorite ones to visit. There was a feeling of chaos that I found fun and entertaining, but also very comforting. Quiet made me nervous and forced me to be alone with myself and my thoughts, which I didn't like as a kid. I envied my best friend Lisa who had two sisters, one of them a mere year and a half younger than us. They hung out in the same cliques and played the same sports, and they had double the wardrobe of everybody! They were built-in best friends who could go home from parties and talk to each other about everything that happened while they got ready for bed and as they tried to fall asleep, since they shared a bedroom. I always wanted a sister I could talk to, hang out with, and borrow clothes from. I thought it would be awesome to have a twin, but my dad said that the world could only handle one of me.

Because my parents had adopted me at a later stage in their lives, one of the upsides was that my dad was quite settled in his career by the time I came along, and they were able to provide me with a very comfortable lifestyle. The downside was that they were a lot older than any of my friends' parents and were often mistaken for my grandparents, which was more than embarrassing and uncomfortable for me. It really shouldn't have bothered me, but it did – especially because my best friend's mom was gorgeous and looked exactly like Meredith Baxter when she played Elyse Keaton on *Family Ties*. My best friend's father was handsome, super funny, and liked the same music that we liked, which went a long way with me. My parents thought my music was "noise," and neither of them was particularly cool or good-looking by teenager standards, which are always very harsh especially when applied to one's own parents.

I should have been grateful for everything my parents did for me and for all the things that were given to me. I had so much, and not only did I take it for granted, but I don't think I truly appreciated it. I was too busy being mad and selfish about the things I didn't have. I didn't want material items because I mostly already had everything I wanted. I wanted things that they couldn't give me, and that was immature and unfair in retrospect. I wanted them to understand me and to actually get me. I wanted to feel a bond with them that no one could break. (I think I had that bond with my dad, but not so much with my mom.) I wished that I had respect for my mom, and I hated that I didn't. I wished that I had siblings who were closer to me in age and in our relationships. I wanted a sister. I wanted to feel as if I could be left to my own devices and that if I was, I would be okay. I wanted my mom and dad to lose weight and wear cooler clothes. I wanted to stop feeling guilty for everything that happened and for all the mean things I was wishing for behind my parents' backs. I wanted to be a good person and for people to recognize me as one. I wanted to like myself. I was a kid and I wanted the world.

Like all the best families, we have our share of
eccentricities, of impetuous and wayward youngsters,
and of family disagreements.

—Queen Elizabeth II

VIII

HAVING TWO BROTHERS who were quite studious, and who were accepted into every college they applied to, set a very unrealistic example for the crazy and wild younger sister who wanted to "major in fun." By the time my turn came, I was under the impression that you fill out some paperwork and mail it in, and then you get a bunch of letters of acceptance which need to be pored over in an effort to choose where you will attend. This was not so for me. My letters came back in a thin, small envelope and all started in a similar vein that went something like:

"Dear Elizabeth, we regret to inform…"

How could this be? What a rude awakening it was as I began to envision myself at our local community college, unable to escape our town and living next door to Mr. Robertson. I was petrified that I would be doomed to community college. What the hell? I must say, I was shocked. My dad said it had something to do with my grades. Hmmm; go figure. He said that I might be able to get a swimming scholarship or, if not, I would need to find a school that wouldn't give me money to swim, but might push to have me accepted so that I could walk on the team. My parents could afford to pay for my education, and they paid for both of my brothers as well. We were all very fortunate to have a dad who believed it was "his duty" to educate us, and that he could afford to do it.

We found a school that was small, private, expensive, and wanted me on the swim team. I couldn't wait to go. It was my chance to get away from home, to swim on a college swim team, and to get my grades up with the intention of transferring into any school I chose. Mostly I just wanted to swim, party, and meet new guys…but the other stuff sounded good to my parents; so off to Niagara Falls I went.

I'm sure my parents thought they would be seeing me in the news, careening over the Falls in a barrel. They had their doubts that I would ever get into any college, so they were very happy and proud that I would be attending Niagara University. NU is a tiny school with as many undergrads in the entire university as there were kids in my graduating class in high school. There was good and bad to be had in such a small college, but being an athlete there was what kept me grounded, on track, and out of too much trouble. Granted, I did jump out of a moving taxicab during one of my outbursts, and threw fits over various things, including when my Buick Skyhawk broke down in the Burger King drive-through. Of course this happened one night on the way home from the bars, which caused me to call my dad at 3:00 a.m. and yell at him for buying me the worst piece-of-shit car ever. It had to be my *dad's* fault that the car broke down, right? My dad got in his car, drove to Niagara, and made sure my car was taken to a service station and running well for me the following day before calmly driving back to Rochester.

When I chose to go out drinking, I still had swim practice at 5:00 a.m. Having to share a lane with me on the mornings after a long night out was never fun for my teammates. In between sprint sets when everyone is huffing and breathing hard, the smell of alcohol that permeated from my body and my breath was a horribly gross distraction. Looking back on it, though, we had a guy who would fart in between sets (he said it was the sign of a good workout), which *had* to be worse than my distillery breath.

Niagara didn't have a pool on campus, so the swimmers had to drive to the pool and be on deck no later than 5:00 a.m., five days a week. We swam for two hours, and then came back at 4:00 in the afternoon for a second session that included a dry land workout and another hour of swimming. This was the time of day that my party friends, or the girls in the dorms, would put off their studies in order to eat cookie dough, peanut butter, pretzels, and ramen noodles while watching soap operas before dinner and then getting ready to hit the bars for the night.

When you are wet more often than you are dry, and you only have so much time to study in between swim practices and classes, it really forces you to get your work done in the little window of time allotted. This was my saving grace. I went out and I found time to get nuts with the party kids, but I always made it to practice and caught every early morning bus for the away meets – even if one of them got held up with me running on board last-minute still in a dress from the formal I had attended the night before. My breath stank of alcohol, and my coach shook his head at me, angered by my lateness. (During my life I have experienced a lot of head-shaking.) But I had the fastest 50 backstroke time on the women's team and he needed me for the medley relay. Conversely, in my freshman dorm, the girls who had too much time on their hands often didn't get their work done, and many of them flunked out. I was often ridiculed for having to swim all the time and for not going out every night. To be honest, by the time I got to college, I had done my fair share of drinking and didn't feel as though I was missing out on anything by staying in to study. I had already "tarnished the family name" enough times while I was in high school that the appeal to continue tarnishing had worn off.

Telling me that I had tarnished the family name was probably the worst thing my father ever said to me. I was never very sorry for any of the things I did when I got into trouble or angered the adults in my life, but disappointing my father made me feel as if I had just drowned a bag of kittens. There was sadness, shame, and remorse when my dad turned to me and said that I disappointed him or that I had made the family look bad. In his defense, it was a much more effective form of punishment than screaming at me could ever be. I actually enjoyed the screaming matches. It was the calm anger from my father that disturbed me the most.

In high school I was an expert at ruining an adult's idea of a quaint evening. I can remember a few open-air concerts I attended in high school where people brought blankets and wine and cheese, only to have me literally dropping in on them unexpectedly. Nothing screams romantic date night like a strange, drunk teenager rolling around on your blanket. Either I had some whacky aversion to outdoor venues (and allowing any spectators to enjoy them) or I was working on perfecting the art of public drunkenness in hopes of paving the way for Lindsay Lohan. I'm not sure, really. I guess if you get these things out of your system early, you don't partake as heartily when you get to college, or at least not to the degree that the kids who didn't drink in high school were doing it.

I thought college would be more grown-up and mature than it really was, since I had done a lot of the stupid "kid stuff" early on. The time I spent in the dorms made me realize that college wasn't all that different from high school, and actually, in some ways, it was a bit worse in terms of being popular or fitting in. In high school I never thought twice about my weight and at our lunch table I was the one who would eat everyone's food plus my own. I was never on a diet and was really carefree about frivolous things like calorie counting and fat grams. Those things didn't even make my radar.

In college, we all lived together and shared a bathroom, and it was a breeding ground for bulimia and anorexia to the extent that if you weren't puking after your meals, something was wrong with you. Because of the self-dread that I carried around, and the feeling that I should be punished because I was not a good person, it was all too easy for me to be sucked into the world of bulimia. The pretty girls who I befriended, and who everyone wanted to be around, were all binging and purging. Once again, I began to study and judge myself even more harshly than I usually did. It didn't take much for me to get caught up in a vicious cycle of binging and purging because I hated myself, and then hated myself more for binging and purging.

I went to every length to hide it and stopped doing it in the main bathroom. I was embarrassed to have people in the stalls or at the sinks hear me. I didn't wear it like a badge of honor as did other girls who did it in the main bathroom no matter who was in there and listening. I filled a bucket with water and would bring it to my dorm room, when my roommate was gone, with a bag of Oreos, chips, or crackers and do my thing in private. Once I knew the bathroom was clear I would dump the bucket in the toilet and flush away the hate and ugliness I felt for myself as a person. This was an unhealthy pattern of behavior that led to other (more physical) issues: my voice was in a constant state of semi-laryngitis; and I began feeling weak during swim practice.

My first year of college was lived in this dichotomy of treating myself badly and then going to swim practice to be a healthy athlete. I was sad and lonely but no one would have guessed it because I was always the life of the party and hid my self-hatred fairly well. I didn't want to live like this anymore and I knew that it wasn't the way an athlete should treat her body. It was a pattern that was so hard to break no matter how much I wanted to.

At one point it became much more than just thinking I ate too much or that I needed to lose weight. For me it ran much deeper than vanity and was actually more about punishing myself. I really felt that I needed to have bad things happen to me because I didn't deserve anything that was good. Anything that was good in my life would probably just end up in the toilet along with the last meal I ate. Sometimes I would get into my ugly, boxy, blue Buick Skyhawk and go through three or four different drive-throughs, ordering normal amounts of food at each one (so that no one would think I was a pig) and eating it all…just to punish myself. After doing that I felt justified to hate myself even more.

One night I got home from a night of drinking and I remember thinking to myself that I didn't want to be hung over, so I should take an aspirin. I had a bottle of ibuprofen and I can remember standing there holding it and thinking:

"If I take *one* I will avoid a hangover…if I take more than one, I will feel *even better*."

I honestly can't remember my thought process beyond that. I don't honestly know if I was trying to OD, or if I was just so used to binging, or what. But I took the whole bottle and then went to sleep…or passed out, depending on how you look at it. I was awake within the next couple of hours, throwing up violently and feeling as if I would die. My roommate was beyond scared. She thought for sure that I wouldn't make it through the night, but I did. I was in bed all the next day with nothing left to come up but severely yellow bile and some blood. She wanted to take me to the infirmary and begged me to let her. She was so afraid that I would go to sleep that night and never wake up. I begged her to let me ride it out, but she saw how sick I was and she knew what I did when she wasn't around. She was literally scared for my life and ended up dragging me to the infirmary. I had to tell them what I did, and they had to label it as an OD. Because of the OD, I was given the choice of going to see a counselor on campus or getting my parents involved, and possibly being sent home.

I chose the counselor, and began seeing him three times a week. I felt that going to see him (and being forced to do it) was both humiliating and weird. This was my first experience of many with any type of psychotherapy and being forced to talk about my past. My swim coach had to be notified of the situation because my sessions sometimes interfered with swim practice. Surprisingly, my coach was actually extremely empathetic and compassionate towards me, because he had a very serious girlfriend who was also bulimic. He "got it," and he wanted to help me. He was actually much better at helping me than the counselor was. I did my time that I had to do with the counselor, and the sessions were knocked down to once a week, and then eventually I didn't have to go anymore. The counselor was significantly convinced that I wasn't a threat to myself or to others, so the forced sessions were at an end. I was thrilled that I didn't have to go anymore, but continued to binge and barf. It would take a lot more than a few sessions with a dry academic counselor to get through to me.

I was my own worst enemy and I knew that I had to begin the slow work and dedication it would take for me to become my own best friend. It would be an extremely long journey, but at least the recognition was there of what I needed to do. It was much easier said than done and I had many relapses, but over the years I was able to finally overcome my battle with bulimia. Deep inside I had an inner strength that I was able to tap into which came from my love of running and swimming and the fear that if I didn't quit, I might not be able to run or swim anymore. Once again, as I made my way down a risky path, it was athletics that held me back by the scruff. The thought of ruining the one constant and very good thing in my life – the thing that could pull me out of any dark place and put me back on track – was terrifying to me and not an option.

I made the dean's list at Niagara University and not only swam for them, but also played on the tennis team and the rugby team. (It was a very small school and they were hard up for tennis players.) Someone recognized that I was a decent athlete and was able to hold a racquet – mostly the only requirements other than a heartbeat and the willingness to be on the team. I decided to give tennis a try and although I embarrassed myself regularly at the matches, I had a blast travelling and playing on the team. My swim team coach actually let me get out of some of our swim practices so that I could attend tennis matches and some of the tennis practices.

Rugby was also an incredibly cool experience and I liked learning about the game, travelling with the team, and attending the crazy parties. I could have done without some of the bruising and the broken ankle I had one season, but those things come with the territory. As they say: "Be Kind to Animals; Kiss a Rugby Player." Being part of these teams helped me focus on myself in a positive way and gave me purpose and a place to channel my negative energies.

By the end of my freshman year my friends had tired of constantly waiting for me to get home from practice before we could leave for dinner or go to the bars. I noticed that the girlfriends I made were more than happy to have me around when it came to borrowing my clothes, but not quite as happy to be in my presence when boys paid attention to me at parties or in the dining hall. I was really outgoing and quite honestly, fairly promiscuous, so it wasn't that tough to get attention from the opposite sex. Since I had always been a jock and had lots of guy friends, talking to guys I didn't know didn't intimidate me at all. I also wasn't horrible to look at in college, and all of these things put together were a recipe for success when it came to meeting guys and a recipe for disaster with the girls I thought were my friends who really weren't. Our little group of girls did everything together (except none of them was on the swim team or athletic in any way) and made plans after freshman year to move off-campus together into a house.

I was so happy and couldn't wait to move into the house where I imagined my best college memories would be formed. I could already picture the fun we would have decorating each of the rooms, and the many parties and dinners we would have there. It would be my chance to feel as if I had sisters who I could always depend on, and talk to late at night when we got home from studying or from dates or parties. I couldn't believe that I was actually going to forge lifelong friendships with the sisters I never had, and I would never have to be alone.

Two weeks before school started, when we were getting ready to move into the house, the other girls sat me down in the living room, where I had envisioned our bonding and heart-to-hearts would take place, and broke the news that they didn't want me to move in with them. They rubbed salt into my wounds by explaining that they all felt that I thought the world revolved around me, and that they didn't like having to wait for me or make allowances for me just because I was a swimmer. They also pointed out that I was spoiled and that my "daddy" did everything for me. They didn't want me in the house and they didn't want me around anymore. I was reeling in the harsh reality that instead of discussing what color our matching comforters would be, my heart was being crushed. My throat instantly grew a lump the size of a grapefruit. The pain I felt went beyond sadness – it was a cut so deep that you could see raw bone. This was honestly the last thing I had expected; but Rejection reared its ugly head and reminded me that I didn't deserve the good things that other people did. Betrayal (always Rejection's trusty sidekick) told me in no uncertain terms that I wasn't worth having around; no one would ever love me; and I would never be good enough for anyone.

When I started at Niagara the initial plan had been to get my grades up so that I could transfer schools. After the slap in the face I had been dealt by people I thought were my friends, my focus became even stronger that I would stay on track and move on. I had to scramble to find a last-minute roommate and a place to live, which landed me back in the dorms. I made new friends and became even more serious about my classes. I also kept a wall around my heart that wasn't going to come down as easily as it did the last time.

Making the dean's list and all my athletic endeavors at Niagara University gave me the chance to basically pick what school I wanted to go to when it was time to transfer after sophomore year. A good friend of mine from my high school swam for American University in Washington, D.C., and after visiting her, meeting the coach, applying, and being accepted, it seemed to be a no-brainer that

American was where I would finish my remaining college career.

Leave it to my oldest brother, Dave, to pose a challenge that changed everything. Dave said I should apply to Miami University because it was a great school and considered by many the "Harvard of the Midwest." He also said I probably wouldn't get in. I had never heard of Miami University before, and had no idea that it was actually in a little town called Oxford, Ohio. So, Miami (which isn't in Florida) and Oxford (which isn't in England) were a challenge that had been posed at the last minute that I couldn't refuse to accept. I applied *and* I got accepted! Miami was the school I chose, but it wasn't the "in your face, bro" that made me want to go there. It was my visit to Miami's campus that clinched it. Dave was living in Cleveland at the time and offered to take me to visit the campus.

Once we drove down the long road lined with farms and corn fields, and pulled into the expanse of green lawns, brick buildings, and big white columns that make up what I felt was the epitome of a college campus, I was hooked. We walked through the quads and all over the campus, and in a cute bonding moment with my brother, he stopped, turned to me, and asked me, "Can you see yourself going to school here?"

The answer was a resounding *yes*!

When I was 8 years old I visited my brother at the University of Virginia and I remember thinking how beautiful it was, even as a little kid. I recognized that it was a great place to be and that my big brother was someone important for being there. Miami University's campus made me feel as I did during that visit to UVA. Not only could I see myself at Miami, but the mental picture also came with a sense of pride. Bye-bye American; hello Miami.

I learned that I couldn't be on the swim team at Miami because of a Division 1 rule that you must "sit" and cannot compete for an entire year after transferring from one Division 1 school to another. Apparently this keeps coaches from recruiting athletes out of other schools. I sat for the year and by the following year, as a senior, I wasn't about to go back to two-a-day workouts and wet hair 24/7. Instead I joined a few club teams, including the lacrosse team and a running club called the Miami Striders. These teams were my therapy without having to go to therapy. The club teams were invaluable for me when I was at Miami, were a great break from school, and helped to take my mind off of negative things. They helped me regain my lost confidence from what had happened at Niagara as well as helped me begin to build a little much-needed self-esteem. I began to hate myself even more deeply than ever for the bulimia and feeling so out of control, and decided one day after throwing up in the toilet and crying in front of the mirror, that I couldn't live my life like this any longer. I stared long and hard into my watery bloodshot eyes and made up my mind not to do it anymore. Ever. I would quit cold turkey and that would be it. I had one or two relapses, and then never did it again. If my love of being an athlete, and all the good that sports brought to my life, wasn't so strong (in turn making me strong too) I would probably still be bulimic today. I wouldn't allow myself to treat my body that way any longer, and that is completely due to the healing powers of running, biking, and swimming; I never wanted to be incapable of doing those things!

This is one of the biggest reasons the *Girls With Sole* programs are so important for girls who have experienced abuse or trauma. They need someone to introduce them to the mind, body, and soul connection.

Once they "get it" they won't ever let it go. But someone needs to show them the way there.

It was at Miami University that I really put together the strong connection between mind and body and how this connection can help a person to push harder; go farther; and overcome obstacles. While at Miami University I tapped into my love for long bike rides and long trail runs. I loved to get on my bike and see how far I could ride it on the never-ending country roads, and I drove out to Hueston Woods State Park to run the trails. I liked that I could say that I rode my bike to Indiana and back. (It wasn't really that big of a deal since we were on the border of Indiana, but I liked feeling like it was.) When I took my car to Hueston Woods to go for a run, I would bask in the healing powers of being at one with the nature that surrounded me. I felt as if I was the only person on the planet when I was in those woods, and thrived on the feeling that I alone had the power that dictated how far I could push myself to go. It was a way to find myself while getting lost in the beauty of the woods.

For most of the time that I was at MU I dated a guy named Tim who believed that doing acid and mushrooms (or any drugs) was a religious experience. It wasn't hard for him to get me into the scene. I never liked smoking pot, and I was afraid to try coke, but hallucinogenic drugs sounded as if they could be just right for me.

I learned after partaking enough times that I didn't "worship" at the same "altar" as Tim – nor did I want to. Once you get a true sense of what the neurochemicals such as endorphins, dopamine, serotonin, and epinephrine can do for you, you quickly realize that feeling out of control isn't as good as you thought it would be. The "running drugs" are capable of bringing feelings of clarity, control, power, and pain relief and they are completely natural, healthy, and legal. Running alone in the woods gave me a chance to take care of mental housecleaning and it was an organic way for me to feel strong and purposeful.

I started to become focused on what my body could do instead of what it looked like. It was me, the woods, and my body. No one could do it for me, and no one could take the joy it brought away from me. I felt a Bohemian type of freedom that I wanted to experience all over the world; not just in Hueston Woods. I began to wish that I was done with school, and the time I spent in class, and not on the trails, made me resent school more and more. I was impetuous and extremely restless. I hated being in that stage between a kid and an adult.

I wanted to rebel against the real world of working and responsibility. Embracing my inner earthy crunchy granola Dead Head, I told myself that I didn't need money or material objects and could find work as a nanny or maybe just live on a beach somewhere and not worry about the material trappings of modern society. So what if I loved Ben & Jerry's, nice clothes, and material stuff; I could get over it. At the end of my second year there, when I was only a few months away from graduation, I called my dad out of the blue and told him I was going to quit school and go to Australia or California. I told him that I just felt as though I needed to get out of there, and there was no need for me to finish. My dad stayed calmer than I thought he would at the news that I was about to quit school to travel the world, but he had a tone to his voice that hit me harder than a wrecking ball when he said through clenched teeth and with a slight note of despair in his voice, "You are going to stay in school and get that sheepskin. You are almost done and it is beyond silly to quit now. Once you get that sheepskin, no one can ever take it away from you and you can go to *Timbuktu for all I care!*"

I stayed and I graduated. I never made it to Timbuktu, but I have travelled to many other places, and had many incredible life experiences, and I must admit that my dad was right. I don't regret having the degree that I earned at Miami University, and it is now one more accomplishment that no one can take from me. My dad was always there for me and he never steered me wrong.

I have come to accept the feeling of not knowing where I am going. And I have trained myself to love it. Because it is only when we are suspended in mid-air with no landing in sight, that we force our wings to unravel and alas begin our flight. And as we fly, we still may not know where we are going to. But the miracle is in the unfolding of the wings. You may not know where you're going, but you know that so long as you spread your wings, the winds will carry you.

—C. JoyBell C.

IX

THIS WILL COME as a huge shock and surprise for many, I'm sure, but when I graduated from Miami University, I didn't have a job all lined up and waiting for me.

I tried to attend the on-campus interviews and gave my best shot at impersonating the perfect Miami student by donning a navy blue power suit and waiting in line, with resume in hand, to speak to the "Powers That Be" at Proctor & Gamble, among other companies, who were looking for fresh-faced young meat for their corporate sausage grinders. Back then it just wasn't my time to shine. I wasn't ready to be put under a microscope. I wasn't capable of having a panel of interviewers and recruiters scrutinize and judge me, and then hold me up and compare me to my better, smarter, and more Eddie Haskell-esque peers. I went to one interview – and failed miserably. How was I supposed to know where I would like to see myself in five years or what my greatest weakness was. I also had no idea why they should hire me; wasn't that something that should be determined by *them*? (Why should I do their work for them?)

Needless to say, it was not in my cards to work at P&G and I couldn't help but feel that it was a personal reflection on me – an outright rejection resulting from a panel of intelligent and smartly dressed corporate types who saw right through me and knew from the moment I sat down that I wouldn't cut the mustard (not even honey mustard-flavored Pringles; a not-so-popular P&G product).

I didn't seem to have a plan and I lacked direction. By most people's standards I was going to lose in the game of life. I had been told this in so many words and so many ways by relatives, Girl Scout leaders, teachers and high school guidance counselors, fiancés, and therapists. The majority of the time I was in full agreement with them.

So, when my parents' dear family friend Winston Konner asked my father if I had a job after graduation (after the belly laughing subsided) my father got himself back together and answered him with the obvious, "No!"

Winston was more than happy to give me both the experience of working in his patent law office in Munich, Germany, and the chance to travel while making a little money to do it. He had a rent-free apartment in Munich that I could share with a young lawyer who worked in his office, named Hans, and a bike I could ride when I didn't take the streetcar or subway. When my dad told me about Winston's offer I jumped out of my skin at the chance to live in Europe and experience it on my own. It didn't occur to me in the least to be the slightest bit scared or nervous. This was long before the movie *Taken* with Liam Neeson came out, and I couldn't wait to go to Germany and start meeting strangers who might possibly change my life forever – in a good way!

Living in Europe helped to open my mind even further when it came to the differences in others, and it expanded my ability to embrace and accept strange cultures.

Recently one of my best friends, Tricia, gave me a card with a quote on the front by J.R.R. Tolkien that said, "Not all who wander are lost."

Inside the card, my friend wrote:

"Dear Liz, To someone who wandered and found everything she was looking for – and then some! Just think of the poor saps who never wandered in the world. Who stayed put without risk. Not you Liz. Not you! I'm cheering you on and find myself so fortunate to have such a great friend."

My dear friend, Tricia, is an extremely intelligent, kind-hearted, and wonderful woman and friend. I don't know where I would be without her and all of our laughs, tears, and laps in the swimming pools of Cleveland, Ohio. We will be rolling each other into the pool area when we are in our 90s – on Scooter Walkers and wheelchairs – to get our swimming in together.

So many times people are given great opportunities, but they are afraid to accept them (or to see them for how great they are) because those opportunities aren't what "everyone" *thinks* they should be doing. At that time of my life everyone thought I should be entering the "real world" of office cubicles and fluorescent lighting with a briefcase in hand and an eagerness to hike up my suit skirt in order to begin the climb up the corporate ladder. Back then, *flouncing* around Europe was not as common for a college grad as it is today, at least not among anyone I knew. A lot of my friends and family were shocked that I wasn't terrified to have to do things on my own in a place so far away from home, where I didn't speak the language or have a set group of friends to hang out with.

I couldn't wait to leave.

I graduated in January of 1991 and was in Germany before February 1st. I truly felt as though I understood the expression, "The world is my oyster," as I flew to Munich to embark on a new adventure that could literally take me anywhere. I began working in the law offices of Konner and Meyer immediately upon arrival. The firm did work with some very big companies in the U.S., Germany, and Japan. I was basically an office assistant who handled the correspondence with clients in Japan and the United States, all of which was done in English. It felt odd sitting in a quaint office in Munich, Germany, typing letters to American companies such as Caterpillar Inc., Eaton Corporation, and Rockwell International. If I had been offered the same position in the States, I wouldn't have been half as excited to take it and probably wouldn't have. Where was the adventure in that?

I also drafted patent contracts from dictation that were then sent to the clients as well as to the European Patent Office. I learned how to review intellectual property claims and their translations before filing them at the E.P.O. Quite often the language of the letter had to be revised numerous times in order to make the client's project inventive. It was my job to review the previous claims, make the revisions, and file them so that a patent could be granted in the designated European countries. It was incredible to me that a file could be over 100 pages long, and all of it was to describe the inventive properties of *one* flange or a connecting tube in an entire Caterpillar tractor. It's rather eerie in a way that as I typed those letters, I had no idea or foresight that one day I would start an organization and its logo and tagline would be Nationally Registered Trademarks in the United States Patent and Trademark Office.

Upon arrival in Europe I wanted to immerse myself in the culture and feel as if I instantly belonged. That didn't happen right away, but I still managed to have the time of my life. My new German roomie was Hans, and his bedroom was separated from mine by a fabric curtain. The apartment was amazing, considering I paid zero rent and it was in the heart of Munich, situated around the corner from the famed Glockenspiel (clock tower).

If I were the type who looked a gift horse in the mouth, I might complain that it was the size of a shoe box, which made it rather awkward when Hans made his Nutella toast and tea in the morning wearing nothing but the tiniest briefs that were smaller than my Wonder Woman Underoos from when I was in first grade. I knew my presence irritated him too, like an itch on the bottom of your foot that you can't get to because you are wearing shoes. He wanted to find a ruler or a pencil or something that he could stick in his shoe to get rid of the itch so everything would be back to normal as it was before. He knew I was a close family friend of Winston's and that he, like I, was not paying to live in the awesome apartment. Hans had a great thing going in the law firm as well, and wasn't going to do anything that might jeopardize his position there such as complain about Winston's American "relative," so he put up with me but would have preferred that I wasn't there. Soon enough, he got his wish, and then he only had to see me during office hours on the days we were actually there at the same time.

Another "first thing" I did when I got to Munich, almost as soon as I unpacked, was to begin my search for a gym I could join and work out in. There weren't as many gyms to choose from over there as I would have thought, and it was funny to me that many of my co-workers thought I was a "crazy American" for wanting to jump around and sweat inside a building as a way of getting exercise. As is common in Europe, and not so much in America, the people that I worked with walked and rode their bikes everywhere they went. They only bought food from various markets in amounts that could be carried in a backpack, and in their eyes to get on a treadmill or run around in the street was as foreign a concept as I seemed to be. I knew that there had to be people who worked out in a gym, and finally found one that matched what I was used to at home. It was called My Sport Lady and was an all-female gym that had every amenity and aerobic machine or class that I could expect here in the States except for a swimming pool. I was so excited and joined right away. Of course, Winston paid for my membership and was happy that I found a place to drink carrot juice and do weird American Jane Fonda-type activities that he knew I loved so much, but also had no comprehension of whatsoever. He just knew it made me happy and more "at home," and he truly wanted me to have the best experience possible while "in his care."

I went to the gym every single day, usually after work. It didn't take long before I was considered a regular and everyone who worked there got to know me and we began to form friendships. One of the best friendships I made while I lived there was an aerobics instructor and personal trainer at My Sport Lady named Claudia. She and I hit it off right away and she shared my love of running and setting goals that seemed just slightly out of reach – literally, since she introduced me to the sport of climbing. I had never climbed in my life, but quickly learned to love it while living in Germany. Claudia and I would ride our bikes to an outdoor climbing wall almost daily once the weather got nice and she taught me about climbing techniques and gear that I knew nothing about, such as bouldering, belaying, chalk bags, carabiners, overhangs, monkey toes, and other basics that everyone at the wall seemed to know but me. It was a whole new sport and culture and I loved it. We would stay at the wall for hours, and then go out for dinner, or she would invite me to her apartment to hang out with her and her boyfriend, Ingo. They were both really awesome people and had such an open and giving spirit which made us all fast friends. We began doing everything together, including camping and climbing up in the mountains, and having dinners and parties with their friends at their apartment.

She and I told each other everything and bonded while running together, riding our bikes, and climbing. She knew that I wasn't comfortable living with Hans, so she and Ingo said that I should move in with them. I was over there all the time anyway, and they had a spare bedroom. They didn't have to ask me twice and by the next day I had a futon mattress on the floor and my clothes moved into the spare room of their apartment. I loved it! We were like a little family, and had so much in common with our love for fitness, our senses of humor, and how we viewed life. Soon after I moved in with them, Claudia asked me if I wanted to start teaching aerobics classes at My Sport Lady, as I was at the club every day anyway. I was so excited, because I was dying to get some real experience as an instructor. She cleared it with the management to pay me under the table and I was dubbed the "U.S. Guest Instructor." This was a high compliment because unlike the world of fashion, in the world of fitness, Europe is a few steps behind us. The latest in the fitness industry at that time was Step Aerobics, which we had been doing for years at home, but in Germany it was brand-new. To them I was an expert, and most of them assumed I was from Los Angeles or New York City, or somewhere very glamorous (from a fitness standpoint). In actuality I had never taught a class in my life, but I took so many of them I knew I could "fake it to make it."

I was put on the aerobics schedule and built up an amazing following. Instantly I was hooked by the energy of instructing the class, and couldn't get enough. I began attending aerobics certification classes on the weekends and learned how to conduct Funk Aerobics classes, High and Low Impact Aerobics, as well as Step. It was an awesome learning experience and so much fun to feel as though I was an accomplished instructor. Claudia was also one of the Corporate Fitness Instructors at Siemens Corporation, and I filled in for her there whenever she had a scheduling conflict. I was brand-new to the scene, but was already working in a corporate fitness center of a major corporation, and in one of Munich's top fitness clubs.

This was what I wanted to do. Sitting at a desk was not for me, but if I needed to do it for a few hours a day, I could suffer through it until I could get to the good stuff.

While in Europe, to lie out in the sun topless was something that I felt I needed to do if I was truly immersing myself in the culture of my surroundings. Every time I did it, whether in Germany or the Canary Islands, people would approach me thinking I was either German or Swiss and begin rattling off to me in German. The minute I opened my mouth to explain that I was American and didn't really understand them, they were astonished that I was from America; because of that they were also surprised that I was doing the topless thing. I don't see what the big deal was. Americans can be really prudish by European standards, but I liked the idea of doing something that I couldn't get away with at home. Some of the people I spoke to ended up telling me that it wasn't that surprising to them that I was from the U.S. and going topless. The shocking part was that I was from the U.S. and I wasn't 300 pounds. Many of the people I met think that a small percentage of Americans look like Hollywood movie stars and the rest are grossly obese. (A visit to most shopping malls or grocery stores across the United States would most likely show that they weren't really that far off.)

Being a resident in a foreign country for an extended period of time is such a different experience from visiting during a week's vacation. It was incredible at times to really feel as though I lived there, and other times I missed the good old U.S.A. I learned quickly that many of the conveniences I was used to in America were nonexistent in Germany. It seemed that I was always behind the eight ball when trying to acquire food. It didn't seem to matter if I was looking to get it in a grocery, small café, or specialty shop; they were always closed when I got there! Shops were closed by 6:00 p.m. during the week, by noon on Saturday, and didn't open at all on Sundays. Many of the cafés were closed on the weekends as well, and there always seemed to be some religious holiday – that fell on a Monday, that I didn't know existed – which meant everything was closed and you were shit out of luck for food until Tuesday. I really have no need to go to the grocery store at 3:00 a.m., but there is certainly a comfort in knowing that you can if you want to, here in the States, that I didn't notice until I moved to Europe. Maybe that is why we have so many oversized people here. Our stores, meals, and therefore, our humans are all super-sized, and we have access to the meals and stores around the clock. I have to admit I missed America and loved Europe equally. It was a strange dichotomy.

I recall meeting a guy through a friend of mine who asked me if I wanted to go out with him. He seemed nice enough, and I was still fairly new to town, so I accepted the date. He took me to a concert celebrating the 200th anniversary of Mozart's death. We got a glass of wine and milled around the elegant and beautiful concert hall before settling down in our seats. Because I didn't know my date very well and I could tell that he was a little more, how shall I say, uptight, than the guys I was used to dating, I did my best to conjure up polite conversation. I decided to go with something very neutral regarding the concert itself and expressed that I didn't realize Mozart had been dead for 200 years already. He quipped, "Of course you didn't. You are American. You have no culture. Your culture is McDonald's."

Then Mr. Suave went on to say, "You must be very happy that we have a McDonald's in Munich."

I told him I probably wouldn't be eating at McDonald's while in Germany, as I didn't even eat there at home; however, I had noticed that there was always a very long line of people at the Munich McDonald's every time I walked past it, and I couldn't imagine that all of those people were Americans. (In my head I was thinking that this dude clearly did not want to get laid.) Thank God not *all* of the men I dated while in Germany had a lack of couth and a stick up their ass.

Munich is a really beautiful, clean, and classy metropolitan city that I enjoyed living in very much. It was so cool when I finally learned my way around and could ride my bike everywhere I went. Shopping was a ton of fun and I found myself in envy of the Europeans and their flair for style. No matter how hard I tried, it was something I couldn't duplicate and they seemed to have it down effortlessly.

I loved touring around and hitting the shops for fashions that I could never find at home. I truly had the best of both worlds when I was working for Winston, because I was earning a little bit of money and living with no expenses, and he fully encouraged me to travel and experience as much of Europe while I was there as I possibly could. Oftentimes he would even pay for me to go somewhere that I wanted to visit and see. This gave me a disposable income that I never had before and will probably never have again. (Yes, people ask me all the time why I ever left Germany!)

During one of my shopping trips I came across the grand opening of a Patagonia store. Usually I only wanted to visit shops that carried brands I couldn't get at home, but with my new interest in climbing, and because we didn't have a Patagonia shop in Cleveland, I went in to check it out. The store was incredible and beautiful, and as luck would have it, the American guy working there was as well. There is always an initial gleam of excitement that goes along with coming across another person from the States when you are living abroad. It's exciting to be from the same country, speak the same language, and know each other's cultures. You can't help but bond with a stranger, if only momentarily, when two Americans meet in a foreign land. I've even seen it when travelling in the U.S. People on vacation in Florida are psyched out of their minds when they run into a couple of strangers who are also from Ohio or Indiana or New York. It must be human nature to want to belong and to know where someone is "coming from."

We chatted for a while and I learned that his name was Timothy, but most people called him "T," and that he was from California. He travelled to various places in Europe to open new Patagonia retail locations and ensure that the stores and staff were up and running properly. He was 10 years older than I was but handsome, active, and fit. I took my time browsing, and of course, buying some of the Patagonia active wear, and realized that there was a spark between us that went beyond that first exciting exchange of "Where are you from?!"

He and I exchanged numbers and went out to dinner as a first date and eventually started seeing each other very regularly. We had a lot in common and both loved athletics and outdoor sports. We had a ton of fun just being together listening to music, drinking coffee, or going out, and the sex was amazingly hot. The difference in our ages was rarely an issue, and only because I was a lot sillier and much goofier than he was personality-wise, but that was one of the things he loved about me. He treated me like an absolute queen and at first I truly loved the attention he showered on me.

I still spent a lot of time working out with Claudia and hanging out with her, but I slept at T's apartment every night. At first we did the whole "drawer" thing, and I went back and forth with my stuff quite a bit, until he asked me to move in with him. I was so excited and also flattered in a little-girl-wanting-to-play-house way. I was young and immature, and although I thought I was taking it seriously at the time, I know now that I wasn't thinking of living together as the first step to something much more serious – at least, not in the same way that Timothy was. Things were great and fun during the "honeymoon" period, but my usual restlessness crept back in and began to make trouble in paradise.

I was hanging out a lot in the Patagonia store while T was there, and got to know his co-workers very well. One of them in particular was a black-haired, blue-eyed Peruvian German named Adler. His dad was from Peru and his mom hailed from Germany. Adler was only 5 years my senior and was very silly and funny and charming. Oh, and by the way, he was freaking gorgeous! His English, as with just about everyone I met over there, was perfect and the banter between us was nonstop and left my stomach muscles sore from all the belly laughing. Adler was in training for the Munich Marathon and he and I began running together.

Things with T were beginning to get too serious. He wanted to get married and have me move to California with him, which probably would have been great had I met him at least ten years into the future. At that time in my life, marriage was the last thing on my mind. I wanted love, and I wanted children…but that was "someday." I also had a huge problem with anyone who adored me that much. Once I detected his adoration in all of its sincerity, there was a direct translation in my mind that there was something innately wrong with the man, and we were instantly on borrowed time. When I went into this mode of thinking I had no idea how much time was left, only that it was limited, and even shorter if there was a hot olive skinned man with thick black hair, an athletic body, and piercing blue eyes hot on my tail.

My time with Adler, running and laughing all the time, further magnified my feelings of suffocation with Timothy. It wasn't really his fault, but I wanted to get out and move on. (And I knew full well that "moving on" really meant *me* moving *on* Adler!) Adler and I started to talk about the way we felt about each other, which entailed a very strong "like" reinforced with an even stronger "lust" on both of our parts. Neither of us wanted to tell T that I wanted to break up with him, and that I also wanted to jump Adler's bones, because he was Adler's boss; and I was too much of a coward to tell him I wanted to move out. It was much easier for me to run away, or cause a big scene over something and use that as an excuse to run away, but T never did anything wrong, making it impossible for me to start a fight. Instead I took the weasel way out and moved out of T's apartment the day he left for Paris on a three-day business trip. I didn't leave a note explaining why I had left, nor had I given any indication whatsoever that I would be gone when he came back. It was a horrible thing to do and I am not proud of it. Luckily, Claudia, Ingo, and I were all still friends, and although they both shook their heads at me in unison over the whole affair, they welcomed me back into their apartment.

Just when it seemed I couldn't be any bigger of an asshole, I promptly jumped into bed with Adler. He kept me a secret from T, who still had no idea why I left him. Timothy tried calling me at Claudia's place, and even stopped in at the law firm, but I wouldn't talk to him. God, I was a horrid creature!

In the meantime I was starting to realize that Adler and I were trouble together. We were both incredibly passionate and hot-headed people who did everything to the extreme. We ran together and had marathon sex sessions together. We laughed hard and fought hard, the few times we argued. I liked the fiery fierceness of it all. Mostly we were just very silly and I liked that as well.

Adler created a name for the two of us together, formally dubbing and referring to us as "The Monsters." I have a photo of the two of us that his mother took one night after having dinner in Adler's apartment. He has his arm around me and we are both smiling with big toothy grins. He had the picture enlarged to an 8x10 and on the back he wrote, "The Monsters 1992." Not long after he gave me that picture, I began to want to run away from him as well. We had so much fun together and the sex remained amazing, but now and then the forcefulness of it startled me. I wasn't scared of him, and he was never abusive, but he liked to get a little rough at times in ways that didn't jibe with me. Sometimes he would hold my arms behind my back a little too long, or he would hold me down from behind just long enough to freak me out. He always stopped when I asked him to, but I guess I didn't like having to ask. I was able to talk to him about what I liked and disliked sexually, but one night he threw me for a loop by saying that he wanted to get me pregnant. I had noticed there were a lot of couples in Europe who intentionally had babies together but never married. That was not *at all* on my agenda, but Adler really wanted to have little "monsters" with me. At first I thought he was kidding, but he was dead serious. He went on to say that if I did get pregnant we would move to Peru and raise the baby there because that was where his family all lived. Crap! What had I fallen into this time? I wasn't on birth control pills, and this guy was actually trying to knock me up. This was a new one for the record books, and although I didn't want to let go of him so quickly, it was Auf Wiedersehen Adler.

After breaking up with Adler I went out with a couple of Wolfgangs. You can't swing a dead cat in Germany without hitting a guy named Wolfgang. I didn't move in with any of them, and we had fun – climbing, running, camping, and hanging out together – but nothing too serious beyond that. I did learn while living in Germany that I prefer a circumcised penis to an uncircumcised one. I guess the turtleneck is OK, but if I had my choice, I would go without it.

During all of these relationships I also kept in touch with a close friend from home named Mick who was living in Amman, Jordan, teaching English in a U.S. Embassy school. He and I grew up in the same neighborhood and had been good friends ever since I cheered for his CYO basketball team in 7th grade. To get to his house all I had to do was cut through my back yard. He was funny and popular, and we hung out as friends in 7th and 8th grade and all the way through our high school years. We didn't really keep in touch when we first went away to different colleges, until we came home for Christmas break one year and met up at a party. He was home from Duke and I was in my last year or so at Miami. As we had always been very good friends, and we both found each other to be very attractive, it only made sense to us that we would make a great couple. During the extended Christmas vacation from school we began dating and became inseparable. We knew the distance thing would be a huge issue, so we kept a semi-committed relationship going when we went back to school that continued on even after we graduated and both ended up overseas after college. One of the best parts of my time in Germany was when Mick came to visit me and he and I travelled around together for two weeks. At times we fought like cats and dogs over stupid things, mainly because of the way I used to get when I began to feel smothered (and it did not take much for me to get there), but it was an experience of a lifetime that I still treasure today.

Mick made his way from the Middle East to Munich to embark on the unofficially official Irondequoit European Tour. He used to sing the LL Cool J song, "(I need an) Around the Way Girl." But he changed it to the name of our hometown and sang, "I need an Irondequoit girl." I liked when he did that. We were best friends turned lovers and testing it out for real in Europe. People wrote books and movies about this type of shit and I was about to live it! Upon his arrival in the Munich Bahnhof we wanted to see absolutely everything we could during our travels, soaking up the experience like a sponge. We wanted to do everything there was to do (that we could afford…which wasn't that much) in every city we visited.

I showed him all the touristy sights of Munich, and we even made a trip out to Dachau to see the old concentration camp. It isn't the cheeriest thing to do but we wanted to experience all that Europe had to offer, including the good and the bad. We figured it would be a meaningful journey into a place that would be both sobering and eye-opening for us. It was all that and more. The day was cold and windy, with skies the color of steel and gun metal. The weather conditions actually heightened the already emotional experience. We could almost imagine (almost) what it would be like to have been there. The things I had endured in my life were nothing compared to what the prisoners of this camp had endured. Being there made us appreciate how good our lives really were, and that we should never take our freedom for granted. It was an emotionally charged day, but a worthwhile experience.

Mick and I both had backpacks that were stuffed with a couple of shirts, sweaters, and a change of jeans. In mine I also had a baseball hat, a toothbrush and toothpaste, and a huge handful of tampons thrown in for good measure. We travelled as barebones as we could. Because of a lack of extensive funds we had no plans to do anything that would require nice or "dressy" clothes. I did, however, make sure I had room for my running shoes and at least one set of running clothes. I never go anywhere without my running shoes. Our first stop was in Nurnberg to visit my Tante Uschi and some other relatives on my mom's side of the family. Tante Uschi is my aunt; Uschi is her first name. My Tante Uschi barely speaks English so a lot of the time spent with her was dotted by head shaking, big smiles, and hand gestures. Luckily my cousin Carina speaks perfect English, and she helped us communicate with everyone as we toured the historical city.

We were extremely well-fed while staying with my aunt. It seemed like a never-ending stream of meals, "tea times," and drinks followed by after-dinner and dessert drinks as well. Tortes and fresh whipping cream around a little table in my aunt's living room took over our long afternoons, and left no room for running. It would have been rude for us to skip afternoon tea for any reason, let alone running, so we skipped running instead, sat with my relatives, and ate all day. Mick and I really appreciated their hospitality but neither of us liked the way we felt. We weren't used to that type of inactive entertainment. We started arguing over silly things because I was getting cranky from not working out, but Mick was much more easygoing about it than I was. Our next stop would be in Paris, where I made him promise me we would find a gym to work out in before I went out of my head.

Some of my friends in Munich told us that we could save money if we avoided using the train for transportation, but instead used the "ride board" services that almost every city had. It was actually a faster and much cheaper way to get around so we were all over it. All you had to do was go into one of the little ride board shops which was basically one room with scraps of paper and phone numbers pinned to the walls, organized by destinations and dates of travel. After you located someone on the wall who was planning to drive his or her car to the same place you wanted to go, you paid the "agency" to give you that person's name and phone number, which was usually written on a scrap of paper like a number you might get from someone you picked up in a bar. After you got the number it was up to you to contact the person, set up a place and a time to meet, and share the trip in his or her car, splitting the cost of gas and any other travel-related expenses. The woman we caught a ride with to Paris was a punk rocker who looked like a combination of Annie Lennox from her Eurythmics days mixed with Courtney Love.

We had plans to stay with two friends of Mick's from Duke. They were a really cute couple who dated in college and moved to Paris together after they graduated (ah, to be young, in love, and a trust fund baby). They had an apartment in Paris and welcomed us to stay with them for the five days that we planned to be there, along with three of their other friends who were also visiting from the States. Mick and I knew that his friends would be out of town for the first two nights we were in Paris, so we were on our own until they got back. The "Annie Love" woman behind the wheel offered to have us spend the night in her apartment. We weren't going to arrive until late at night anyway, and she didn't mind if we crashed there. She was rather odd but harmless, and although her apartment was rather dark and scary, it was free and the floor was comfortable. It only had two tiny "rooms" and it was decorated with ripped-out pages from magazines. Her English was pretty good, but she started every sentence with the phrase, "It isn't funny."

So things became really funny when she said things like, "It isn't funny when you have to go to the bathroom." Or "It isn't funny when the bar closes and you have nowhere to go." And "It isn't funny to sneeze when you get your hair cut."

Mick and I smiled and agreed with whatever she said wasn't funny (all the while finding it to be very funny), but we decided it would be best if we slept in a youth hostel the second night.

We didn't have a lot of money, so we got baguettes, wine, and cheese and walked around in awe of the gorgeous City of Lights on the second day we were there. It was easy to take up an entire day taking in the incredible sights and city streets. As we had sworn we would do while stuffing ourselves in Germany, we found a phone book and tried to locate addresses for gyms or fitness centers. We found one, so we wrote down the address and eagerly sought it out. The address took us to a very old building that seemed to combine some apartment housing with a few offices. We cautiously made our way up the old, narrow staircase and found the door we were seeking. We stopped and looked at each other in a way that confirmed we were both on the same page. There was no way that a full-blown fitness facility could fit into the space behind the tiny worn wooden door before us, but our curiosity had been piqued, so we had to go inside and see for ourselves. The "gym" was one room, dusty, and empty, aside from the man who opened the door and a large wooden table with whacky old cables and rings attached to it. We told the guy we had the wrong address and ran down the stairs laughing our asses off. Instead of finding a gym, we opted for an outdoor run through some beautiful Parisian parks.

In the hostel that night we were separated by men's and women's bunks, so we couldn't sleep in the same room. Neither of us really cared about that as we weren't in the room for anything more than a few hours of sleep. The small room was cold and sterile and was only big enough for its two sets of bunk beds, all of which were occupied. I had the top bunk and slept in my clothes. The other bunks were taken by three lesbians who were travelling together from Germany. They were nice and wanted to know why I was alone. I told them that I wasn't alone, and that my boyfriend was in the men's bunk. They just looked at me strangely and shrugged, and we all laughed nervously.

The next morning Mick and I had breakfast in the large cafeteria of the hostel and then hit the streets of Paris. I couldn't believe a youth hostel would have such amazing café lattes. Only in Paris. During the days that we spent visiting his friends, we did all the usual things such as visit the Eiffel Tower; the Arc de Triomphe; the Notre Dame Cathedral; the Musée d'Art Moderne (where I got in big trouble for snapping a photograph of a famous Matisse painting); and the Louvre Museum, so we could see the Mona Lisa. I couldn't believe how small the painting was; I was picturing something much more grandiose, and with a lot less Plexiglas surrounding it.

We took a boat ride on the Seine River, rode the metro, and even visited Jim Morrison's grave. It was crazy how many people were in the historical graveyard just to see Jim Morrison's tombstone. It was like a tiny outdoor concert scene with guys playing the guitar, cassette tapes of The Doors, women dancing, and people milling about with candles and fresh flowers. Some were burning incense and others were partying. A strange, gypsy-looking guy who spoke very little English tried to sell something to Mick that looked like a thin dried-up strip of beef jerky or tree bark lying on a wrinkled piece of tin foil, saying that it was hash or something like it. Mick didn't buy it, but he did find a bowl in his pocket that he had forgotten was there. We didn't have any pot with us, and had no desire to find any, really, but the bowl in his pocket was along for the ride.

At night, Mick, our five other friends, and I made dinner in the tiny apartment that was only big enough for two people, and we ate, drank, and laughed. When we went to sleep at night, we unfolded the bed from the wall, and four people lay next to each other across the width of the bed while the other three people slept on the floor surrounding the bed – one at the foot, and one on either side of it. We called it our "happy tenement."

Our next stop was Italy and we couldn't wait to visit Florence and Venice. Since we had such a great experience with it the first time, we decided to use the ride board again, and got a number for a guy named Pierre who was planning to drive to Florence the same day that we wanted to go. We got his number and called him. Pierre gave us an address to meet him the following day, and when Mick and I showed up he was waiting for us with an old beat-up white Peugeot hatchback and another guy from Paris, who claimed not to speak any English.

Pierre was all smiles as he propped the hatch back up with a wooden beam in order to throw our backpacks in with all the other junk he had back there. Mick and I couldn't believe his name was actually Pierre. It was too cliché, but we went with it. We both decided immediately that with his old brown suede jacket, black shirt and jeans, and his small stature and scruffy black goatee and shaggy hair, he looked just like Bob Dylan, circa 1970. The gentleman in the front seat never got out of the car and didn't turn to look at us when we shoved ourselves into the back seat of the Peugeot, which was covered with bits of white plaster and some old painting clothes. He was tall and lean with a Euro-artsy appearance that was popular in the 80s. He looked a lot like the Mike Myers character on *Saturday Night Live* named Dieter, who hosted the show *Sprockets* and always asked if you wanted to pet his monkey. He was almost comical in his apparent disdain of our presence, which neither of us cared about because we were going to Italy, baby!

We met Pierre and "Dieter" late in the afternoon, which meant that we would need to drive throughout the night to get there. After we began driving Pierre laid into Mick right away for being some kind of pussy to be travelling with a woman. He also let us know how he felt about Americans in general, particularly how ridiculous we were for visiting a country for a few days and believing that we actually saw it and experienced it. Mick just laughed it all off and said that he liked being "in the company" of women. Dieter simply stared forward while Pierre turned around in the driver's seat, offering us a brown paper bag full of boiled potatoes, as if they were potato chips. Just after chastising us he donned a big smile and in a friendly voice asked, "Potato?" We politely declined and said he should probably keep his eyes on the road, to which he replied, "You think I drive bad now…wait until I am tired."

He was right about that, and by about 1:00 a.m. we were up in the Alps with Pierre speeding like a nut on the dark, winding, gravel-strewn mountain roads while Mick and I shivered in the cold back seat, huddled together, fearing for our lives. When we reached the border into Italy we were relieved to have made it in one piece, but our peace of mind was soon shattered by the reaction we elicited from the border patrol.

Apparently it isn't too common for a Parisian Bob Dylan and Dieter to cross the border at 1:00 in the morning with two young Americans in a beat-up, dirty Peugeot. The officers began to ask Pierre a litany of questions, as Dieter sat silent, rigid, and guilty-looking in the passenger seat. We were then told to pull over, and two of the officers took Mick and me inside while two others tore apart the car. We were led to an interrogation room complete with bright fluorescent lights and smooth steel tables and chairs. The cops spoke Italian to each other, as we stood petrified in the hallway in front of the type of room we had only seen in the movies up until then. We were sure that our asses would be thrown into some Italian jail never to be heard from again, especially as Mick had that stupid bowl in his pocket and nowhere to get rid of it. We were, as they say, fucked; and we knew it.

I wondered what the hell Pierre and Dieter were doing outside. Were they being hauled away to prison – or did they drive off and leave us there?

The border patrol police looked menacing in their uniforms at night in the small but brightly lit space, and I must have looked pathetic standing there waiting to be told what to do. One of them came over to me, holding my backpack, and told me I would be first, ushering me into the room with a swing of his hand. Mick was told to wait where he was standing in the hallway. I looked at him briefly, thinking it would be the last time I would see him.

I stepped into the room and stood in front of the steel table as the officer dumped the contents of my backpack onto the table while standing on the other side of the table with his fellow gendarme. I was travelling very light, and the things that spilled across the table were not exactly frilly, girly-type items. They included some dirty running clothes, a raggedy sweater, baseball hat, and a pair of jeans; along with a handful of tampons, a toothbrush, hair brush, a few ponytail holders, and a folded-up envelope.

The first thing he said as he stared at the heap was, "You dress like a boy."

Then he and the other officer looked at each other in a way that told me they "had me." They locked onto the white envelope that was folded into a neat, small square. The one who didn't like my taste in clothes lifted his eyes, giving me the once-over, and then hurriedly grasped at the envelope and began to unfold it. The envelope contained a little wax paper bag with something bulging inside of it. They were positive that this was it and I was done for. I watched his eyes as he opened the wax paper and pulled out the rosary I had purchased for my mother while touring the Notre Dame Cathedral in Paris. I knew my mom would adore receiving one, so I went out of my way to not only purchase one, but also to have one of the priests there bless it for me. His eyes grew as large as a little kid's on Christmas who just got his first bike from Santa, and a smile crept across his face. He turned to me and as he held the rosary up in the air for all three of us to see, he pressed his thumb and middle finger together on his other hand, held it up in the air, and waved it back and forth in quintessential Italian style as he said, "Ah… you Catholic! You a *good* girl! You go!"

He then proceeded to re-wrap my mom's rosary and stuff the rest of my belongings back into my backpack. As he shuffled me out the door, Mick stood in confusion and relief, realizing he had somehow escaped interrogation. We stepped outside and our pals Dieter and Pierre were still standing near the car in the cold, uncomfortably shivering and smoking cigarettes as the border patrol finished searching the car. Nothing illegal was found in the car and the other cops must have told them that I was a "good girl" so we were told we could leave.

When we arrived in Florence we were not sad to say goodbye to our travelling companions, and we went our separate ways. Mick and I walked around the city until we found a reasonable hotel called the Apollo and checked in. In my typical way I was getting antsy and restless inside, resenting Mick for liking me more than I liked him. It was immature and bitchy, but I began to get pissed at him and at myself because I was in these romantic and beautiful cities such as Paris and Florence, and I wasn't in love with the guy I was with.

I was angry at myself because I placed too much importance on sex, and I didn't enjoy sex with Mick. I beat myself up internally for not loving someone who was funny, cute, kind, and who loved me. I thought about that song by Berlin called *The Metro*, and repeated the line over and over in my head that went: "I remember hating you for loving me; Riding on the Metro." I looked out the window of our hotel and saw couples on Vespas speeding along the Renaissance streets. I leaned over the stone wall, taking in the beautiful Ponte Vecchio Bridge where people stood around and kissed, and I just stewed.

It was stupid of me to be that way, and then I got even angrier at myself for being someplace so incredible and not truly appreciating the experience. I wanted it to be like a movie, and of course, nothing in real life is like it is in the movies. My hair was dirty; we had been wearing the same clothes for days; and I was cranky because all I could think about was that Mick and I were good as friends but not as lovers. I knew that he was picking up on my quite overt, bitchy vibe, and although he tried to make the best of it, it was starting to wear on him. He dealt with it by writing about me in his journal, which he had been keeping religiously during all of his time overseas. I wanted so badly to see what he had written in it because Mick is an incredible writer with a sharp, sarcastic wit, and because I am nosy as hell and wanted to know what it said about me. I have still to this day never seen the journal, although I got close a couple times while Mick was in the shower, but he did disclose to me long after that trip that there were some unfavorable pictures painted of me with his prose. I deserved it and then some; and there was no reason at all for me to be mean to him just because I was unhappy with myself.

We toured the city and saw the beautiful Duomo from afar, photographing it from up above the city, as well as up close. Even though our money was super tight we both wanted to see Michelangelo's "David," so we splurged on the Accademia Museum. The statue was truly spectacular and impressively beautiful to see. I was amazed that someone had actually carved it out of stone, and by the details of the hands and the muscles of David's smooth statuesque body. (I know what you are thinking, and being horny had nothing to do with my amazement of the statue! It really *is* very beautiful!)

We didn't want to spend all of our money in Florence since we still had a couple days left to go in Venice. We decided to hang out for a while in the main square, Piazza della Signoria. It was a fun environment with shops and street performers as well as caricature artists. The artists came on very strong and were not shy about trying to talk people into sitting in their chairs to have a drawing done. Mick and I got sucked in by one very boisterous and persuasive artist who said he could draw me, and his friend would draw Mick, at the same time. Mick was really into the idea, and thought it would be a great keepsake souvenir that we would both treasure for years to come. I think he had visions of framing the picture for a future home that existed in his dreams, filled with memories from his travels around the world. I didn't want to spend the money on it (which is weird, because I *love* to spend money), but I was imagining more tasteful and prettier souvenirs in Venice that I knew I would like better.

I am a sucker for a good sales pitch and I have a hard time saying no, so I quickly gave in and sat down in the small director's chair after paying the artist. Mick was sitting in a chair off to my right and we smiled at each other in excitement to see the masterpieces when they were done. The guy drawing me kept saying over and over that he was going to draw me "sexy" and that I was a "beautiful" woman. Mick's guy had finished his drawing first, so he jumped out of his chair and excitedly held up his caricature for me to see. He was clearly pleased with it, and from where I was sitting, it looked great. I started to get excited to see mine as well. I decided Mick had been right, and that this would be a great thing for me to have that I could show my kids someday while reminiscing about the cool travels of my youth. Mick tightly grasped his rolled-up white scroll and made his way behind the artist drawing me so he could preview his work. I saw the change in his expression and a look that resembled fear, replacing the excited happy look from only a moment ago. I asked him what was wrong and he said, unconvincingly, "Nothing!"

After the picture was finished I stood up and practically snatched it from the artist's hands as he said (now laughing), "I draw you sexy!"

I looked down at the caricature in horror, and I felt the hot pins and needles of anger flow upwards from my toes and wash over my shoulders and ears. The artist drew me so that you could see my face and my long flowing blonde hair as I stood naked, looking back over my shoulder. In this "sexy" pose he had me slightly bent over with my ass in the air (cheeks perky and protruding), and my breasts were sticking out like scud missiles and had been drawn to look like headlights on a car with the high-beams on.

Usually I think things like this are funny, but I was so upset and livid. We didn't have enough money to eat dinner, yet I spent money on this crappy naked comic strip drawing of myself. I stomped away with Mick running behind me, trying to convince me that it wasn't that bad. I was so mad that I had spent the money on it and that it was not a special souvenir at all. I told him how pissed I was that he talked me into getting it done, and that I was going to throw it away. I was just about to toss it in a public garbage can, when Mick was able to calm me down. He said that I might not see it now, but someday I would find it funny and I would regret throwing it away. Begrudgingly I rolled it up into a scroll and stuffed it into my backpack.

We went to Venice and toured the maze-like streets, stopping for cappuccinos and visiting stores that carried the famous paper maché masks. We didn't have enough money to eat in the restaurants there or ride in the gondolas, but I didn't care about that. We actually found a Wendy's and ate at the all-you-can-eat salad bar, even though all-you-can-eat there meant you could haul away as much as you could in one trip! We built up our plates higher than the leaning Tower of Pisa and took our seats in the green-painted walls of a Venetian Wendy's. Before we left we got a glass of wine and drank it standing up in a small, crowded bar.

The trip had been an incredible experience all the way around, and in the end, Mick was right. I still have the caricature of myself in my "sexy" pose, and I find it hilarious. It makes a good story too. I haven't shown it to my kids yet, but I am sure I will soon, and they will laugh and want to know about the guy I was travelling with who isn't their dad.

When we returned to Munich, we had one more trip to take before Mick returned to Amman. My boss, Winston, decided to surprise me with two plane tickets and some money so that Mick and I could go to Prague for my birthday. Who were we to say no? We got on the plane in excited anticipation of a city neither of us had been to before, but couldn't wait to see and experience.

We found a room that was a pension of sorts in an apartment with a woman and her ten-year-old son. The woman didn't speak any English, but her son had been studying English in school and it was actually quite good. His name was Tommy and I felt sorry for him because he was overweight and seemed lonely. He didn't go outside to play at all and he stayed in his pajamas the whole weekend – the hot stuffy air in the apartment leaving a permanent smell of burnt toast on the boy. He showed Mick and me to our funky, psychedelic room that looked more like a leftover sound stage from the TV show, *Laugh-In*, than it did a bedroom.

After Tommy closed the door behind him, we plopped down on the downy comforter of the small bed and laughed. The whole room was decked out in bright fuzzy orange and lime green, white plastic furniture, and a gorilla head sculpture for its décor. It was like a bad 70s porno on acid, and we loved it. We went out to see and do as much as we could in two days. Crossing the Charles Bridge was like being at a Renaissance fair and the entire city looked like a page out of a fairytale book. We had a great time looking in the shops at the lead crystal and had drinks at a jazz club in the late afternoon. We walked through the red light district and couldn't help laughing when they tried to lure us in (knowing we were American tourists) by yelling things like, "Live Sex!"

As tempting and enticing as that "hook" would usually be, we declined the live sex shows because they were expensive and we weren't quite sure what was really happening past the darkened doorways. We ended up settling on a show at a Black Light Theatre. We didn't understand the language, but because of the Dr. Seuss-like quality of the costumes, color, and illusions, it was very mysterious and entertaining. The theatre was dark inside and had dark black curtains and a dark stage. A black cabinet and black ultraviolet lights were used and paired with fluorescent costumes and other visual illusions to make the entire show quite spectacular in a childlike and imaginative way. I thought it was the perfect thing to see when you didn't speak the language, because there was so much to look at.

After returning to my normal life for a few weeks, I decided to take a couple more trips, only these were done solo. I went to Greece for two weeks by myself, which really scared my dad because he was convinced that I would be abducted into a harem and never seen again. I told my dad that he watched too much TV and off I went. I flew to the island of Santorini which was incredibly breathtaking with whitewashed buildings that looked as if they were dripping into the bluest waters I have ever seen.

It has a volcanic landscape with black beaches and is quite possibly a little piece of heaven right here on Earth.

I stepped off the plane and expected an airport of sorts, but instead there was a cart with our luggage and we had to dig through it to find our own bags. I grabbed my little bag and was instantly surrounded by men and some young boys who had pictures in books and plastic coverings with them of their pensions. All of them called out instantly to me to look at their pictures and stay with them. This was considered a normal practice and is how many families make extra money.

Two boys who looked to be around 9 or 10 years old and probably brothers were the most innocent-looking of the bunch, so I gravitated towards them. They shoved the pictures at me and begged me to stay with them. I told them I had chosen them, so they happily showed me to a car that was parked off to the side, where, I suppose, their dad was waiting. We all got into the car and I blindly let these guys drive me to wherever they wanted to go. We got to their house, and my pension was in the back – separate from the family home by a few steps in the back yard. They opened the door for me and I couldn't believe my eyes. It was small, but clean and beautiful with white drapes blowing into the room from the soft breeze off the sea. It had a tiny little balcony that I could barely step out onto, but the quaintness and beauty of it made my heart leap. I couldn't believe that I had found this place in the way that I did at the airport with the kids, the pictures, and the creepy car ride.

I decided to go for a little run, and took off into the heat of the day. At first I figured I would run straight for as long as I could and then turn around and go back to keep from getting lost. This isn't something you can do on a small island, unless you only want to run for two minutes. I began taking turns left and right, promising myself I would remember how to get back. I went up steep hills, passing old men walking their donkeys on a rope and old men sitting in the sun drinking Ouzo. There were women and children and a few tourists scattered about, and everyone just looked at me as though I was an alien from Mars. I decided to go back to my room and quickly realized I was lost. A very dry and thirsty panic set in, and I feared I would never find the place I was staying because I forgot to write down the address and all the places looked exactly the same. About two and a half hours later I was cooked, but I found my pension.

I showered up and went to the nearest café to get my soon-to-be new favorite drink, the Greek Frappe. Who knew that I would enjoy Nescafe so much? I sat there sipping my Frappe and couldn't help but overhear the people at the table next to me speaking English. I couldn't figure out the dynamics of the trio because there were two guys and one girl. The girl was brunette, in her late 20s or early 30s, and very petite and pretty. She had a runner's build and tanned muscles, but was very girly and feminine. One of the guys looked as if he was the same age as she was – nice-looking, athletic build, and a face like a young Mel Gibson. I couldn't tell but it seemed as though they were a couple. The other guy was definitely American, like they were, but he had much darker skin, with long black hair to his shoulders, and a ripped-up, rock-hard, muscular body. He looked to be Italian, Greek, or American Indian. I couldn't tell which.

I leaned over and said, "I don't mean to eavesdrop, but I have been eavesdropping on you anyway, and couldn't help but notice that you are American." They thought my intrusion and introduction were funny and asked me to pull a chair over and sit with them. We ended up sitting there for most of the day, and I found out that

Kostas was the one who looked Greek, and he was raised in Greece for most of his life and still had family and friends there, but had moved to the United States in his early 20s and resided in Florida. Kostas was 42 years old with the body of a 23-year-old. Julie and Mark were a married couple who were very good friends of his, and the three of them were travelling together to see Greece and Kostas's "homeland."

All of them were really into health and fitness, and Kostas was a personal trainer in Florida, as well as an artist and painter. The day seemed to fly by and they asked me if I would like to join them later for dinner, so I did. It was amazing because Kostas took us to a restaurant owned by people he knew, so we were treated like family and drank retsina wine that tasted of pine needles until the early morning hours. We had such a great time that the three of them asked me to go to Perissa Beach with them that afternoon, where we laid in the sun on the black volcanic beach and jumped off a cliff into the sea and swam to shore.

We all had such a great time together, and I could tell that Mark and Julie were hoping that Kostas and I would become a couple. I was staying there for two weeks and so were they, so they asked me to go island-hopping with them on a friend's yacht. Of course I said, "Yes!"

Maybe because I was young and stupid and up for anything, and maybe because I had been through some really bad things as a child, I figured there wasn't too much else to be scared of out there; but still, I should have known better or at least been leery of all of this. But I wasn't, and amazingly, it all turned out all right in the end. I had the most incredible time island-hopping on the yacht and visiting Kostas's friend named Risto who had a gorgeous villa and some beautiful olive and apricot orchards. We had an incredible time in Kos, Mykonos, and Rhodes. I didn't want to go home, but I didn't expect things to get as serious as they did with Kostas either.

Kostas and I began sleeping together (of course), and although I liked him and I thought he was hot, there were things about him that I knew I wouldn't dig in the long term. For instance, he always had a mean look on his face. It was a scowl. I wouldn't describe him as a warm person; in fact, if you didn't know him he was rather scary-looking, even though he wasn't scary and was a good guy. He was also rude (almost mean) to waiters and waitresses, and that is a quality that I can't stand in anyone. I could also tell that he was a bit on the controlling side, and noticed that he wanted to tell me what to eat and how to work out, and insisted that I go on a plan that he created for me. I enjoyed the true Mediterranean Diet that we were eating while I was there, and I had a blast going to his old *Rocky*-type Greek Gym, but I didn't like having him tell me what I needed to be doing and having him hover over me to be sure I was doing what he said. I told Kostas that I wanted to visit Athens because I wanted to see the Parthenon and the Acropolis. He winced at this because Athens is smoggy and dirty and he saw no reason to go there. Before I knew it he had chartered a plane and the two of us were flying to Athens so I could see the sites I wanted to see.

While we were in Athens Kostas took one of the Greek drachmas I had been admiring to a jeweler, where he had a hole drilled into it and then placed it onto a pretty gold chain. He gave it to me on the way home in the airplane. When we got back to the island, we spent some time seeing it in a way that the tourists never could, because he knew about things that other people didn't know, and the people in the village treated me as part of the family. The night before I left to go back to Germany,

Kostas told me that he wanted me to move to Florida and marry him. He said we would live half the year in Florida and the other half in Greece. I told him I had to think about it, but I had nothing to think about. God help me, the offer sounded like the greatest thing in the world; but the thought of marrying him rather scared me, and if I was going to be honest with myself, I couldn't stand one more minute with the controlling man, no matter how hot his body was. Besides, he was 20 years older than I was. I was impetuous and goofy, but I knew I wanted whomever I was going to marry to be able to get it up for at least 20 years into the marriage.

I went back to Germany and kept in touch with him by writing letters for a little while, and then slowly stopped writing.

The last major trip I took before coming back to the States for good was to the Canary Islands, off the coast of Africa. I was still feeling empowered, and quite cocky, after my flawlessly executed trip to Greece, so I travelled in the same unplanned, un-booked style to the Islas Canarias, confident that all would turn out beautifully. It was a beautiful trip, and I met incredible people, saw sand dunes that looked as though they went on forever as if I was on a different planet, and saw cactus plants taller than most buildings in Ohio.

I rented a moped and drove it around until it died on me, and I had to get someone to drive me back to where I got it to tell them it was dead on the side of the road. I even went on a camel ride and was tricked at the end by one of the tour guides, who convinced me to give the camel a kiss by feeding him a bottle of soda and then putting my face next to his mouth, which resulted in the camel jamming its tongue down my throat and thunderous laughter from the whole crowd. I laughed too, but it was seriously gross and scary.

The week I spent on Gran Canaria at the beach of Playa del Inglés was not as memorable, however, as when I first arrived at the airport and realized I was much further over my head than I would have liked to admit. I was expecting the same low-key airport as Santorini, with the luggage cart being pulled up to us by a donkey, perhaps. Instead I was horrified to see that the airport looked to be the size and the same level of frenzy as O'Hare! I reeled my initial panic back in and told myself this was no problem. I would find a cab driver who could take me to a holiday beach town, and after I got there I would just find a hotel among the masses to choose from.

I walked around the airport, almost afraid to move too quickly. Everything around me seemed to be going at warp speed, including people's conversations in Spanish. I don't know a lick of Spanish, except for *agua* and *uno*, *dos*, *tres*, and *cuatro*. That was as high as I could remember from *Sesame Street*. (That darn Maria and Luis. They were too busy getting busy to teach me anything useful.)

After what seemed like an hour, I found my way to the front of the airport and exited where it looked like I would be street-side. There were about 50 yellow cabs lined up and waiting for someone who knew where they were going, or who spoke Spanish. That wasn't me, but I made my way over to a cab driver and he gestured that he could take me where I wanted to go, so I hopped in the back. I was happy that I would soon be sitting on the beach; maybe I would go for a swim too if it wasn't too late when I arrived. The driver got in behind the wheel and looked at me in the rearview mirror, waiting for me to tell him where I wanted to go. I smiled and said, in English, that I wanted to go to the beach. He looked at me and shrugged and said something that indicated he didn't understand. I told him that he should just take me to the beach. Even if he did speak English, this would have been hilarious, and I was the hugest idiot because there are tons of beaches on the island, and I hadn't researched any of them, let alone booked a hotel or anything. I shrugged and smiled a lot, and shrugged and laughed. I did the "swim" in the back of the cab by doing the crawl stroke in the air, followed by holding my nose and pretending to go underwater. Then I said *agua* a bunch of times, because I didn't know the word for beach.

I was so sweaty and began to get a little panicky too. I looked around and I noticed that with my blonde hair down to my butt, I stuck out like the sore thumb, idiot tourist that I was. I was the only blonde for miles, and I was giving us all a really bad name. He pulled away from the curb and pointed his index finger in the air, telling me that he a) wanted me to pull his finger; b) he had a great idea; or c) he wanted me to look at the gray felt that lined the inside roof of his cab.

I was hoping he had a great idea. I stared out the window and listened to Jon Secada belt out *Just Another Day* on the cabbie's radio. I started to hope I would meet a guy here who looked like Jon Secada and then scolded myself for digressing. What was wrong with me? I was on a road to nowhere with a guy who spoke no English and I didn't know one thing about the large city I was in, or where I was going.

We pulled up to a hotel that was near the water, but not exactly in a resort-looking or touristy part of town. The cab driver told me to stay put with a hand gesture and went inside the hotel. I felt as though I was a science experiment gone wrong and he was running to find help with the big mistake sitting in the back of his cab. When he returned he had with him a guy in a maroon and navy blue hotel uniform who asked me what the problem was. I wanted to say, "My brain" but instead I explained quickly that I hadn't made a hotel reservation anywhere, but I was looking for the beach resorts. He explained that the resort beaches were about an hour away and I could reach them by bus in the morning.

The tour bus place was closed for the night, but I could spend one night in the hotel and be on my way first thing in the morning. I thanked them both, paid the cabbie, and went inside with the hotel front desk clerk. He checked me in and showed me exactly where I needed to go to check out the bus schedules in the morning, and the rest of the night was up to me. I walked around a bit in the city and found a place to eat. I felt very out of place, a tiny bit nervous, and very alone. I made it through the night and caught a bus to Playa del Inglés, which is Spanish for "Englishman's Beach." They weren't kidding! I was the only American there and seemed to be surrounded by people from England and a sprinkling of Germans. I wasn't alone for long, and started up a little fling with a bloke named Lee. I might stumble, but I always get back up again!

One day at a time – this is enough. Do not look back and grieve over the past for it is gone; and do not be troubled about the future, for it has not yet come. Live in the present, and make it so beautiful it will be worth remembering.

—Unknown

X

PEOPLE ALWAYS ASK ME if I am bothered that, as an adopted child, I don't know my birth family history, especially in terms of my medical history and diseases that might run in my family. Having a medical history that is a blank slate is actually quite liberating, and I believe that all should take the utmost care of themselves and take a proactive approach to their health no matter what they know about their genes. Of course, having a hereditary predisposition to certain diseases can be helpful to know, but too often I feel that people use the information as an excuse for choosing to live an unhealthy lifestyle. Others ruminate on the disease that seemingly looms overhead, creating angst and negativity towards the possibility of being able to change their genetic make-up for the better.

Living in constant fear that a disease will strike surely cannot be good for your health, and might even lead to what is feared in the first place by way of a self-fulfilling prophecy of the worst kind. I like the freedom of not having something hanging over my head or lurking around every corner. I live a healthy lifestyle, have regular physicals, and I don't concentrate on, or expect, anything bad happening to me.

In my early 20s, when I first moved back from Germany, I worked in a few fitness centers in downtown

Cleveland in addition to the Athletic Club. On average I taught nine aerobics classes a week (not including weekends) with my days beginning at 4:00 a.m. and ending at 10:00 p.m. Every day I opened one of the clubs at 5:00 a.m. and then worked the morning shift behind the front desk. After working the front desk I taught aerobics in the afternoon and evening, and finished up in the third gym of the day where I washed towels and closed it up for the night. When you are in the fitness industry, especially as an instructor, you have to teach many classes (and usually at multiple places) in order to make any money at all. I was young and in great shape, but I still felt as though I was burning the candle at both ends. This is why it didn't seem all that unusual when I felt a little dizzy in my early morning Step class. I figured I was fatigued and needed to do a better job at properly hydrating before and after class.

One day while I was instructing, I couldn't help but notice that something wasn't quite right. It felt as if someone had turned the lights down on a dimmer switch, and then turned them back up again – but no one had touched the light switch and there was nothing wrong with the building's electricity. This was a particularly unnerving sensation which even I couldn't ignore. I went to a doctor to find out what was happening and he suggested I see a cardiologist. My father had had a quadruple heart bypass at the Cleveland Clinic, and he made sure that I went to see his cardiologist to find out what was wrong. I never would have guessed that the lights went dim because it was *my* wiring that was faulty.

The cardiologist told me right away what he suspected it to be, but just to be sure I was put on a Holter monitor for 48 hours to track my heart activity. The Holter monitor is a portable device that you wear around your neck, and the electrodes are attached to your chest so the doctors can observe your electrocardiography and see the arrhythmias and their patterns. I felt like a science project, and as I was living with my boyfriend Craig at the time, he probably felt that way too. It felt a little funny knowing the doctors would be able to see when we were having sex as indicated by my elevated heart rate at, say, 11:00 p.m.

The Holter monitor confirmed the doctor's initial diagnosis that I had what is known as bigeminy, which is pronounced somewhat like "By Jiminy." When I tell people about it they usually laugh and joke about Jiminy Cricket from Pinocchio, until I tell them that it means I have a heart arrhythmia and that my heart will literally skip a beat. Sometimes my heart has a "premature ventricular contraction" followed by a pause, and then another premature ventricular contraction. If premature ventricular contractions occur too often, very low blood pressure is a likely consequence as other bodily organs are affected by the heart's reduced capacity to pump blood. This explained my dizziness and weakness, and why the lights were going dim on me during class. There are times that after my heart pauses, I can feel it jump start itself, and I get a weird flutter in my chest that I describe as a "baby heart attack." It doesn't hurt, exactly, but it does make me very conscious of my own heartbeats. Sometimes for short periods of time I have trouble breathing, but then it goes away and I feel fine. I don't like to call attention to this condition, and I certainly don't let it hold me back from doing anything.

Since the time I was told that I have bigeminy I have had two stress tests (about five years apart) and both times I made it through the entire test. After I stepped off the treadmill, one doctor said I was the only woman he had ever seen who made it through the whole test. Each doctor I have spoken to about the arrhythmia has told me that because it isn't causing me pain, and I am able to complete Ironman triathlons and run marathons without difficulty from my heart, it is simply a matter of how my body is wired and I shouldn't be worried about it. So, I am not. I don't tell many people that I even have it because I often forget, and also, because I don't want people to think I am looking for attention or using it as an excuse or a crutch of some sort.

Our minds are very powerful and our bodies listen to them, so I rarely even think about it. This approach shouldn't be confused with burying my head in the sand like an ostrich. I just don't choose to concentrate on it or worry that I have it, because neither will do me any good. If anything, worrying about it will only make it worse.

I did make the mistake, however, of forgetting to tell the hospital where I had my bunion removed that I had bigeminy. The anesthesiologist thought he had lost me on the table when my heart rate reached extremely low levels and decided to take a rest break. The poor guy was probably freaking out about his malpractice insurance, and needless to say he was plenty pissed at me for not telling him. When I came to in the recovery room he was waiting there for me the minute I opened my eyes so that he could rip me a new ass. (No anesthesia that time!) I apologized for forgetting to mention it, but I don't think the apology was accepted.

Sport has the power to change the world. It has the power to inspire. It has the power to unite people in a way that little else does. Sport can awaken hope where there was previously only despair.

—Nelson Mandela

XI

WHEN YOU THINK about it, it is truly amazing how the mind can get the body to go along with just about anything. When I was teaching indoor cycling classes on a regular basis, I always liked to emphasize this to the people in my class, particularly during a difficult set of quad-burning sprints or "runs" on the bike. To help keep them focused and motivated I would often remind them (mid-sprint) that our legs or our asses (or whatever body part was being pushed to its limit at the time) are really not very smart. I reminded them that the legs will do anything the mind tells them to do. They aren't too bright in that regard. If your mind tells them to keep going then they will keep going! If your mind tells them to give up, they will do that too. I would tell my students that they need to reach down deep, pull out something tough, and kick some ass, and it worked every time! The power of mind over matter is staggering and should not be underestimated.

I could have seen a thousand therapists to help me with my battle with bulimia, but if I wasn't ready to be done with it in my heart and mind, and finished with letting it have a hold on me, I wouldn't have been able to quit. I had made up my mind that I could not and would not live like that anymore – so I didn't. You quickly learn as a survivor of trauma and as an athlete that nothing is impossible and if you believe it you can achieve it. The key is to remember this on the race course and in life.

Doing an ultra-distance triathlon such as Ironman, Rev3 Full, or Great Floridian is a fast track to learning this important lesson. I have done four of these ultra triathlons to date, and each one has brought its own set of fears, obstacles, lessons, stories, and journeys that go way beyond the 2.4-mile swim, 112-mile bike, and 26.2-mile run that compose the mileage of the race.

The very first Iron-distance triathlon I completed was in Clermont, Florida, and is called the Great Floridian Triathlon. Its tagline is, "Are You Tough Enough?"

It was 1995, which aside from training for and completing this race, was not my best year or one that when reflected upon brings good memories or prideful moments for me. I was 26 years old and working full time as a membership sales representative at the Athletic Club in Cleveland. The Athletic Club was a starting point for me in many ways. I began teaching aerobics there when I returned from Germany; it was my first real sales position; and it was the place where I was introduced to people who encouraged me to "go for it" when it came to doing my first triathlon and marathon.

In 1993 I was in the pool one day doing my laps when a really friendly face introduced itself as Brady. (When you are in a pool, in the deep end holding onto the wall, you only see a floating face. The remaining portion of the person you are speaking to is hidden beneath the water line.) Brady was an attorney by profession, but his true passion was not only triathlon and Oreo cookies, but also getting other people to be passionate about triathlon and hopefully also Oreo cookies. He once ate so many Oreos that his tongue swelled up to twice its normal size and he couldn't talk, which was a *really* big deal to Brady, because he *loves* to talk. In true Brady fashion he introduced himself and then told me I was a good swimmer. He wondered if I was a triathlete and if I wanted to do swim workouts with him. I told him that I wanted to do a triathlon, but that I didn't have a bike, and that I would love to do swim workouts with someone for a change of pace.

Because I had been a competitive swimmer for so long, I was accustomed to having a coach tell me what to do when I got in the water. Without that structure to my swim workouts, I would swim for about 40 minutes to an hour and then get out. I didn't do speed work or sets of anything in particular, and I was rather bored by simply swimming back and forth. Brady always had a planned workout that was structured, challenging, and fun. Soon we also started running together, and soon after that he had me signed up for my first triathlon as well as my first marathon! The triathlon was in the Columbus, Ohio, area and the marathon was in Las Vegas. I borrowed a bike for the triathlon from Brady's girlfriend and rode it for the very first time at the race. I placed first in my age group, and I was instantly hooked on triathlon.

The sport of triathlon can be extremely expensive and I didn't have a lot of money, but I knew I needed to get my own bike. Brady told me about a bike shop where I could get a decent used bike or "last year's model" for a great price, and he went with me to make sure I got what I needed and nothing I didn't need. I walked out of the bike shop with a screaming banana-yellow bike, equipped with aerobars and clipless pedals. I was officially a tri-geek and couldn't have been happier.

That winter was the Las Vegas Marathon. It was a February race, so training in Cleveland was always dicey. I did most of my runs (even a 20-miler) on the treadmill at the club. Brady and I did the 20-mile indoor run together. We stuck PowerBars on the side bars of the treadmill, and had friends run with us in shifts of about an hour or whatever they could do in order to entertain us and help pass the time. At that time of my life, 20 miles was by far the furthest I had ever run, and I probably wouldn't have ever tried it without Brady's encouragement and inspiration. We were both "talkers," so we never shut up once our feet started pounding and our heart rates were elevated. We became great friends and training buddies, and although a lot of people suspected other things might be going on, nothing beyond friendship and training ever did.

Running is a time during which your soul is both purged and rejuvenated. Running with a good friend is the best remedy for what ails you that a person could wish for, as your sweat washes away the sludge built up in your mind and your heart. It's as if your problems somehow sweat themselves out of your pores, becoming dried-up salt that you can simply brush away.

Strangely, and unbeknownst to me at the time, the desert highway we were running on during the marathon was the same one I would be driving one day, from my brother Paul's house in Los Angeles, to visit a boyfriend on the Vegas Strip. If someone had told me on the day of the marathon that I would be doing that, I would have laughed in their face in disbelief. But then again, I never thought I would be finishing a marathon in about four hours and four minutes in Las Vegas either! I also never imagined I would get married there, but I did that too.

For Christmas that year Brady bought me a training log to keep track of my workouts and write down anything I was doing, feeling, and planning – in racing and in life. We both talked a lot about doing our first Ironman, and on the inside cover he had written a little note to me that said, "Liz, Best of luck in the New Year and with your Ironman goals! Go for it; and don't forget that great souls have great wills, but feeble ones have only wishes!"

Because of Brady's encouragement, and my lifelong dream to tackle what I considered the ultimate in the world of triathlon, I set the goal to do the Great Floridian in 1995.

This was a lofty goal in many people's eyes, as I was not a seasoned triathlete and hadn't done much in terms of distance racing besides one marathon.

But my mind was made up, and although I was petrified on the inside, I wasn't about to let other people's doubts bring me down. Jumping into uncharted waters with both feet and no life jacket was something to which I was well-accustomed. I was lucky, as I wouldn't be jumping in alone. There was a small group of athletes from the Athletic Club who also had the Great Floridian on their racing calendars that year and who would welcome the company on their long swims, bikes, and runs.

No my friend, darkness is not everywhere, for here and there I find faces illuminated from within; paper lanterns among the dark trees.

—Carole Borges

home with his two daughters, but because he didn't "see color," that made him a great and virtuous person, above all others, and therefore the adultery would be excused.

I found out that he would tell his wife he was working late and would meet the woman at a bar, and then go to her place to have sex. Before long she was pregnant with his child. I don't know if it was true, but he told me that the child was a little girl and that she was born blind. She was given his last name and was put on his health benefits. For obvious reasons, his marriage went even further south and then ended in divorce. In the midst of it all, he was diagnosed with testicular cancer. He went through radiation as well as the eventual removal of one of his testes.

The voices that tried to scream at me that I would never overcome these roadblocks and hurdles were always shut down and quieted by Danny telling me that I would never find anyone who would love me.

We fought often and I was almost always the one who started it. He would get very angry with me, and although he could be scary when he was yelling at me, he was never physically abusive at first. Not sleeping all night because of the fights, followed by the make-up sex, was raw and exciting for me. We would have these ups and downs all the time, all the while training for an Iron-distance triathlon. Sometimes we would break up and get back together in the same day, just like junior high kids.

He must have been worried that I was getting stronger (mentally and emotionally), because after a few of our bigger fights and some longer lengths of time in between our little breakups, Danny started talking about marriage and said we should look for rings. I was hooked in with the excitement of starting a life with someone, albeit someone who had a child from an affair and two children with an ex-wife; and who was an "abuser" and an excommunicated Mormon. Hey, beggars can't be choosers.

I always had a strong desire to have children, and I really wanted to experience having a baby of my own, which I feared had a huge risk of never happening for me if I married a man with only one testicle. (It was a really big one, but still only one.) I wouldn't wish cancer of any type on any person, and I feel horrible for anyone who must go through a battle with the beast known as cancer. In *any other situation* I would have had nothing against a person who had a testicle removed; however, marrying Danny with all that I knew and all that I wanted for myself was a different story. It became a life-altering decision that went far beyond how many he had hanging. Much was "hanging" in the balance with this precarious relationship.

Danny told me that he would be able to have kids because he was able to ejaculate sperm if he took medication. (Without the medication, he was able to have an orgasm, but nothing ever came out.) I was so conflicted about all of this, and worried that I would resent the shit out of him if we got married and he had three children with two other women, but couldn't have any with me.

Another part of me felt that I was being horribly self-centered and judging a person for his past, which I, of all people, had no right to do. I was no angel. I had a lot of emotional baggage, but I prided myself on being open-minded and free of prejudice. There was also a part of me that worried Danny was right about me. No one would put up with me and my outbursts and my insecurities. I might be passing up on Curtain Number One for Curtain Number Two, which would reveal nothing behind it but a pen full of muddy pigs or some other dummy prize.

This conflict was on my mind daily, and Danny and I fought almost as often as that. I was on the verge of working up the guts to break up with him when, while training in the pool one afternoon, he made it really easy for me. I was in a lane with a friend of ours, Ray, who was also doing the race in Florida, and Danny was swimming in the lane next to us. We were doing some fairly long sets, and because Ray and I swam at almost identical paces, we stayed side-by-side for every lap. Our flip turns were timed so perfectly it almost looked as though we were doing a water ballet routine instead of a swim workout. In between sets while hanging on the wall, Ray and I would make the long, hard sets more fun by cracking jokes and laughing at how similar our paces were. I told him that I hoped the alligators in the lake in Florida would get him before they got me, and he teased me about the gators being more scared of me than I was of them. It was all silly banter in between sets to help take our minds off being on our second workout of the day, and swimming on a Friday afternoon, instead of starting the weekend off like the "normal" people of the world were. Neither of us had any idea that Danny was getting angrier by the minute. He got out of the pool during one of our sets, and stood over our lane waiting for Ray and me to touch the wall at the finish of another 1,000-yard swim. We touched the gutter of the pool in unison, and like a flash of light, Danny bent down as Ray lifted his head out of the water, and punched him dead in the face out of nowhere! Both of us were in complete shock, but Ray much more than I, I am sure, as his goggles had been knocked off his face, and his eye was trickling blood into the pool.

We both pushed backwards off the wall instinctively and treaded water while trying to figure out what had just happened. Danny was pacing the deck like a wild animal while screaming at Ray to get out of the pool so that he could "finish him off." Ray said he was a Buddhist and he refused to fight. (He wasn't kidding around; he really *was* a Buddhist.) I was screaming at Danny, asking him what was *wrong* with him? I got out of the pool and ran through the locker room looking for someone to help stop the fight that I believed would soon break out in the pool area.

By the time I found someone to come back to the pool with me, Danny and Ray were both gone. Ray had refused to fight back and was able to calm Danny down. He also said he forgave Danny for punching him. Apparently, Danny apologized to Ray while they were in the men's locker room and explained his actions away with a lame story that he thought we were laughing at him for not being a good swimmer. He told Ray that he was really stressed about the swim portion of the Ironman, and that he knew people didn't think he would even make it out of the water at the race.

Danny explained that he got violent because seeing us swimming together and laughing made him so mad he lost his temper. I didn't care what he said or whether Ray accepted it; this was way too much for me. I drew the line at the violence he had displayed and broke up with him about a week later – right before we were to leave for the race in Florida. It took a lot of rearranging, but I found a way to get down there and a place to stay that didn't involve him.

Pre-race drama such as this is far from ideal and *not* the way a person should be approaching an endurance race like Ironman. You need to have all of your energies and emotions focused and you need to be in a positive state of mind from the start. There can't be outside negative influences weighing you down and causing stress if you expect to have the mindset necessary to perform and persevere through the tough miles and mental roadblocks that race day will bring.

I hadn't been sleeping and I missed Danny, but I also knew we shouldn't be together. I was in the airport waiting to fly down to Florida in order to attempt my first Iron-distance Tri and I was a mess. I called Danny from a pay phone to hear his calming (almost hypnotic), confident, and deep-toned voice. He proposed to me over the phone and the weaker side of me accepted his proposal. A woman with an ounce of self-respect would not accept a marriage proposal from a pay phone conversation in the airport, especially after all I saw and knew about him – but I did.

It was game on all over again. He got down to Florida, and we showed up for the start of the race. It was dark, windy, and unseasonably cold for Florida in October. High winds created waves in the lake that crested at three and a half feet and blew around a couple of the giant orange buoys that marked the swim course. I wasn't that worried about the waves, because the fear of having my leg taken off by an alligator far surpassed any other aquatic concerns. I was going to do this race and I was going to be married! There have been many times during my life when fear and excitement were synonymous. Everything surrounding this event was very exciting – the extreme stuff that I lived for. I *thrived* for exciting and extreme situations – unfortunately, not in a good way.

The gun went off and I proceeded to attempt some semblance of a rhythm in my swimming stroke as I battled what felt like swimming in a washing machine with about 200 other women. The waves picked me up and then dropped me like a hot potato, causing my teeth to clash together as I tried to take my breaths. It was really dark, stormy, and windy, but I loved it! At one point I popped my head up to get my bearings and I noticed that another competitor was doing the same thing. Together we laughed about the waves, as we figured out which way we thought was forward. The buoys had been blown off course, so it was hard to determine the course. Once we were sure which way we should go, we wished each other luck and put our heads back down into the waters that closely mirrored the relationship I was swimming in at the time. Even with the craziness of the waves and the stops needed to site the 2.4-mile swim course, I crawled up onto the beach in about an hour and seven minutes – only to run directly into Danny! I was so shocked to see him there! I knew that there was no way he could have completed the swim before I did and to be simply waiting on the beach for me.

I was told much later after the race that he hadn't made it a half mile out into the churning water before he panicked and was pulled from the dark, gray water. The race officials met him on the beach after he was brought back to shore by boat, and told him in no uncertain terms that his race was done for the day. In typical, charismatic, smooth-talking Danny fashion, he was able to convince the officials to let him continue – if for no other reason than to support his fiancée with whom he had been training for almost a year. He told them that I would need him, and he simply had to accompany me on the course. Unbelievably, they agreed, and so there he was – waiting for me to get out of the water so we could head to the bike transition and get rolling "together."

On the bikes he told me the whole story, and before I could determine if I really wanted to be stuck with him for the remaining race, he was already gone. He took off on me and never looked back. He completed the 112-mile bike and the marathon – and had the nerve to jump up in the air with a triumphant fist flying high in excited accomplishment as he crossed the finish line. I saw the race finish photo later and was simply astonished that he would do that, knowing that he hadn't completed the whole course. After the race, he proceeded to tell everyone that he not only finished the Ironman but that he beat me in the race. The last time I checked, the swim portion of an Ironman is a lot farther than a quarter of a mile, but hey, what do I know? I've only done four of them.

I was blinded by the light that sparkled off the diamond ring Danny bought me and the excitement that revolved around getting married. A big part of me was happy that I could say to myself, and to the world, that someone actually wanted to marry me. Under the surface, down deep inside of me, I had to know it was a horrible mistake. But on the surface I liked feeling loved enough by someone that he would buy me a ring and want to be with me no matter what.

The whole time, there were two sides of me that constantly fought an internal battle. The side that seemed to favor Danny and listened to his nonsense often beat out the side that urged me to be strong and move on. I knew in my heart that I would be miserable if I stayed with him, but part of me was afraid to leave him because I was a "freak;" I was "crazy;" and "nobody would ever love me or put up with me the way I was."

The night I realized I was stuck in an ugly downward spiral – that back then I felt I would never overcome – was also the night I decided to stop balancing on the edges of the madness and just dive in. I went into the bathroom to look in the mirror. I stared deeply into my own reflection and cried. In the mirror I saw a horrible person who would never be able to change. As strange as it may sound, I could empathize with Frankenstein's monster. I knew what it is like to feel like a monster, and I often thought of myself as one. But it wasn't the monster's fault that he was created. He didn't want to hurt anyone; he just wanted to be loved.

After much turmoil and heart-wrenching deliberation, I got in my car and drove to my parents' house.

While I was at Miami University, my parents had moved back to Cleveland. My personal items had been moved from my childhood house in Rochester, so I came to Cleveland after I moved back from Europe and made it my new home. My parents and I only lived about 10 minutes apart, and it was not unusual for me to swing by their house for food, money, advice, or "all of the above." My parents had never liked Danny very much and, therefore, I stopped telling them about it when he and I fought or when things weren't going well in our relationship. (It didn't take a rocket scientist to notice that I spent more time at their house when things weren't going well at home with Danny.) We all knew why I was spending time at my parents' house; we just didn't talk about it.

I knew my mom always had a big bottle of Tylenol PM because she often had trouble sleeping. I figured I could stash it in my pocket and take the pills home, to wash down with a bottle of wine and some beer. When I got home, I swallowed the pills one by one while sitting at the kitchen table in the apartment I shared with Danny.

After I had finished them off, I walked through the living room and the bedroom to try to decide where to lie down to die.

It was then that the athlete in me spoke up and screamed out against the nonsense: "You are stronger than this! You don't want to die."

"You have unfinished business in this world and you can overcome anything," the sole survivor in me screamed.

The athlete in me was right. I was not about to give in. I panicked and called the shopping mall where I knew Danny was doing his Christmas shopping, and begged them to have him paged. I told him what I had done, hung up the phone, and passed out. I woke up to the EMS guy taking my blood pressure and my sister-in-law's face looming over me. Danny had called my brother Dave to tell him what I had done and my sister-in-law drove to our house to help me. I still don't know who called the ambulance, but I *do* remember having to pay the bill for that ride for a very long time!

The next thing I knew I was in a hospital bed on the night before Christmas Eve with a hard plastic tube coming up from my throat and out of my nose, and there was yucky black charcoal smeared all over my hands and hospital gown. My throat was killing me but I was afraid to move because of the tubing. Nurses milled around and professionally – but coldly – administered their duties. It's funny, but they aren't quite as cheerful to you after they pump your stomach because you overdosed on pills and alcohol as, say, when you are not sick from trying to harm yourself.

I couldn't be released from the hospital until I was cleared by the psychiatrist. He wasn't in but was on his way. There was a bad snowstorm in progress so he would be very delayed. Schools were closed and everyone in the hospital was talking about how bad it was outside.

It's funny how much you can take your life for granted until you seem to be frozen in time and unable to participate in it, but the rest of the world goes on without you. Lying there in the cold open room, I listened to the background noises that define a hospital – beeping machines, voices on loudspeakers, nurses chatting, people's footsteps echoing in the halls, and the sound of the elevator. I had never felt so sad and alone in my life. I was supposed to be at work, and I asked to use the phone so that I could call in "sick." Ironically my boss didn't believe me, and gave me a hard time for calling in sick right before the holidays. At that moment in time, missing work was the least of my worries. In a state of stiff discomfort, I lay perfectly still while I felt my whole world spin itself even further out of control.

What would happen to me? How could I change the path of self-destruction that I was on, and get to a better place that deep down I *hoped* I deserved. How would I convince the shrink who was on his way to see me (and whose day with his kids and hot cocoa had been disturbed because of me) that I wasn't crazy and it would be okay to release me back into the world? It seemed as though half my life was spent trying to convince people that I wasn't crazy (as they were tossed around in the wake that my crazy behavior had created).

I remember the loud "ping" of the elevator reaching the floor I was on, and then the sound of my parents' voices in the hallway. My brother promised me that he wouldn't tell them what I had done. I wanted so badly to hide and not have to look at them or talk to them, but I was confined in the blue-gray gloom of the hospital bed.

Bring on the shrink.

Suddenly it seemed much easier to me to have to deal with the shrink than with my parents. Within the next few hours as I lay there, my father mapped out my near future. Movers were hired and my things were promptly taken out of the house I lived in with Danny and moved to the other side of town onto the third floor of my brother's house. It was bad enough to be the crazy sister who would never get her act together, but now I was also the crazy sister who needed to sponge off her big brother.

My nephew was about 4 years old at the time and my niece was a newborn. I know the situation wasn't ideal for my brother and his wife either, but I always felt as though there was a certain satisfaction for them that they had to swoop in to help the family fuck-up. I do appreciate that they were kind enough to let me stay with them, but it bothered me that I had no say in the matter. Even though I was the one in the hospital bed who had just overdosed, I was still an adult – yet no one included me in the decision to move my belongings into my brother's house. My dad must have said that I had to get out of that house immediately, and because there was nowhere else for me to go immediately, my brother had little choice but to let me stay with them.

I halfheartedly tried to stay abreast of the conversation taking place between my brother and my father next to my hospital bed – all the while staring down at the stiff, blue-hued blanket, and the lumps underneath that made up my legs. My mother said nothing. All the talking was done by the men. Danny was nowhere in sight, because my father made sure he knew he was not welcome. It was also made clear that I was not to see him anymore and that my things would be moved out immediately. (My belongings were literally being moved as I laid there.) My father and brother weren't talking to me directly, so I began to tune them out.

Have you ever been in a situation where people are talking about you as if you aren't in the room, but you are? Take that feeling and multiply the awkwardness and the uncomfortable weirdness by about a thousand. Then throw in that you can't even call them out on it by saying, "Shit, you guys…I'm sitting right here! Jeez!"

Of course I was grateful that my brother could help me out and that I had a place to live, but I felt pathetic, sad, and very alone.

I wondered if Danny was going about his day as if nothing had happened. He was probably at work, and would get a workout during his lunch hour while the movers tracked dirty snow onto the carpet at the house we no longer shared.

One day I was in my brother's kitchen before my shift at the restaurant where I was working, and I was crying. My nephew Seth came in and asked me what was wrong. I wanted to laugh as I considered spilling my guts to my little nephew, but instead I chose to say, "Seth, I just wish I had a friend. I really just need a friend."

He said, "Like a doggie friend?"

(He was going through a stage in which he constantly pretended he had a dog with him or that he himself was a dog.) I stopped crying and my heart warmed to him as well as to his innocent question, and I answered, "Yeah…like a doggie friend."

Seth said, "Lucky for you, Auntie Whiz, I have a *Sheppahhd* that you can buy!"

Leave it to a child to make you want to go on during your darkest hour by offering to sell you some swampland in Florida. It really was the sweetest thing in the world, and he made me feel so hopeful.

I lived with my brother and his family for a few
months – getting up early every morning to swim or run. I
worked two jobs, saved a little money (never my strong
suit), and moved back out on my own. I got an apartment
on the west side again. Danny had been calling me at my
brother's house, but of course no one would let him talk to
me. He began leaving tape-recorded messages on the
windshield of my car while I was at work. I would come
out after my waitressing shift and find a hand-held tape
recorder sitting on the windshield of my car with a tiny
cassette of him rambling on and on about getting back
together. He called my sister-in-law at her job so many
times that she told the receptionist never to put a call
through from anyone named Danny. To get around this, he
told the poor woman who answered the phone that his
name was Ken, and was put through a few more times. He
even showed up at a hair appointment I had one evening,
and was sitting in the parking lot next to my car waiting for
me to come out. When I walked over to my car, he came
charging over to me, and he was *drunk*! Do you know how
weird it is to have your Mormon ex-fiancé hammered out
of his skull, telling you that he is going to kill himself if
you don't get back together with him? I was both mortified
and scared. I got him into my car and took him back to his
apartment, where he proceeded to vomit and act violently
towards himself in the tiny bathroom. I was so pissed off at
him, and also scared, but somehow I talked him into getting
back into my car. I told him we needed to get him some
help and that I couldn't do it myself. I drove him to the
emergency room entrance of the nearest hospital and got
him out of the car. He said over and over that he would kill
himself if I didn't get back together with him, and I cried at
the lunacy of my life as I drove away and left him there.

Danny was very persistent in trying to get me back,
and he worked hard at explaining to everyone, including

me, how hard it was for someone to be with me, but that he loved me and wanted to help me. A good friend of mine, and mutual friend of Danny, had gone through all of the ups and downs of our relationship, and had remained friends with both of us throughout it all. At this point Danny started to convince her that he was innocent of all of my insanity, and that if he didn't love me so much he would walk away from me once and for all, but the good-hearted man that he was wouldn't allow him to do that. A lot of people liked him, and the story he spun seemed plausible and easier to believe than the truth about Danny, because he would never reveal that to them.

My family, however, didn't believe his crap, and my dad was actually convinced that Danny was the devil. They told me to stay away from him and not to get back together with him again. I was lonely and didn't like being alone with my own thoughts, sadness, and anger, which to me felt like a constant reminder of how right others were when they called me crazy. But, I was staying strong and not letting Danny back into my life, until one night he kept ringing the buzzer of my new little apartment until I couldn't take it anymore. He left his finger on it from outside the building, until I thought the deeply shrill buzzing would push me over the edge. It was late at night, and I tried to block out the never-ending buzzer by holding pillows over my ears and pulling the covers over my head. I kept telling myself he would go away if I just waited long enough. It finally became quiet and I let go of the tension in every muscle, breathing a sigh of relief – until I realized that he didn't go away.

He broke in through the window of my first-floor apartment and he attacked me.

At first it was mostly a verbal affront, asking me who I thought I was, and then answering his own question by saying that I was nobody without him. I screamed back at him and told him to get out. I knew that to hurt him the most, the insults needed to be both sarcastic and religious in nature, so I belittled him for being an adulterer and a fornicator. He went ballistic as he threw me down on my bed and pinned me down by kneeling on my chest with all his weight. His nose was almost touching mine and the look in his blue eyes was crazy and frightening. With his face held a centimeter from my own, he said, "I'm going to hurt you the way you have hurt me, so you can see how it feels."

I was screaming at him to let me up and thrashing on the bed. In a moment of his typical cockiness, he leaned back and sat up, allowing me to connect my foot into his one, lone ball. (Balls-Eye or Bulls-Eye: either way you looked at it, I nailed it.) As he sunk to the side in pain, I rolled off the bed and grabbed at a pair of my shoes that were on the floor, thinking I could get them, run out the door, and keep going. He grabbed me by the ankle and screamed at me in bewilderment as he pulled my body toward him – incredulous that I could be such a bitch as to kick him in the nut. My legs are very strong, though, and I kicked hard enough to shake him off. I stood up and ran into the living room towards the front door. He grabbed me from behind and punched me over and over on my right shoulder, harder than I thought he could. I screamed in pain, "Stop hitting me!"

Before I could get another word out, the front door to my apartment burst open and a mountain of a man was standing there before us, telling Danny that he had better leave immediately or else he was going to have to *help* him leave. The man in my living room was my new next-door neighbor who had only moved in a few days earlier, and who I didn't know beyond a hello in the hallway. He was about seven feet tall and had shoulders like Paul Bunyan's.

Danny tried to weasel his way out of it with his usual litany of explanations that just about everyone else bought from him. He looked up at the man, who needed to duck to get into the room and who seemed to take up the whole apartment with his presence, and said, "You don't know what she's like, man!"

Paul Bunyan answered, "I don't care what she's like; you *never* lay your hand on a woman. Now, you can leave on your own, or I can help you leave. It's your choice."

Danny left on his own and slowly faded out of the picture. I had bruises that reminded me he was there, but they eventually faded as well. The hurtfulness of my friends who took Danny's "side" over mine and who didn't believe me that he had hit me (even when I showed them the bruises) eventually faded as well. I decided to continue on, living my life in what I felt was the right way and working on myself diligently. I couldn't worry about what other people were doing, saying, or believing. I knew Danny's true colors would eventually surface and reveal themselves to those who didn't believe me, and they eventually did. Only a few years ago, because of something that occurred between Danny and her, my friend came to me and she apologized. She said he had exhibited certain behaviors almost exactly as I had described them, and she felt horrible for turning her back on me.

I am too happy with myself today, all these years later. I don't hold a grudge over something that happened in a chapter of my life that resides in a dusty old book which, long ago, was closed and placed high upon a shelf. I forgave my friend and she and I are still friends. I hardly ever take that book down from its shelf to thumb through its pages, and it now seems as though the stories in it are about a fabled character. But those stories are chapters of my life which made me the person I am today, and which brought me to a wonderful place. Those chapters are my history. I wouldn't want to be that person again, but I embrace every bit of the history that made me who I am.

There is a great sense of pride and gratefulness I have for myself and for the benefits of being an athlete. Being an athlete kept me holding on and helped me recognize and believe that I deserved better than to be in an abusive relationship. Being an athlete empowered me and reinforced my inner strength and my tenacity to persevere. Everything I needed was already inside of me. I just needed to believe in myself and begin to love myself the way I wanted others to love me.

Holding on to anger is like holding on to a hot coal with the intent of throwing it at someone else; you are the one who gets burned.

—Buddha

XIII

I SUPPOSE that every household on Earth has a room or a place where all the serious conversations and life-changing decisions take place – or at least this is what I thought for most of my life, because the only place in my house where crucial matters were discussed was at the dining room table. It's actually rather funny to think about it, but certain pieces of furniture in our house expressly stand out in my mind as playing prominent and significant parts in the way I grew up. The bookshelf and my mother's prayer chair are two resounding examples, as is the dining room table. Every important or momentous discussion took place at one place and one place only – the dining room table.

Whenever I had a problem or needed help from my parents in some way, it was understood that a discussion would take place at the dining room table. This was a standard practice in my childhood home that continued even after I was an adult and no longer lived with them. These discussions were held completely separate from any meal time, but were still always held around the cherry wood table. When it was deemed necessary, I would drive over to my parents' house, and it was as though they had both cleared their schedules to make time to sit down together with me. My mom always sat in on the conversations, but hardly ever took part in them verbally. My dad was the "boss" of the house (who, for as long as I can remember, referred to himself as "the head of the household") and any time my mom chimed in, my dad would get upset and cut her off dismissively with a wave of the hand and a stern, "Would you please?!"

It would never occur to any of us kids to sit in my mom's or dad's designated chairs at the table for a meal or for one of our discussions. Just as when we were kids, my mom had the head of the table nearest to the kitchen so she could jump up and get things that people needed, such as more milk or ketchup; my dad had the end opposite of my mom, which was considered the primo, head-of-the-table seat; and I had the chair on the side that was in between them. If they were both talking to each other and I cared to follow the conversation, I would have to turn my head back and forth like a spectator at a tennis match.

During these particular "meetings," however, I usually just looked down at the tablecloth or at my hands with an occasional glance at my dad. These discussions were usually called for when things were really bad, and I was often in tears for the majority of them. Many times they would be held because I was in need of money or advice. Sometimes we had them because I was living with a boyfriend with whom I was fighting about something, and I needed someplace to get away. My parents would often get visits from guys I was dating, living with, or breaking up with. My poor father would end up having to speak to the bewildered men (at the dining room table, of course) who thought things were fine and couldn't understand why I was leaving, or who didn't know what to do about my hot and cold mood swings. One of them sat there and asked my dad what he thought was "going on in my head." My dad told him that if he wanted to figure out what was going on in my head, he should just ask me. To that the guy replied, "I don't think a room full of psychiatrists could figure out what is going on in her head."

My dad made him leave the house. No one was going to put down his daughter in his own house – at his dining room table – and get away with it.

At the dining room table I noticed that not only did my mom have an affinity for lace tablecloths, but also that my parents were there for me to listen to my problems no matter how big or small they were or how many I seemed to have. My parents called me one day to have a sit-down at the table so I could explain my crazy behavior to them once and for all. My dad wanted to know in no uncertain terms why I did the things I did. They wanted to know why I tried to overdose with alcohol and pills. My dad was at his wits' end; he was getting older and he was not in the best of health. He was physically tired, and probably also tired of worrying about me. When I answered his question truthfully, in a straightforward manner, I suddenly realized this was the first that my father was hearing about what had happened to me as a child. I was completely shocked.

I will never forget the look on his face when I said, "I'm sure that the things I do, and how I act, has something to do with Mr. Robertson."

He looked at me with a squinty and confused expression and said, "What *about* Mr. Robertson?"

As giant pools of tears welled in my eyes, blurring my vision and threatening to spill over onto my mom's lace overlay, I studied my father's face very closely and intently. He *really* didn't know! I looked at my mom. Shame sprinted across her face and she immediately went into martyr mode.

I explained to my dad what Mr. Robertson had to do with it all, and as I did, I literally saw the vein near his temple begin to bulge out of his head and pulsate. He was livid. He said that he hoped I knew that if he had known about it at the time he would have helped me.

My mom burst into tears and cried, "Oh fine – *I'm the bad guy! I'm the bad guy!*"

Somehow all of this always ended up being about her. Once again (just as when it actually happened), it was as if I was the adult who had to buck up and handle the trauma for the sake of the child, instead of the other way around.

My mother's little tantrum about being the "bad guy" was probably the closest I had ever seen from her resembling acknowledgment (or remorse) for what had happened and for how she had handled it, but it didn't last long. My dad didn't like dealing with my mother being upset, and the things we discussed at the table were quickly swept back under the carpet in my mother's mind. Actually, none of us ever spoke of it again, including my dad.

On a separate occasion my brother, Dave, asked me, "How can you be the way *you are* when we both grew up in the same house?"

I couldn't believe such an incredibly intelligent man could ask me such an incredibly stupid question. It hurt me, and I wanted (once again) to try to explain myself. I wrote my brother a five-page letter (front and back) explaining that we may have grown up in the same house with the same parents, but we each came from very different beginnings. I explained to him in the letter that I have never felt sorry for myself for being adopted, but having as many traumas as I had before the age of 10 years old could cause a huge difference in a person's behavior.

I don't think the letter was as important to him as it was to me.

I asked him what he thought of it, and he said it was "psychobabble." About a year or two later I made the mistake of asking him if he still had it. (I wanted to read it and see if I was in a better place than when I originally gave it to him, as a way to track my own progress.) He said he had thrown it away. I'm sure that most people probably would have tossed it, but I had had a crazy notion that it would have meant more to him than that and that he would have saved it.

My father's health deteriorated rapidly, and he was often in and out of the hospital or in twice-a-day dialysis sessions. As a result of his diabetes, his leg had to be amputated and he had too many other issues and health complications to be able to come back from it. Every time I went to visit him and I asked him how he was doing, he would always say, "Never mind about me – how are *you*?"

My father always put me before himself.

About a year later, after he had passed away, I was helping my mom pack boxes at her house because she was moving into a retirement home. As we wrapped newspaper around glasses and dishes, the TV was tuned to *The Montel Williams Show* and played in the background. Montel's guests were describing abuse they had endured as children. After one of the women talked about the sexual abuse she experienced, and did her best to tell her story through tears and nose-blowing, my mom looked right at me and said, "Can you even imagine what that would be like?"

When my mom said those words to me (and she actually meant them), I realized she had literally talked herself into believing that nothing like that had ever happened to me, and I shamefully admit that I snapped.

I can honestly say that although I did have a very explosive temper when I was young and up until I was about 25 years old, I am not a violent person. At that moment, however, I found myself being physical towards my mom, for the second time in my life. It's so strange, but it happened exactly the way it had when I was a teenager and I had pushed her down onto her bed. She was standing in front of the couch, so I pushed her to a seated position and yelled into her face, "What is *wrong with you*? How could you even *say* those words to me!?"

I stood up straight, and stepped away from her.

She cried, but I didn't.

I was furious, and stormed out of the house.

I didn't see her or talk to her for two months after that, but after I couldn't avoid her any longer and I let her back in, the subject was never mentioned again.

I learned that when it came to this part of my life with my mother, I would always have to be the bigger person. I had to forgive and forget because the only other option was to be estranged from her and my brother and his family, just as Paul was. This would affect a lot more people than me, and I didn't want to live with anger and hate in my heart for the rest of my life.

Over the years, with a *lot* of work, a lot of tears, and much anger…I have learned to let it go. I am a survivor and I can't worry anymore about other people's demons, as mine have been enough for me to work through. Swimming, biking, and running have helped me work through the anger and focus on accepting that my relationship with my mother isn't ideal and it isn't the kind I had always wanted, but it is the best that can be expected, and I can no longer hold on to the anger that once plagued me.

I also don't feel as though I have to prove to anyone anymore that I am a good person – or that I am not crazy. I know that I am good, and I know that I am crazy, but in a good way! My actions speak louder than words ever could and my joy in helping girls in need radiates from within me – no explanation required.

Far better it is to dare mighty things, to win glorious triumphs, even though checkered by failure, than to take rank with those poor spirits who neither enjoy much nor suffer much, because they live in the gray twilight that knows neither victory nor defeat.

—T. Roosevelt

XIV

I THREW MY WEDDING DRESS out of the second-story window of my parents' house. It was nicely packed away in an airtight box to keep it clean and preserved, so even though it was now waiting for me to pick it out of the shrubs on the side of the house, the dress was not any less perfect or beautiful. It was brand-new and never worn since I had bought it to wear for my wedding to Danny. That wedding cost my parents a good deal of money, considering the actual day never came; I never wore the dress; and Windows On The River would not refund the deposit for the reception. I guess people don't expect you to cancel a wedding two weeks before you are to walk down the aisle, but I never seemed to do what people expected. I knew deep down that if I married Danny I would be miserable. Our relationship was extremely volatile and tumultuous to say the least. That it would be embarrassing to cancel the wedding at the last minute and I would have to return the gifts from the wedding shower were not good reasons to go through with a marriage I knew would never work.

I wanted so badly to start a life with someone, and to have a family…but I also knew that if the engagement ring outshined the relationship, it was time to bail! Surprisingly, people weren't that upset about it and they didn't even want their shower gifts returned. I had fully prepared to give all the gifts back and expected people to be upset. I guess when you have lived your life turning and burning the men in your life, not a lot of stock is placed in any of your relationships and nothing is shocking anymore. (Or so people thought!) Never underestimate my ability to shock, or the need for extra room in what my brother had dubbed "Liz's Hall of Shame." The Hall of Shame included all the boyfriends of my past. It seemed as if they were in a revolving door, and after a while, my parents stopped bothering to try to get to know any of them because I usually got rid of them by the time they did. I had a few "serious" boyfriends, four of whom I had lived with for various lengths of time. In my mom's and dad's eyes this was a sin, but they hoped it would at least lead me to marriage and settling down "honestly."

There were also a lot of guys with whom I had relationships (or relations) who I wouldn't exactly call boyfriends and might not be able to recall their names either. I was very promiscuous, and I began this behavior at a young age. I'm not proud of it, but I think for a long time it was my way of demonstrating some type of power over guys, and the "attention" from them made me feel somehow validated as a person. I liked the initial thrill of winning their affections almost as much as I enjoyed tossing them away once I had them. There were only a few guys I deeply cared for, which brought on an overwhelming sense of vulnerability that I couldn't handle. There was always an unbearable fear of having my heart ripped out – and a rug yanked from under my feet – which caused me to push those I cared for away, and then beg them to stay when they tried to leave.

I wanted so badly to be loved, and when I started to feel close to someone, there was a kind voice somewhere deep inside of me which said it would be okay to allow myself to be loved. The voice would talk me into letting my guard down and believing that everything would be fine. Before I could settle too far into the warm comfort of this feeling, the depraved and wicked voice inside of me would wake me up from my foolishness. Like dumping cold water over someone in a deep sleep, this voice made me conscious once again that my heart was left open, defenseless, and exposed, and that just wouldn't do. That was when I either left with no goodbye, or went into what most guys would refer to as "psycho-mode" to ensure that they would leave and never come back (that old *sabotage* thing again). This defense mechanism allowed me to keep my heart safe and protected, but it also ensured that my heart remained empty and lonely. I decided I would need to do something drastic if I ever wanted to change the way things were going for me in my love life. I made up my mind to marry the first nice guy who came along; to marry quickly after meeting; and to start a family right away.

The old joke my dad liked to tell (over and over) was that my mom flew in through the window on her broomstick at the Halloween party where they met, and they were married four months later. Pretending that my mom was a witch was my dad's idea of comedy but for everyone else it was just corny. It is rather humorous, however, that I met my first husband at a Halloween party and married him *three and a half weeks* after we met. Ironically, no one in the family found that to be funny either. It was just after Halloween when I stopped by my mom's house to say "Hi" on one of those incredible gorgeous and sunny fall days – the type of day so beautiful, that if you actually loved someone, you would want to go apple-picking with that person. I have strange barometers for love.

Days like that in Cleveland, when the summer holds on by its fingertips, make you love living here; and because they are so few and far between, they are almost magical when they occur. I knew exactly what I would do before I even got to my parents' house on Pond Drive. I went upstairs while my mom was making me something to eat. I went into the spare bedroom and opened the closet in which I knew the wedding dress was being stored. The dress was on a shelf in its big, special, white box. There was also a very beautiful headpiece with a small veil attached to it which went with the dress. I had purchased the dress at a well-known bridal boutique on the east side of Cleveland in Chagrin Falls, which cost my parents around $4,000. Wouldn't it be a great shame if it was never put to use? At the rate I was going, I knew I would never have a conventional relationship, courtship, or wedding, but that didn't mean I couldn't sport this gorgeous dress with my Converse sneakers in Vegas! So, out the window it went!

I told my parents that I was going to a wedding that weekend in Chicago, which was the truth to a certain extent because I *was* going to a wedding. Okay, I got the city and state a little mixed up, and I left out the part that it was *my own* wedding I would be attending, and that it would be to an almost complete stranger. So? What's the big deal? And, unfortunately, no one was going to pay me a million dollars to do it either, like on those television game shows. For me it was more like that Bruno Mars song, *Marry You*: "It's a beautiful night/We're looking for something dumb to do/Hey baby/I think I wanna marry you."

I went to a travel agent and booked the flight for Joel and me to Las Vegas, and then we went to the mall and put a couple of wedding rings and a small engagement ring on a payment plan with my credit card. Because Joel had lost his driver's license as a result of his second DWI, I took the wheel (quite literally) and firmed up all the details. We were set to go with no one in the know except for Joel, a friend of his who lived out in Vegas who agreed to be a witness at the ceremony along with his girlfriend, and me.

It was so exciting and fun to be on a crazy adventure, to be getting married, and to be doing it all on the sly! I didn't care anymore about waiting to find the perfect person. I knew there wouldn't be one for me. I had resigned myself to believing that true love and beautiful fairy tale lives were either not real, or they were only a reality for *other* people. They were not for me and never would be. I would have to settle for someone who was at least nice, and who "loved" me. I had those two things with Joel and it would have to be good enough. I was 28 years old – about to turn 29 – and I wanted to have a baby before I was 30. Sometimes you have to take the bull by the horns…even if that means you might end up with a horn in your ass down the road. I didn't care. I was willing to marry a guy who had two DUIs, no driver's license, and an unsteady house-painting job, if that's what it would take to change the direction my life was going.

My impetuous behavior often upset my family and confused people around me, but when you are called crazy your whole life, and people consistently tell you that you are nuts and you make poor decisions, you begin to go along with it and just live up to the low expectations. I'm not saying this behavior is right, or that it should be used as an excuse for poor decision-making, but if the self-esteem isn't there, it is very easy to fall into a mode that will keep you behind the eight ball for your entire life. Sometimes, having the life you want takes serious action, and sometimes you have to really shake things up to make a change and to achieve what you want. Living the same way day in and day out by other people's standards of what is right was getting me nowhere (nor was believing that I was crazy and would probably accomplish very little in life). So I had nothing to lose! I had already been hospitalized for overdosing; I had been moved out of my apartment by my parents while in the hospital; forced to see an anger- and emotions-management counselor; told I was bipolar; told I was unlovable and crazy; had been in and out of an abusive relationship and in a relationship that went south because his family said I was crazy; had gone to bars and had threesomes; and done other risky things that made me feel dark, empty, and lonely. I felt bad about myself and thought I would be alone for the rest of my life. I was forced to sit down and tell my dad that I was abused by the neighbor, when I thought he would have already known what happened to me. I felt as though my whole family thought I was some type of "case" that they all had to supervise. And I was sick of it. I was done with it. Getting married in Vegas to a person I just met would seem small in comparison to the many other inductees I brought into the Hall of Shame.

I guess that's why I decided to overlook it when I saw the envelope in Joel's stuff that was marked "Paternity." My heart sank into my stomach as I opened the letter and read the outcome of a test that said it was 99.9 percent positive that Joel was the father of a baby named Veronica. When I asked him about it he said that he barely knew the woman who he had got pregnant. They had hooked up twice after many drinks at a bar. He said she was separated from her husband, and she had been sleeping with him as well. When she came to Joel and said she was pregnant, he didn't think it was his baby and he told me he had already made it clear to her that he wanted nothing to do with her. She said the baby was his and that he needed to take responsibility. He said he would take the test and if the baby was his he wanted her to have an abortion. The test proved that he was the father, and she refused to have an abortion. Joel explained to me that he wanted nothing to do with this woman, but when he found out that the baby was his, he agreed to pay child support but refused to have anything else to do with the child's life.

All of this was revealed to me right before we left for Las Vegas. The bags were packed, the tickets were on the dresser, and the story that was unfolding before me should have been something I was reading in *Us Magazine* on the plane, but instead it was the new life I was heading into. I wasn't happy with the news that Joel had a child, let alone one with whom he had nothing to do except for financial payments.

The whole thing was just another piece of the white-trash puzzle that was my life. Piece by piece I was living out what I thought I deserved, but in my heart I knew I wanted better. I asked him over and over if he was sure that he didn't want a relationship with his daughter. He said he didn't even know the woman and that he told her a long time ago that she was psycho and he wanted nothing to do with her. He didn't feel he needed to have a relationship with her or the baby, and he wanted to keep me completely separate from them both. We were starting our own life and our own family, and they didn't have any part in that. It was before he met me, and he didn't have any type of relationship that he felt bonded him to anything beyond a financial responsibility. It was not one of my proudest moments, but I agreed with him. Because he said he had never met the baby, and there was no longer any contact with the child's mother, I agreed that keeping things that way was the best thing to do. Our plans were set to go and I didn't want to call off another wedding. There would never be a perfect scenario for me, and even though my heart said Joel's situation was wrong, his mistakes were all made before I met him. I wasn't going to hold them against him, since I had so many mistakes of my own. We made the trip to Vegas with my smuggled wedding dress and a secret plan that was our shot at happiness.

When we arrived in Vegas, Joel and I walked up and down the Strip and scoped out the seemingly endless number of wedding chapels. We were excited to get our wedding underway in an inexpensive but not too cheesy manner. I wasn't that picky about where we held the nuptials, but I didn't want to do a drive-through and I knew I didn't want Elvis to officiate. We settled on the Shalimar Wedding Chapel. The $129 package had everything a blushing bride could want, including limo service from the hotel to the place where you get your marriage license...and then to the chapel for the ceremony! It even included 12 photos (we got to keep the roll of film), three hand-tied roses which I was allowed to keep, and a matching boutonniere for the groom to keep, as well as music, the minister, and a VHS video of the ceremony. It really is the best deal in town for the most important day of your life.

The Shalimar Wedding Chapel itself is rather cute, small, and, I suppose, "modern" in design. To me it leaned a little heavier on the funeral parlor side of things than perhaps the wedding chapel side, but maybe that is supposed to be part of the allure – like a little play on the age-old clichés such as the end of your single days; the ball and chain; the death of your freedom. I don't think that was the intended look, though. Whoever designed the Shalimar probably thought the archway at the front of the chapel, flanked on either side with flower-adorned candelabras and draping billowy white curtains, as well as stained glass window facades designed in hearts and flowers were the perfect décor for the beginning of a couple's life, instead of "the end." But when I looked at it, I could more easily envision a casket than a couple of newlyweds under that archway.

All things considered, however, it really was fairly tasteful and sweet. I mean, it isn't as if we selected being married in a drive-through, by an alien, or by Elvis!

I wore my special dress, and although it was wrinkled from being jammed into my suitcase…it was beautiful. My Converse sneakers underneath couldn't be seen, but they were white and comfy. For *that moment in time* we were a very happy married couple with a future that was brighter than the Vegas Strip at night. After we were pronounced husband and wife, we went back to the hotel to change our clothes and then hit the town. We partied on the old Vegas Strip at old-school places such as the Golden Nugget and enjoyed the free champagne we received for being newlyweds.

The next morning I felt I should call my parents and let them know I was married. I don't know if it was guilt or excitement, but I needed to tell them what I did. On a pay phone outside the New York-New York Hotel, I watched the roller coaster as I made the collect call to my mom and dad. My mom answered the phone and accepted the charges. She could hear that I was someplace loud and crazy, and when I told her that I had to tell her something…she knew right away to start screaming for my dad to pick up the other line. Any time my parents spoke to me or my brothers on the phone they always insisted on both being on two different extensions at the same time. They were really into the party call. I'm fairly sure this started because everyone went to my dad, and if my mom wasn't on the other line she would miss out on the conversations altogether and wouldn't know what was going on. My dad probably didn't want to have to repeat the whole thing to her, so it was easier just to wait until everyone was on the line before we began talking.

In a shrill banshee-like manner (with a German accent), my mom was calling out *"Dad!"* In between yelling for him, she would come back to me on the phone and tell me, "Hold on" and "Don't say anything yet."

I knew the drill so I stood and waited while I stared at the roller coaster, listening to my mom freak out and smiling at Joel, standing next to me. My dad picked up the other line and in an exasperated tone asked my mom, "What is it!?"

My mom said, "It's Liz. She isn't in Chicago, and she has something to tell us."

The line was dead quiet and I watched the people on the roller coaster put their hands in the air and scream as they tipped over the big hill. I thought about how weird Vegas is when you really think about it. The fake mini-cities that never sleep and the themed casinos without any clocks are all very strange when you stand back and really think about them. I had been there a few years before my wedding to run my first marathon with my training buddy, Brady. As I had never run a marathon before, doing one in the desert made *loads* of sense. Ignorance is bliss, as they always say. I recalled how on race day we got up at 4:00 a.m. and made our way through the lobby munching on bagels and sipping water in our running clothes. All the "normal" people were still awake – partying, smoking, and gambling – from the night before. We were looking at them as if they were crazy and they were looking at us as if we were freaks. Everyone was right.

My parents were waiting for me to drop the bomb. They knew something was up and because it was me they were dealing with, there was no telling what I was about to say. I told them I was in Las Vegas and that I was now married! The silence was deafening at first, until my mom started crying. My dad asked me if I was kidding. I said no. Then they wanted to know who I married, as I wasn't really dating anyone. They ventured a guess or two that included my old boyfriend, Craig. (That was a good guess, actually, as Craig and I often broke up and got back together, but he had married in the meantime, I think.)

"Nope. Not Craig!"

One of the strangest wedding experiences I have had, other than this one in Vegas, was with Craig and took place in Pittsburgh at his best friend's wedding. This was sometime back in 1993, I believe, when the sport of triathlon was still very new to me, but it was my latest passion. I had been training for the Cleveland Triathlon and had my heart set on doing the race, of which Craig was well aware. The wedding, of course, fell on the same weekend as the triathlon, and it was made quite clear to me that as his girlfriend it was my duty to skip the triathlon and attend the wedding. I really did not want to miss doing the race. This was probably very selfish on my part, but to be fair, his friend did not like me very much to begin with and in the "old Liz days" it wasn't considered very wise to force me into a situation in which I didn't want to be. I had many conversations at the dining room table with my dad about this wedding dilemma, and he agreed with me that I shouldn't go. He reminded me how angry I could get when I felt pushed, and opined that Craig wanted me there in order to "show me off to his friends." (My dad was always proud of me and complimentary no matter how much I didn't believe him.)

As usual, my dad was right.

I blew off the triathlon and went to the wedding, which ended up with Craig and me in a huge and very public fight, and me catching a cab home...to Cleveland! I didn't tell him I was leaving Pittsburgh. I simply went back to the hotel, packed, and called a cab. The driver thought it was hilarious that I wanted him to drive me from Pittsburgh to Cleveland, but my mind was made up and I wasn't about to stay there a minute longer. He told me he would do it for $250, which was a bargain, as I would have agreed to any price. I went to an ATM and took out half the amount to pay him up front, with the remaining half to be paid upon arrival. We reached my parents' house at about 1:00 a.m., when my poor dad was not only awakened to the surprise of my being there, but also that I was delivered by cab *and* he owed the driver $125!

My parents thought maybe I had married my last boyfriend. Again the answer was "Nope!"

This game was fun!

"Well, who is it?!" my father demanded.

I told my parents it was no one they knew, because I had just met him about three weeks earlier. Needless to say there was not a lot of joy and elation on the other end of the line. My mom was upset that my dad would never walk me down the aisle, and my dad was upset that I was doing something crazy which would inevitably cause me pain, and in turn, would cause him pain as well (and most likely that pain would come in two forms: emotional and financial).

My dad was a smart man. Joel and I didn't have a pot to piss in, but we had each other! (Eeek!) I told them they would meet their new son-in-law when we got home, not to worry, and I would see them soon. I hung up and Joel called his family. Joel was raised by his grandparents because his mom and dad had him when they were 19 years old. His mom took off soon after she had him, so he lived with his father and his uncles at his grandparents' house. It was as if his grandparents were his parents; his mom was out of the picture, and his dad and uncles were like his brothers. His father remarried and Joel had a stepsister and stepmother, who I met once or twice in the two years we were married. I never met his mom, although Joel said he would run into her once in a while when he was out at the bars. He said she worked at the DMV, and that was about all I ever knew about her, except that Joel said she was of Italian descent and had dark hair and olive skin. Joel's phone call took half as long as mine, and after he hung up we walked over to New York for a slice of pizza. It was time to go home and start our new life together.

At Thanksgiving dinner that year, after our October nuptials, I introduced my family to my new husband. I wouldn't say they were extremely warm, but no one was mean to him either. They all did that thing where they looked at me with pity and as though I was crazy – maybe even a little scary – but I was used to that look! Thanksgiving dinners, and holidays in general, have always been rather strained for me with my family because I always felt like an outsider. I knew that the extended family, such as my aunt and my cousins, often heard from my mom about what a nut I had been all year, so when it was time for a holiday dinner, I knew I was being looked at like a sideshow freak at the circus. Joel and I really didn't care, and I was used to being looked at by my family as the helpless crazy loser (or at least that is how I felt with everyone always asking me if I was okay, and tiptoeing around me as though I was some type of land mine). At the moment we were happy to have each other, and we decided to try to have a baby right away.

By the time Christmas rolled around I wasn't feeling well, and by New Year's Day I knew I was pregnant. That we had only known each other for a few weeks when we got married made what I felt was a clear statement that we hadn't married because I was pregnant. We hadn't been together long enough for me to get pregnant, or at least to know if I was. Regardless, people assumed that was the reason we were together, as we didn't know each other for very long before tying the knot.

Not everything is the way it seems, however, and this included my new groom. I knew that marrying someone I didn't know could potentially reveal things about that person which weren't exactly ideal. For instance, maybe he snores or leaves the toilet seat up. It didn't take too long for me to begin to see things about Joel that weren't exactly pretty. There were some major issues that began to reveal themselves more clearly, and I told myself I was prepared to deal with them...right after I had the baby.

When you are an athlete, you are accustomed to being in tune with your body, in control, and in harmony. When I got pregnant, that all flew out the window and my body's harmony sounded more like a needle being scratched across a spinning record, bringing the music to an abrupt halt. I went from being an Ironman athlete to gaining more than 80 pounds and being told by the doctor that I shouldn't be running because of the risk to the baby. I had "morning sickness" all day long and horrible, debilitating migraine headaches caused by fluctuating hormones. I couldn't take anything for the migraines because of the baby, and even if I could have, I would have barfed it up anyway. Feeling sick all the time bothered me a lot.

It didn't bother me that we didn't have much, and that our apartment was the upstairs of a rented duplex in Lakewood with no air conditioning. It didn't even bother me that we didn't have a bed. We had a mattress and box spring on the floor. I liked to think of it as Bohemian. This was something that bothered my dad a lot! He bought us a bed saying that no daughter of his, pregnant with his grandchild, was going to sleep on the floor. I borrowed maternity clothes from friends and bought one or two pieces that I wore over and over. I may have been a lot of things in my time, but being jealous of the things other people had which I didn't was never one of them. I had friends who had money and could afford multiple cars, nice homes, vacations in Hawaii and Europe, dinners out, nannies, and a plethora of other things that I would never have. Thank God none of that bothered me at all. I was always happy for other people who had nice things and accepted that they just weren't in the cards for me. I had a baby setting up shop inside of me, and that made me feel as though I was plenty rich.

The things I had on my mind were much more important than what other people were doing or how much money or clothes they had. I had to worry about my health and my baby's health, and I was fairly sure I would have to worry about these things on my own. I knew I needed to be there for my baby and never let him down, and that frightened me immensely. I didn't feel in control of my body, or my life for that matter, and I couldn't do what made me feel better and gave me strength, which was running and working out.

It was really scary to come to the realization that I would have to be on my own, taking care of and supporting a child, when I felt I couldn't even support myself. There were a lot of tears and a lot of visits to my parents' house when Joel wasn't around, which was most of the time. Of course I was aware that everyone looked at me and my poor life choices with the same old "there she goes again" attitude, but I had to get over that and get through the obstacles one by one… the way an athlete would. The obstacles I had to overcome were really just normal everyday things for most people, but at that time in my life they seemed to be challenges of catastrophic proportions. I had a very difficult pregnancy and a job, in human resources and recruiting, that went from good to bad faster than you can say "pickles and ice cream" – resulting in a pregnancy discrimination lawsuit. Joel wasn't working, and had also invited a friend of his who I had never met to stay with us until he could find someplace to live because his wife had kicked him out.

I also slowly began to realize (and accept) that Joel was an alcoholic.

The painting company he was doing some work for was part-owned by one of his best friends, but things changed organizationally, which meant Joel needed to find a new job. He ended up taking a job in a mortgage company, but the position was strictly commission-based – no draw, no salary, and certainly no benefits. He did get some nice business cards which said he was some type of manager, and that made him happy. I didn't care if he was the elephant poop-shoveling manager at the zoo if it brought in a paycheck, which, sadly, his job did not. We talked about the need for him to get a second job in the evening, at least until he started making commissions. This was a done deal (in Joel's mind) because the same friend with whom he was painting also owned a coffee shop where he had worked part-time in the past. As luck would have it, his friend was happy to have Joel come back and work some night and weekend hours. I tried to encourage him to find a job that wasn't 50 minutes away from where we lived and didn't cost more in gas than he could bring in from the tip jar. (I guess it was worth it to him to drive to the coffee shop where he could hang out with his friend and sip booze from a coffee mug behind the counter.)

My job at the time was with an occupational and physical therapy placement firm that recruited therapists and placed them in nursing homes, hospitals, and other OT and PT facilities. It was rather funny (or at least I thought it was) that when I interviewed for the job I was single and not even dating anyone. I knew it wasn't legal but didn't make a big deal when, during my interview, the owner of the company asked me if I was married or if I had any kids. When I told her that I wasn't and that I didn't, respectively, she asked me if there was anyone at all in my life who would be upset if I worked long hours or if I got paged at all hours of the day or night. I should have jumped up and ran, but I needed the job and I prided myself on getting an offer from every job I had ever interviewed for, so I affirmed that it wouldn't be a problem as I didn't even have a boyfriend.

The job was mine and I was to start in about four weeks. On my first day of work I came in and no one recognized me. For some odd reason I had decided to dye my blonde hair a dark black! It really looked horrible, but I didn't have time to get to the salon to change it, so I went to work looking like a half-dead gothic zombie. After the initial shock of my new look, there was also the shock of my next bit of news, which I casually threw out as:

"Oh, and by the way – I don't know if this matters – but I got married, so my last name is different now."

My boss thought that was weirder than my new hair color, but she didn't make too huge a deal out of it at the time. All she said was, *"What?* I thought you weren't dating anyone?"

I answered with: "I wasn't when I interviewed, but we met after the interview and got married in Las Vegas, so my last name is different from what I told you."

I worked really hard and did my job well. She was pleased with all that I was able to accomplish and with my tenacious drive, which she attributed to my being a goal-oriented athlete who could run marathons and do triathlons.

She had me doing everything from picking up the South African therapists at the airport and driving them to the corporate condo at all hours of the day and night; to getting them their social security cards; teaching them to drive; conducting their human resources training and coaching them to interview well; to making 50 cold calls per day; doing site visits; and securing placements so we could bill for their hours. I even brought a group of newly arrived therapists to my family's Thanksgiving dinner, because they were brand-new to this country, didn't have anywhere to go, and they had never eaten turkey or celebrated our American holiday. It was fun having someone at a holiday dinner who actually felt more "foreign" than I did!

When I became pregnant, everything changed and my boss was quite visibly upset. It wasn't a secret in our tiny office that she and her husband had been trying to have a baby for years and that she had had more than six miscarriages. I would never wish this on anyone and I felt sorry for her, but I also had no idea that she would take out her sadness, anger, and frustration on me for getting pregnant in the blink of an eye. Even if I wanted something so badly and couldn't have it, I wouldn't begrudge another person for having what I wanted. It has never made sense to me to get angry at other people for having something that I couldn't have or being able to do something that I couldn't do.

Suddenly, *almost* out of nowhere, my required cold calls went up to 100 per day, and my pager would go off at 5 a.m. or midnight. When I called my boss back after being paged, she would yell at me for doing things that she had specifically told me to do the last time she paged me. No matter what I did, I wasn't doing my job up to her ever-growing and changing standards. She was setting me up for failure by piling on more and more outlandish goals and duties. It was a ludicrous work environment, and, at first, I couldn't understand why it was happening. I began "investigating" a bit by talking to a co-worker and found out that all three of the other women in the office (including the woman who gave me this information) were also not able to have kids, and that they had all been asked about it during their interviews as well. This was a huge eye-opener to me and could not have been a coincidence as far as I was concerned.

My days at work and my time at home became more and more miserable. I knew my boss was trying to push me out but I also knew that I wasn't in a position to look for a new job while I was pregnant. I also couldn't leave Joel yet, even though I didn't want to raise a baby in a house with an alcoholic with whom I knew I wasn't in love, so I tried to stick out all of it.

The day finally came at work when my boss sat me down with all of her "documented" wrongs that I had committed and told me I was fired for not being capable of completing my work or doing my job. She wanted me to sign a statement that I agreed with her accusation that I was incapable of fulfilling my job description and duties. I told her that she purposely made it impossible for me to fulfill my job "requirements" because they changed on an hourly basis, rendering them impossible for anyone to accomplish. I refused to put my signature on the paper she pushed in front of me. She said she would withhold my last paycheck if I didn't sign the document. I explained that withholding a paycheck was illegal and she laughed at me. I know that in her eyes I was weak and had no power or money, and she was the complete opposite. There is nothing more frustrating to me than a person who tries to take advantage of someone in a lesser position – financially, emotionally, physically, or otherwise. It is disgusting.

I got up from the table and left. I didn't have a cell phone, so upon leaving the office I found a pay phone and dialed an attorney's number while crying my eyes out. I called my friend Todd, who I knew from when I worked as a sales rep at the Athletic Club and who practiced law and would be able to calm me down and tell me what to do next. We had always been buddies and often ran together or went to concerts or movies and hung out. Todd had a big crush on me that he didn't try to hide from anyone. The whole fitness club knew it. On my birthday he left a tape-recorded message that included *Birthday* by the Beatles as well as a mix tape and some other goodies on my desk so I would be surprised when I arrived at work. Other actions that told me he rather dug me more than just as a friend included the gifts and flowers he often gave me, as well as when he would see me come out of my office he would fall down on the floor in the middle of the lobby near the front desk (literally) and clench his heart, feigning that the mere sight of me gave him a heart attack. I loved spending time with Todd because we had a ton in common and he was really funny and obviously silly, but we were never more than friends. I made it clear that it would never go beyond friendship, and I guess he went along with it in hopes that I would change my mind someday. Todd cared about me and he "got" me, but I just wasn't attracted to him and didn't want to marry someone my parents actually liked. He didn't practice employment law, but I figured he could help me and maybe refer me to someone who did. I called him slightly hysterical and crying, and told him quickly what had happened, but with some very specific examples. I broke down and let him know what a horrible place I was in personally and professionally.

He said, "I hate to say I told you so, *but* – you had to know this would happen when you married *the coffee shop guy*!"

(The coffee shop that Joel worked at was in Todd's neighborhood, so he actually knew Joel before I did! This world is *way* too small sometimes!) After he got out his "I-told-you-so's," Todd made time for me to come see him in his office. When I got there, I could see it on his face the minute he set eyes on me. He looked shocked that I was no longer the fun and pretty happy-go-lucky girl from the Athletic Club who could run for miles and miles. It had only been a year since I had last seen him, but I had cut my hair really short, which accentuated the fullness of my tired face. I was not only pregnant, but also fat, and I looked worn out and sad.

The combination of surprise and pity that I saw in his eyes as he looked me over made me feel even worse than before, but I swallowed my pride and vanity and embarrassment because I had bigger things to worry about than any of that. I figured if he had ever fantasized about the girl he never had, but wished he did…that fantasy was killed instantly upon my arrival. We had always been good friends and underneath it all he cared about me and couldn't help wanting to help me, even if I was stupid enough to marry an alcoholic coffee shop worker. He referred me to the wife of one of his partners, whose name was Rebecca; she was not only an employment attorney, but Todd said she was also known as an "Ice Queen." He gave me her contact information and said she was someone he would want on his side, and that she was the best. Within days of my visit to Todd's office, my father and I were sitting in front of Rebecca, telling my story.

Rebecca was as no-nonsense as they come, but she was also very kind. She was tall and thin with dark hair, brown eyes, and a Long Island accent. You don't hear many of those in Ohio and I liked it. She listened to everything I had to say and informed me that I had a case. My father agreed to pay her retainer and hourly fees. It was yet another "mess" that my dad seemed to have to help me out of...but at least it was agreed upon by everyone that this time it wasn't really my fault. My father was always my rock that I could turn to and he supported me in every way until he died. I was much too old to need his help, and he probably should have shown me "tough love" by making me figure it all out on my own, but he couldn't do it. I was a mess and it wasn't in him to not do everything he could to help me. Even at my worst my father always saw potential in me to be something great. He believed in me in the same way that I believe in all of my *Girls With Sole* kids.

I had a child on the way I would need to take care of, but I felt I couldn't even take care of myself. I knew I wouldn't be able to count on Joel for anything, but I couldn't worry about him at the moment. Every time Joel and I had an issue which required money to solve it, his answer to the problem was to go talk to my dad. He didn't even pretend that he was pondering other solutions before immediately pulling out the "dad" card. He didn't try to get a job that paid money, and he was drinking during the day and night. I needed to get my life in order for my baby and myself and worry about divorcing Joel later. I wanted so badly to force it all to work and to have an instant family. I didn't care that we would never have money; that was not the issue and I was okay with that. The problem at hand was twofold:

Number 1. I couldn't be married to someone who wouldn't try to help himself and wouldn't at least get a job (any job) to help his family.

Number 2. I refused to raise my son in a house with an alcoholic who refused to get any help.

If I had learned anything at all from my father it was to "take one thing at a time" (he said this to me over and over like a broken record) and to tackle a problem in steps in order to keep from getting overwhelmed. This advice has been extremely valuable to me and I have used it throughout my life, repeating it like a mantra.

I organized a mental checklist of the steps I would need to take that would get me out of the position I was in and into a life that would be best for my son and for me. I climbed the steps one at a time, trying very hard not to worry about what happened in the past or what might happen in the future. My checklist wasn't long, but that didn't mean it would be easy. It looked like this:

Find a new source of income.

Have the baby.

Recover from the pregnancy.

Divorce Joel if things don't improve.

As my father and I prepared to leave her office, Rebecca said she wanted to ask me something but she didn't want to insult me. I am not insulted that easily, so I told her to ask away. She said she realized I was a college-educated person, but she had recently lost a nanny who had to go back home to Alaska and was looking for a new one to replace her. She didn't know me very well but said she could tell during our meeting that I was a good person and was wondering – if I didn't have another job and if she wasn't insulting my intelligence – whether I would like to work for her and her family until I had my baby. Rebecca had three little girls. At that time they were 9, 7, and about six months old. They lived about 45 minutes away from where I did, and I was about four months pregnant, but as I didn't have a job and probably wouldn't find one in my state, and my husband had a job but he didn't get paid – I took it!

It was almost immediately after I accepted the nanny position for my attorney that I slowly but surely lost any remaining crumbs of respect for Joel. And in *any* marriage, that is the kiss of death. He made no efforts to find a paying job, and spent a lot of time at the coffee shop and then out at the bars drinking after he clocked out. On the nights that he was home, he would stay up and drink after I went to bed. I wasn't used to being so tired all the time and went to bed fairly early because I had to get up early to be over at Rebecca's house before she left for work. She liked to have me at their house fairly early in the morning so I could tend to the baby while she worked out and then got ready for work. My baby was growing bigger and bigger inside of me and by the time I was five months pregnant, I was so huge that people thought I was having twins. I worked all day watching my attorney's kids, taking them to camp and picking them up, doing their grocery shopping, and folding and putting away their laundry.

Rebecca began paying me to clean their house as well, so I could earn extra money. I was happy that she was able to help me out and I was willing to take on any jobs she could give me. I don't know what I would have done if I hadn't been able to work for Rebecca and her family. Joel and I still had trouble making ends meet so sometimes if Rebecca was hard-pressed to find a baby sitter on the weekends, she would have me do that as well. When she and her husband came downstairs after getting ready to go out and they looked so nice and had somewhere cool to go, I felt a twinge of sadness knowing that I was a 29-year-old baby sitter. But I was able to push the thought out of my head. I had to do what was right for my family and not let a thing like pride get in the way of that.

My parents and I started looking for a house for my new family to live. I was surprised they wanted to help us, but also, not surprised. They weren't crazy about Joel or his lack of motivation, but they wanted their daughter and grandson to live in a decent house that, unlike the one we lived in, wasn't smelly, crowded, and hot with really awful and mean landlords.

Looking back on it now, I'm sure the landlords we rented from were most likely not that mean at all. In actuality we were probably the worst tenants on the face of the planet, and they had the misfortune of owning the duplex, renting to us, and living right below us! One night they called the police on me for what they thought was a domestic violence dispute. I was nine months pregnant with my son Jake, it was a stiflingly hot August night, and Joel was at his friend's coffee shop on the east side of town "working" and then stopping off at the bar on the way home. We had no air conditioning in our apartment, so it felt as if it was the temperature of the Earth's crust. The smell of the cat's litter box was killing me, but because pregnant women are restricted by their doctors from being near cat feces, I couldn't clean it out, and Joel never did it either. I was the size of a house and felt every bit of it. To add insult to injury the swelling in my feet felt as though I was constantly stepping on pins and needles when I walked, and all I wanted to do was eat French fries and lie on the couch.

My pregnancy was considered high-risk (so I couldn't work out), and I was worried that I would go into labor while Joel was out getting hammered almost an hour away from where we lived. Needless to say, I was miserable, and when you mix the ingredients together of a fat, hot, and hormonal pregnant woman with an unemployed, drunk, delusional husband, what you've got on your hands is a recipe for disaster. I called Joel at the coffee shop and let him know how angry I was that he was there, drinking, and that he didn't care that I could be having the baby any minute. I was pissed I was working so hard to try to keep us afloat and that all he seemed to do was drink until his teeth were floating. Our "conversation" turned into a screaming match, which, in turn, resulted in my throwing everything he owned out the window and onto the side lawn below. There was quite a pile of clothes, and a radio, mixed in with knickknacks accumulating in the darkness and green of the lawn beneath the window. I told him that all his shit would be waiting for him outside when he got home, and my loud and angry diatribe must have sounded like two people fighting instead of just me throwing things out the window and yelling over the phone.

After hanging up on Joel and stepping back for a minute, the reality of the situation hit me like a bucket of ice water on that hot and steamy night, and snapped me out of the rage I was in. I couldn't believe this was my life. I was *that* person – the person I didn't ever want to be; the person who ran away from marrying Danny so I *wouldn't* be that person. I had to reel it in and be better than my anger for myself and my son.

Immediately, I began making trips up and down the stairs of our apartment, scooping up piles of Joel's belongings, along with some grass and dirt, and creating a giant pile of all his shit in the middle of our tiny living room. I wasn't going to put all his crap away for him (let's not get crazy now), but I would at least make the effort to get it all back inside. I realize now how sad it is to admit this, but at the time I truly felt that making the effort to pick everything up and bring it back upstairs was a valiant overture.

I was exhausted and sweating so I took off my clothes and went to bed, and that was exactly when there was a thunderous pounding at the door. I put on a pair of underpants the size of a tent and a "wife-beater"-type undershirt, went to the door, and upon opening it was face-to-face with two huge cops. They had an unusually large appearance because there were two of them and the stairwell of the old double was narrow and cramped. Their police radios crackled, echoing off the hallway walls, and their night sticks seemed menacing and intrusive in the small quarters that, awkwardly, we all stood in together.

They asked me if I was home alone, and I said yes. They asked if they could come in and I said yes. They stepped inside the apartment and told me they were there on a domestic disturbance call as they made concerted efforts not to look at me in my underpants and bra-less undershirt. I explained everything to them in detail and after seeing the pile of men's belongings in the living room, they believed what I said and realized that I had been there alone the whole night. One of the officers said, upon leaving, "My wife is pregnant right now too. I understand where you are coming from."

I was happy that they understood, but I still felt completely mortified that I was even in that situation. I felt as though I was some type of trash that the cops had to come and attend to. I felt as though there were now two more people in the world who looked at me, my situation, and my behavior and walked away shaking their heads. I hated that.

After that night I was more motivated than ever to find a house to move into and to keep moving forward on the path that I could follow one step at a time to a happier place.

The pregnancy discrimination suit against my ex-employer settled out of court, which granted me a little bit of money after paying my dad back for floating my legal fees. I owed him much more than I had paid him back, but he wanted me to keep some of it and probably knew I would end up coming back for it eventually anyway.

I came across a really cute house in the city of Cleveland on West 135th Street, and after touring the inside, I knew it was the one. I rushed right over to my parents' house and begged them to go see it. My mom and dad would be co-signing with me and putting the money down on the house, so they had to see it before anything else could go forward. My dad absolutely hated it when I sprung things on him unexpectedly (spontaneity was not his thing) and he didn't want to rush over there to look at it, but I made him. They took a look and immediately dubbed it "the doll house." It was small and sweet and they knew I could make it a home for my son and me – and Joel too, if he lasted that long.

The three of us purchased the house together, with my parents and me on the deed, and Joel on the mortgage. I was the proud owner of a home, and things suddenly looked as bright as a sunny day.

On September 1st, 1998, six months before my 30th birthday, I gave birth to Jake. My mom said it was important for her to see Jake being born, since she wasn't there on the day I was born. My mother and Joel were both in the delivery room. They stood – one on either side of the bed – each of them holding one of my legs and pressing so that my knees were up towards my ears as I pushed. At one point, my mom wanted to see what was happening on the front lines, so she let go of the leg she was holding and let it drop with a heavy and unexpected plunge. My leg suddenly felt like an anchor that was heaved off the side of a boat, and I probably looked like a greasy, plucked chicken with a broken wing. She left her post next to the bed, but surprisingly, I didn't yell at her – or Joel – during any of it. I just needed to get through it, and to bring Jake into the world without any anger.

I cried a lot during the labor, and I felt as though I wouldn't make it. My doctor kept telling me that I was an Ironman and I could do it. I told her I would rather do five back-to-back Ironman races instead of what I was doing right at that moment. She told me to push hard – so I did – and then she suddenly yelled, "*Stop!*"

Jake had arrived and I was told by my doctor that the tear he created was the largest she had ever seen. (She was not a new doctor – it was a 5th degree tear.) Jake's shoulder had torn through my rectum. I was in a lot of pain from all of the stitches and I felt an exhaustion that made the Ironman race I had done feel like a walk in the park.

But all of the pain and exhaustion disappeared as if it were sand that blew straight out of my mind the moment the nurses brought Jacob into my room so I could feed him and snuggle him. (Much like the way you can be hurting and aching during a long race, but the minute you cross the finish line, the pain evaporates and is replaced by euphoria.) When I looked at Jake, I knew that he and I would have a special bond, and that he had, in essence, saved my life. I would never be the same, in a good way, because of him, and my heart instantly tripled in size just like the ending of *How the Grinch Stole Christmas*. (Mine wasn't two sizes too small to begin with, but it was definitely missing something, and that something was Jacob.)

When it was time to bring Jake home, Joel and my parents arranged to come and pick us up at the hospital together, so they could come over to have dinner with us and help us get settled in. We all piled into my dad's maroon Buick, and he proudly drove his new grandson home for his first night in his new house. As he pulled into our driveway, the first thing Joel said was, "Where's the Jeep?"

Joel's red Jeep Wrangler (for which he had never fully paid his friend when he "bought" it from him in the first place) was no longer in our driveway where he had left it. He assumed it was stolen, when in fact, it was repossessed. I guess it didn't dawn on him that in order to keep the car he needed to make payments on it. In his typical fashion, Joel went directly to my father for help and my dad, in turn, got it out of hock and also paid it off for him with the understanding that Joel would need to make the monthly payments to my dad. He agreed, thanked him profusely, and then never paid him back a dime of it. After my father passed away, Joel could have made attempts to pay back the money he owed for the Jeep to my mom, but he didn't do that either.

That night, after we ate and they hung out for a while, it came time for my parents to go home. As I watched them go out the door and down the driveway to their car, I think I cried harder than I did when I squeezed the baby out of me. I was terrified and felt overwhelmed that everything pertaining to the health, safety, and care of this child would be up to me and basically me alone.

About a week after coming home with Jacob and falling deeper in love with him by the day, I knew I had to leave Joel as soon as possible. I was breast-feeding Jake and because of some plugged milk ducts, I had developed double mastitis which, by the way, really sucks and is apparently not very common. Mastitis in one breast is common, but to have it in both at the same time isn't. I didn't even know what mastitis is, so I had no idea why I had a spiking fever, and my boobs were both rock hard and felt as if they were on fire. The pain felt like hot pokers in both boobs and my fever made me so delirious it was as if I were speaking in tongues. Joel took me to the emergency room where the intern proclaimed the utmost need for a spinal tap as the only way to rule out spinal meningitis. I was so out of it, but screamed in terrorized pain when he stuck the needle into my spine, removed it, apologized for doing it wrong, and then stuck it in a second time. It was then that I could honestly say I could take a "stab" at what it might feel like to be tortured.

The good news was that I didn't have spinal meningitis, but the bad news was that the improper manner in which my spinal fluid had been removed resulted in the need for what the doctors called a "blood patch." A leak in my spinal cord had been created which changed the fluid pressure around my brain and spinal cord, thus creating a searing headache that felt as if it could melt steel. I didn't know that such a thing existed, but couldn't even think about it with the excruciating headache I was experiencing. On a positive note, at least the headache was a great distraction from my red, inflamed, and painful boobs. I couldn't lift my head from the pillow and the pain was more than I could stand. I was told that the blood patch was the only way to remedy the problem, and that the doctor would need to draw my blood, stick yet another needle into the same place where the leak was created, and then inject the blood into my spinal cord. When the blood clots, it seals up the hole, which is why they call it a blood patch.

I have no idea how I was able to sit up and bend over for this procedure, but I knew that I had to do it because my son needed me at home! I had to get better and get out of that hospital. I don't know which was more painful – the procedure, or having to be away from my newborn who I had begun breast-feeding, but now had to pump and dump because I was on antibiotics that I couldn't pass on to him. I missed him so much and cried nonstop. My boobs, head, back, and worst of all, my heart, all hurt so much it seemed almost unbearable.

After I was home, fully recovered, and back on my feet, the first thing I did in order to regain some much-needed mental and physical strength was begin to work out again. I started with walking and was running again before I knew it. I took long walks with Jake in the stroller and took him to my mom's so I could squeeze in a run or a swim.

Within two months, I secured a new job as a recruiter in the human resources department for a company called Premier Farnell. For the next couple of months I settled in happily at my new job and felt proud to be working there and even prouder of being a new mom. If there was a glimmer of hope or an instant when I wanted to try to be a "complete" family and give my marriage to Joel a chance, it was quickly shattered one night when he came home drunk and started a fight. It was a fight over the same old things, but it escalated to something new and scary that I had never seen in him before. I yelled at him about all the usual things that made me angry or that I didn't like about his lifestyle, and he retaliated by running upstairs into Jacob's nursery and ripping him out of his crib where he had been sleeping soundly. I ran upstairs, petrified, and begged him to give me the baby. He said he was going to leave me and take Jacob with him. I didn't care if he left – and in fact, wanted him to, for good – but not with my son. He had nowhere to go, and he was drunk.

Jake was now wide awake and blinked his brown eyes at me over Joel's shoulder in a way that I took as bewilderment. I was beside myself and crying hysterically, as Joel stumbled down the stairs with my son in his arms. I ran for the phone and instinctively called my father. My dad had a calming influence on people which was also stern enough to lend an edge, causing the person he was counseling to realize that he had better listen to him or there would be serious consequences.

I woke my father from a dead sleep and rattled off the situation with lightning speed. He responded with, "Give the phone to Joel."

I ran to the door as Joel was trying to get it open and take Jake outside to his Jeep, and I grabbed his shoulder while I pressed the phone to his ear, simultaneously swiping Jacob from his arms. I don't have any idea what my father said to Joel, but when he hung up the phone he didn't try to take Jake away from me, and he apologized for what he did. I told him that he needed to leave and that I wanted a divorce. He literally had no place to go, so I let him sleep on the couch for a couple of weeks until he could find a friend who would take him in.

I was taking control of my life and getting stronger by the day. I had already set the goal to run the next Cleveland Marathon and it helped me gain strength and alleviate stress. It would be Jake and me against the world and I was not only ready for it, I embraced it. I knew it wouldn't be easy, and because Joel was still Jacob's biological father, I would have to grant him rights to see him, but having him out of the house would make things easier for me to raise Jake in what I felt would be the best and most healthy environment.

As dictated by our shared-parenting agreement, Joel was able to have Jacob spend the night with him once during the week and every other weekend. Those were the hardest nights for me to get through, and the sight of his empty crib ripped a hole in my soul. I had to remind myself that it was better for Jake to live in a happy home than in one that had Joel and me in it together, fighting, and unhappy. I vowed that I would let Jacob know the truth about why Joel and I weren't together when he was old enough to handle it. I wanted him to know that we had only known each other for three weeks before we married, that Joel had a child before he met me, and that Joel had a problem with alcohol. I believed that when Jake was old enough to handle it, he should know these things and I would not hide them from him. When I shared these beliefs with Joel, he took them as a personal attack and screamed at me, threatening that if I told Jake anything about him, he would tell him I tried to kill myself. The threat was idle, however, because I was not planning on keeping my past from my child; I didn't believe in it. Again, if Jake was old enough to handle information about me and my past (and the circumstances around it), I was okay with him knowing about it. This infuriated Joel and he started to blame me for all of his problems.

As Jake got a little older, he was able to tell me what he did when he slept at his dad's house. The scenarios he described were cause for serious concern on my part about what went on during the times that Jake slept away from home. The bits and pieces I was getting from my almost four-year-old son indicated that he was being left alone in the apartment while Daddy went to "McDonald's" or to "the store."

By this time Frank and I were married and had been blessed with Morgan. We had a very happy home that was a safe and secure environment for Jake. Over time we deduced that Joel actually was leaving Jake alone in his apartment so he could go out and drink, and that most of the time he actually was in the apartment with him, he spent sleeping while Jake watched age-inappropriate movies such as *Carrie* and *Jaws*.

Based upon what Jacob had told us, added together with odd behaviors and issues Frank and I had noticed, we confronted Joel, and initially he denied all of it. I went through very detailed and specific examples of things which I could only know about if in fact what Jacob was saying was the truth. I asked Joel hundreds of questions about what they did when Jake slept over there, and why Jake would describe the movie *Carrie* in detail from beginning to end, and how Jake knew that Dad went to McDonald's to get breakfast for them, but he didn't come back until the *Barney* tape was already over.

The litany of questions and accusations was enough to make Joel trip and fall, too exhausted to keep on denying after he stood up and brushed himself off in the dusty heat of a mother's defensive fury. Frank and I explained to him that we were not trying to take Jake away from him, but we couldn't in good conscience let Jacob sleep at his place. He could come over and get him, spend time with him, and then bring him home again. Strangely enough he agreed to not having Jake sleep over at his place. He didn't fight it and almost appeared relieved as he acquiesced. This was a good solution which didn't require the courts, and one that worked well for a brief period of time.

Sadly, the problems associated with Joel's drinking escalated, so Frank and I had to approach Joel again and tell him that we couldn't let him pick Jacob up anymore, or spend time with him anywhere but in our home or our presence. He didn't put up a fight at all because he knew that we could go to court, and armed with the things we knew about and could prove, he might never see Jake again.

Many things had happened that led to this point, but the one that stands out hauntingly in my mind was the time that Jake called me from Joel's cell phone and said that Joel left him in the car in a parking lot, that he didn't know where he was, and that he had been gone a very long time. I went into a state of panic and asked Jake to describe where he thought he was. He kept me on the phone for about 30 minutes, and I drove in the direction of the places where I thought he might be. It was nighttime, and Jake wasn't sure which one it was but he knew he was in an empty Giant Eagle parking lot. He said Daddy told him he had to get something in the store, but that he was gone for a very, very long time. I had almost reached the parking lot when Joel got back to his car, and I told Jake to give him the phone. I unleashed the wrath of a mother bear protecting her cub and let him know that he would not be able to see Jake anymore as long as he was drinking. It was up to him if he wanted Jake in his life, and I was okay with it, but he had to be sober.

Time had gone by and it was difficult to do, but because Jake was still too young to handle it, and we didn't want to "bad mouth" Joel to him, we kept him sheltered from a great deal of what was really happening. Joel was changing jobs and residences so often that I stopped keeping track of his addresses. I didn't need to know where he was living, because Jake wouldn't ever be there. Time went on and we all lived our lives. Jake only asked now and then why "Daddy Joel" wasn't around.

One day while I was at work I received a phone call from someone who said he worked with Joel and was calling me because I was Joel's only emergency contact. Joel had just started a new job and was in Florida for some training. Frank and I were happy that he would be working because it meant he might be trying to better himself, and we might begin to receive child support which was over $8,000 in arrearage. Those hopes were dashed as I stood in my office at work and listened as the man on the other end of the phone explained that Joel was in the hospital; that he had had a seizure, had hit his head on his way down to the ground, and had two more seizures in the ambulance on the way to the hospital. My throat dried up like the Sahara and I felt anguish and anger percolate somewhere below my heart. I asked the man as calmly as possible if Joel had been drinking. He said the seizure took place at 9:00 in the morning, but that Joel did hit his head on the hotel bar. He said Joel had been drinking heavily the night before with the group, and he thought Joel might have gone to the hotel bar during a break in his training.

I knew that if Joel had reached the bar about a minute sooner, he might have had the chance to get alcohol into his system and could have fended off the seizure. It didn't play out that way, however. Joel was in the hospital in Florida and I was standing in my little office in Cleveland trying to figure out what I could do about it.

Joel told the man, who I found out was his new boss, that he didn't have any family (which is very sad but also true, as they do not speak to him) and that the only person he could call was his ex-wife. I told the stranger on the phone that I was not a vindictive person, but what I was about to tell him was so the company could get him the help he needed. I told him Joel was an alcoholic and that he needed to be put into a rehab program. That was Joel's first stint in rehab, and I was positive that what happened in Florida was Joel's "rock bottom." Let it be a lesson to me that "rock bottom" is very personal and unique for everyone, and it can only be determined by the individual experiencing it.

It scares me to say that as of today, Joel has not hit his yet.

All I could think of when I hung up the phone was Jacob. I didn't want to tell him about what happened, and the mere thought of having to tell my son that his father had died petrified me. If this wasn't Joel's rock bottom, then it was definitely mine. Jake was around 8 years old at the time and I didn't know what else to do. I had to tell him his father had a drinking problem and begin educating him that although it wasn't ideal, it was something we would deal with together and it was in no way whatsoever his fault.

I don't know what I would have done if it weren't for my long runs and swims with my best friends. During our swim sessions (which usually included kicking about 5,000 laps with the kick board so we could talk), my dearest friend Tricia heard the heartbreak in my voice and saw it in my eyes as I conveyed the stories. She strongly and supportively suggested I go to an Al-Anon meeting. She told me that Al-Anon and Alateen could be very helpful for me, and maybe even for Jake. I decided to give it a try and sheepishly went to the meeting at a church near our house. We had moved out of the doll house and into the suburbs by then, and the church was a beautiful building I had passed many times, never thinking I would ever go there, especially for the reason I did. I spent the first meeting very silent and didn't share anything with the group. I just listened, but it made me feel much better, and I was glad to get out some of my tears and my fears in a place where people understood me. I picked up a book at the end of the meeting titled *What's "Drunk," Mama?* which was written to help explain alcoholism to an innocent child. It was perfect, and I couldn't wait to thank Tricia for pointing me in such a wonderful direction. I told her how great the meeting was for me, and she urged me to check out the Alateen meetings for Jake. He wasn't a teen, but I was at my wits' end and needed help and support. I went to speak with the Alateen leader, an incredible and wonderful person, and he encouraged me to bring Jake to the next meeting. Both the Al-Anon and Alateen meetings were held at the same time, so I could drop Jake off in one room while I attended the adult meeting in another room down the hall.

I began taking Jake to Alateen meetings regularly, and he quickly and affectionately earned the nickname "Alakid," as he was the youngest in the group by a good five years. The other kids welcomed him warmly and Jake seemed to like going to the group, but mostly because of the big kids and the cookies. I went to the meetings down the hall and opened up to the group that I was there so my 8-year-old could attend Alateen and that I was sure his father was going to die or do something to scar my son's life for good. For the next few months I didn't make it through a meeting without crying my eyes out. Afterwards I would try to gather myself back together as I made my way down the fluorescent-lit hallway to the room where Jake was. We always talked about the broad topics presented in his group, but I didn't push him to tell me anything specific that he might have said. One night on our way home from the meetings, Jake wanted to know why the kids in his group talked so much about all the yelling and screaming. He said he didn't get that part, because there was no yelling and screaming in our house. I explained to him that the kids in his group were living in the midst of their parent's alcoholism, and he wasn't. I explained to him that I wanted us to live apart from Joel so he wouldn't have to grow up hearing the yelling and screaming.

He understood. The connection was made.

For a very long time, because Frank and I had married when Jake was so young, Jake thought Frank had been there from his birth. He actually asked Frank one day (as a little guy) if he had picked the name "Jacob" for him or if Mom picked it. He honestly didn't know life without Frank in it, and I think that is very fortunate for all of us.

Frank is such an amazing and wonderful person, who loves Jake like his own son – so much so, that he often took care of Joel when he needed it, out of, and because of, his love for Jake. Frank kept up with Joel and checked in on him by phone to make sure he was doing okay (and he still does today, over five years later). He put his reputation on the line with various contacts, who agreed to talk to Joel about hiring him for jobs. He also connected him with one of his co-workers who is a recovered alcoholic and agreed to help Joel find a good AA group as well as help him with anything else he needed.

Joel spoke to Frank often and it seemed as if he began to view him as a father figure instead of his ex-wife's husband. Some time had passed and the Joel front was quiet...too quiet. Frank said he hadn't heard from him in over a week, and neither had his co-worker. They were worried, so Frank went to Joel's apartment. He was there and had been on a week-long drinking binge. Because he hadn't been to work in a week, he had been fired. He could barely walk or talk and had drunk more vodka than the Russian Navy. Frank told him that this was *it*. He was taking him directly to rehab and checking him in. Frank made it clear to Joel that he was not going to tell *our* son that he was dead, but that if he didn't clean up his life he would end up in jail or in the morgue. Frank poured Joel into his car, called his office to let his assistant know he would be out of the office all day, and drove Joel to a rehab center on the other side of town. He filled out all the paperwork for Joel, and made sure everything was in order for him to be checked in before leaving him there.

Joel stayed there as long as he could before he could no longer pay for it. He left rehab after being dried out and put on various medications. He needed a job badly, so a friend of his hired him to work at his commercial paving business. About a week later, Joel was drinking again and had a seizure in one of the parking lots that he had been hired to pave. Someone found him passed out, face down in the lot, and Joel had cracked his head on the pavement.

Jake knew his dad was an alcoholic and beyond that I didn't need to tell him much more, because over time he saw it all on his own. He saw behaviors that he didn't like and noticed that his dad didn't show up for very many events, and that Frank and I were there for everything. We were his parents and gave him a loving and supportive environment which I hoped would be enough to help Jake grow up to be a confident and wonderful person. He is now 13 years old, and he is both of those and much more. Jake and Joel talk on the phone, and get together to grab ice cream or a burger now and then, and that is about it. He loves his dad, because he is a loyal kid and he isn't going to turn his back on him; however, completely on his own, Jake began calling Frank "Dad" and referring to Joel as "Joel." To me this says it all, and speaks volumes about the state of their relationships.

I have found that if you love life, life will love you back.

—Arthur Rubinstein

XV

OFTENTIMES I HAVE SAID that running has saved my life. So I suppose it is only natural that I should meet the love of my life while running a marathon. It was April of the year 2000, and I had registered to run the Cleveland Marathon and wasn't about to let my recent divorce hold me back from running and racing. I was a single mom with a full-time job and full responsibility for paying for my son's day care, diapers, and all that went into caring for him as his residential and primary parent. Running kept me happy, healthy, and sane.

The marathon was a short six months after I was finally able to get Joel to move out of the house and go ahead with the actual divorce proceedings. It took longer than I had wanted it to, more out of lack of motivation on Joel's part than anything else. I don't think he wanted it to be over, but the simple truth was that he also had nowhere to go. He didn't come into the marriage with anything but his clothing and a dresser, and we didn't accumulate anything together except debt. The one and only (and most wonderful) reason we were absolutely meant to be together was to bring Jacob into this world. Once we had accomplished that, we had nothing else.

Everything that has happened to me in my life – and the choices I have made, including those that most people would consider very bad ones – is what made me who I am today and shaped my life as part of a well-charted plan. It may have looked "nuckin' futz" to people on the outside, but I knew if I kept persevering and moving forward, my heart would not lead me to a bad place.

I was meant to have my Jake, and while I was creating him, I was also unwittingly biding my time for when I was to meet Frank and create Morgan and our life together as a family. I know that almost nothing I have done, or the way that I did it, could ever be considered conventional, but just because I do things in my own way doesn't mean that my way is bad. Good things have come to me because I followed my heart and continued to set physical goals for myself that kept me strong and healthy in body and mind. The good things, like love and happiness, peace, and virtue were the things I knew I deserved and would eventually find. If it ended up being just Jake and me, I was okay with that, too. I would be the greatest mom to him and I didn't worry for our well-being. We would have a great life together, on our own, if that was what was in the cards for us. (There was a little feeling inside of me that told me it wasn't.)

It was in October, about six months before the marathon, that Joel had made arrangements to move out of the house while Jacob and I were in Marco Island, Florida, at my parents' time-share. It was good timing as they had a few weeks booked every October, and I could spend time away with Jake. When we got home Joel would be gone, and we could begin our new lives together.

The week in Marco was really nice and actually only slightly stressful. Jake and I played in the pool and spent time down by the water in front of my parents' pink condo. I would set Jake down on the beach and watch him marvel at the biggest sandbox he had ever seen in his short

13 months on this planet. The sun seemed to bounce playfully through his big loopy curls while he investigated the new surface like an astronaut who discovered an unknown planet. His vast, deep brown eyes radiated great warmth that rivaled the Florida sun, as he lifted a shell and held it up to me in wonder. This simple gesture from my baby boy made my heart (which had been hardened as of late) feel as soft and supple as the sand itself.

As Jake played, I looked out at the ocean and thought about life for us from here. I didn't worry about us being alone for the rest of our lives, as long as we had each other. I wasn't concerned about ever getting married again, and I knew I would be able to find a date if I really wanted one. I was already dating a guy at work. He was a nice guy, and I was really attracted to him, but I wasn't in love and knew he wasn't someone with whom I would want to share my life. This was all fine with me, as long as Jake and I were together, healthy, and happy.

But then my romantic side and the spiritual person in me couldn't help looking at the water and talking to God, silently, in my head. I privately pondered if I would ever find someone to love, who would not only love me, but love Jake, too. I asked God if there was someone out there for me who would be with us forever, and could be my best friend and my lover all in one. I asked the Universe if I could have some help in finding someone – and then quickly picked Jake up, wiped the sand from his hands, and carried him back up to the condo, which was on the 7th floor and had a great view of the beach. When I got inside, my mom was out on the balcony with her binoculars, looking at something on the beach near the area where Jake and I had just been playing. When she saw that we had come back she quickly waved me over to the balcony to show me what she had been looking at.

"You have to see this! Come over here and look at this wedding on the beach; it's beautiful!"

I was freshly divorced with a baby in diapers, and my ex-husband was moving his crap out of my house back in Ohio, probably at the same time that she and I were standing there on that balcony. It was beyond me what on Earth about *that* picture would make her think I would want to partake in a snapshot of someone's wedding day bliss on the beach. I told her I didn't want to see the wedding and left the balcony shaking my head at her.

Let's fast-forward to the day of the Cleveland Marathon. I almost didn't make it to the starting line of the race, because I had missed a flight in Chicago the night before and "shot my wad" while sprinting through the enormous airport. I was there to get some training for a brand-new job I had accepted at an IT recruitment firm. The frustration of missing my plane, and being yelled at by Joel for having to watch Jake longer than he had expected, made me consider scrapping the marathon altogether. I pushed the anger out of my head and figured I might as well do the race since I had already trained for it and had made plans with a friend to meet me at the halfway point so she could run me in the last half of the race.

The next morning, bright and early, my boyfriend dropped me off at the starting line where I took my place with about two thousand other runners waiting in anxious anticipation for the start of the race. No matter how many races I do, or how relaxed I am before a run, I can never escape the pre-race jitters, especially in that time just before the gun goes off. Once the gun does go off, and we all take off running, the jitters melt away and are replaced with a Zen-like euphoria. At that moment there was no one to yell at me, no worries to be had, and nothing on my mind but running and looking for my friend at the halfway mark. I had no idea that the person about to "run" into my life, and change it forever, already had quite a different mind-set, as well as a plan to approach me and introduce himself.

As usual, I had to pee, so I took an immediate detour at the first sight of a port-o-potty at mile three of the marathon. Comfort while running is key, and in marathons my finish time means very little to me, so I take the time to use the port-o-potties in lieu of the hard-core method of peeing on myself while continuing to run the race. This threw a wrench into my "secret stalker's" plans, as he was just about to approach me when I ducked into the potty to relieve my nagging bladder.

My unexpected turn into the port-o-potties threw him for a loop. He didn't know what to do with himself while I was in there. If he continued running he would most likely lose me and wouldn't be able to strike up the conversation that he was banking on getting him through the race, and maybe more. That was a risk he wasn't willing to take, so he stepped into the potty next to mine. Because he didn't have to go to the bathroom he suddenly felt very self-conscious, as he could hear me peeing next door. He quickly stepped out of the port-o-potty and jogged slowly, watching for me to pass him.

He was working on Plan B, and I still didn't even know he existed. I ran past him, happily comfortable again and looking down at the road in front of me when I realized there was someone running beside me, and a voice was asking, "Is this your first marathon?"

My initial thought was, "*Oh* brother, *what a cheese dick.*"

I told him, "No, it's my fourth."

We began to chat and he told me his name was Frank and that he was up from Columbus to run his first marathon as a result of what could be construed as a dare. Hey, I'll talk to anyone (especially on a race course) and this guy was entertaining *and* not bad to look at, so we stayed together and continued our running chatter. He explained that he had always been into weight-lifting, and at his size and stature was often taken for a football player instead of a runner, let alone a distance runner.

Some of his buddies in Columbus not only nicknamed him "No-Neck-Ferro," but also dared him to run a marathon. He accepted the challenge and that's why he was there that day. Being a big guy at 6-foot-2-inches and about 200 pounds is a disadvantage in its own right, but Frank also went out the night before the race and got hammered. We were running along and talking about ourselves. I told him I was just divorced and about my son Jake – perhaps to see if he would sprint away?

He told me he was an insurance salesman and that when he started training for the marathon he had given up drinking for a solid four months. He came up to Cleveland to stay with a friend who took him out for a good pasta dinner the night before the race, which ended up being a drink-fest until 2:00 a.m. A short four hours after he got home and went to bed, he got up to run the marathon and threw up. He felt like hell, took a shower, and forced his buddy to drive him to the race. His friend wasn't feeling great either and tried to talk him out of doing it. Frank said he couldn't go back to Columbus and face all the people who had said he could never do a marathon, even if he *was* dehydrated, had basically no sleep, and his longest run before this was only 14 miles.

I listened to all of this and laughed. I told him it would have made much more sense for him to have kept drinking during the four months leading up to the marathon, and simply given up the one night before the race (just a thought, there, big guy). We continued on together and I told him I had a boyfriend, and that at the halfway point I needed to look for my friend who was planning to jump in and run with me. When we reached the 13-mile mark, I panned the crowd for my friend, Chrissy. She had already seen me approaching long before I saw her. She and her husband saw me running towards them with a tall, muscular guy sporting a clean-shaven head and sunglasses. They laughed and shook their heads, chuckling that I was already with a guy, and predicting the last 13 miles would be plenty interesting and entertaining.

Chrissy said goodbye to her husband with a knowing look and jumped into the race, immediately introducing herself to Frank. We had a long way to go, so there was plenty of time to get to know each other and to laugh away the miles. Chrissy and I did the laughing and talking at that point, because Frank was mostly delirious. We kept pulling him along, and Chrissy would cheerfully encourage him with a loud "Come on, Frank!"

She and I kept him going and told funny stories and goofy jokes. Frank grunted a lot, but didn't say much.

I had started the race that day with a tampon in, but it was at the very end of my period, so in the port-o-potty at mile three, I took it out and tossed it away. I didn't want it in there sucking out any fluids from my body if it wasn't completely necessary. All of a sudden on the course, I felt a strange sensation which indicated it may have been a mistake to take that tampon out after all. Sometimes having to deal with running and periods can be a very slippery slope, and I worried that a gusher would soon be cascading down my leg in a horrible and embarrassing stream of red.

The only way to put my mind at rest was to go in and "check the oil."

I told Frank I needed to check something and that he shouldn't look. He saw me slip my hand into the front of my shorts, and didn't look away as I put my finger inside and pulled it out to look at the result. Everything was good to go, thank God! Chrissy (who could tell that something was brewing between Frank and me) was the first to acknowledge it by saying, "I bet you thought you wanted to date this girl until you saw her do that!"

Frank didn't skip a beat and replied, "After seeing that I don't want to date her, I want to marry her!"

At mile 18 my boyfriend was on the course and yelled to me as we ran past, "I love you, Liz!"

I smiled and waved to him, and for an awkward split second, all three of us silently knew that he was soon to be replaced by a big bald guy. Just before the finish, somewhere around mile 22 or so, I started to feel really nauseous and crappy. All runners have a race now and then when they bonk or feel like shit, and that one was mine. When we reached mile 24 or 25, a woman friend of Frank's from Columbus was waiting for him and jumped in to run him into the finish. She could sense immediately that Frank had the hots for me and that something was going on between us. Obviously she was there for him because she really liked him, but as it turns out he only liked her as a friend. Her claws came out, and although it was unwarranted, she was very unfriendly and borderline mean to me. At that point I didn't care at all what she thought. I barely knew the guy; I had a lot going on in my life; I had just run 25 miles; and I felt like dog shit.

I slowed the pace way down and told them to just go on ahead without us. Frank was hurting badly as well. He just wanted to finish the race, and to get away from any weird drama that his friend brought to the dynamic of the group. They took off and when he stepped across the finish line, in the midst of his delirium, all he could do was ask person after person for a pen. He needed to find a pen and paper so he could give me his email address and he wouldn't give up until he found one. When he saw me cross the finish line, he came up to me, handed me his email address, and said, "We should train together sometime."

When I emailed him a couple of days later, I said I assumed he wanted to do more than just train with me and he answered with, "You are correct."

I broke up with my boyfriend, and Frank and I started dating each other exclusively. When I went down to visit him in Columbus for the first time, I did my usual snooping about in his little apartment, which was actually a renovated garage behind another house. I saw a framed photograph of some people that looked as if they had been married and were posing with family members on a beach, with the water and setting sun in the background. It was a beautiful picture with a very happy bride and groom, as well as some children and Frank. After looking at it for a second I said, "Hey, I know this beach! That's Marco Island."

Frank said, "Yeah, it is; how did you know that?!"

I told him that my parents have a condo at the Surf Club in Marco and we go there every year in October. I told him that I was just there, in fact. He just stood there and looked at me as if I had grown an extra eyeball. He said, "This picture was taken in October two doors down from the Surf Club. It was at my brother's wedding."

Whether a person believes in Fate or in God or the Universe or Mary having a predetermined plan for us, that Frank and I are together is a great argument that these things are real. My mother had watched the wedding that *Frank* was *in* on the *very* beach where each of us had separately looked out into the water and asked to find the love of our lives. Within six months of making those requests, we were both standing in a crowd of thousands of people at the Cleveland Marathon and found each other.

We got engaged three months after we met and decided we would begin trying to get pregnant right away. Frank was 36 years old at the time and had no children from his first marriage. I was 31, and we weren't sure how long it would take for me to get pregnant. So we went for it.

As it turns out, it took no time at all, and because I was pregnant by July, we bumped up our wedding plans to October. We knew people would think we were only getting married because I was pregnant, but we didn't care. We both knew that bets were being taken on how long our marriage would last because neither of us had the best track record, and the over-under was set at about six months.

Frank would be the first to tell you that he burned through women, and he also had a strict policy to never date anyone who had children. Yet, there I was, this person with a baby in diapers, who burned through the men in her life, and was four months pregnant at our wedding. It couldn't have been more beautiful.

We got married by a judge (who used to take my Step classes downtown and also continually asked me out back then *and* who kissed me after he performed the nuptials!). Frank thought it was weird, because he didn't kiss any of the other women he married before us, but we just laughed it off. For the actual wedding, my mom was there, my brother Dave and his wife, and Chrissy and her husband, since they were there when we met.

It was a gorgeous, warm day in October with blue skies and a light breeze off Lake Erie that moved our hearts as well as the fall leaves of gold and russet. Afterwards my mom took us out to lunch, and that night we had a small reception at the Baricelli Inn in Little Italy, Cleveland. The Baricelli was a 25-year-old landmark in Cleveland and was housed in a mansion where you could stay overnight and enjoy the fine dining for which it was famous. We had a private room in the mansion for the nine of us, and then Frank and I stayed overnight in a quaint room upstairs.

Everyone at the ceremony was at the dinner reception, with the addition of the friend Frank had stayed with (and partied with) the night before the marathon, and his girlfriend. It was odd to have nine people, instead of an even ten, but my father had just passed away, leaving a big gap in my life – and at the table that night. He would have been nervous about my impulsiveness, but also happy for me and excited about little Morgan, who was also in attendance for the wedding, reception, and honeymoon!

We had a great meal and lots of laughs, and Frank and I even danced to "our song," which I played from a little boom box. As it is for most couples, our song is *very* important to both of us, and Frank even inscribed part of its lyrics on the inside of my wedding ring. The song is *I'll Be* by Edwin McCain, and on the inside of my ring is inscribed: "Your greatest fan." The lyrics of *I'll Be* still mean so much to Frank and me and to our relationship today. After more than a decade of marriage to my best friend and my greatest fan, I am greatly moved by the words and music of this relevant and meaningful song.

I like being unconventional.

—Florence Griffith Joyner

XVI

MY BROTHER PAUL is 5 years older than I am and as kids we didn't exactly get along. He collected antique wind-up Victrola record players and old 78 records which he played on them constantly in his basement bedroom. We called his room "the dungeon." I used to spy on him while he sat in the dungeon until I couldn't stand the scratchy-sounding old-fashioned music any longer. My parents were very supportive of his interests in music and encouraged his differences with fancy private cello lessons and tickets to various operas. Most of the teen boys I knew had a poster of Farrah Fawcett in the famous red bathing suit with her scud missile nips standing at attention. Instead my brother had posters from the *Threepenny Opera* and one that said "Dare to be Different" which featured an orange amongst a bunch of apples.

When I was in 8th grade I swam for the varsity team at the high school. The high school was located right next door to the 7th and 8th grade middle school, so I walked over there for practice every day after school. It didn't really occur to me to be afraid to walk into the high school and past all the older kids who probably wondered if I was lost. I got to know a lot of the upper classmen (boys and girls) because I would chat everyone up in the halls before making my way to the pool area.

After people found out my last name, they just about fell over. Because the physical and personality traits between my brother and me were so different, no one could believe we were related. People always wanted to know what was up with my brother Paul because they thought he was very odd, and practically no one knew I had another brother because of the nine-year age gap. By this time, Paul had just graduated from high school and my brother Dave had already graduated from University of Virginia (in three years), gone to grad school in Syracuse, and was off working in New York City as a bond analyst.

When I wasn't at school or at swim practice I was busy at home terrorizing my brother Paul and my parents. Paul had been accepted into the Culinary Institute of America in Hyde Park, N.Y., but had to do an externship in a restaurant near home before attending classes. He was always at home if he wasn't at the restaurant. I used to love coming home from practice and immediately finding ways to get under my brother's skin. If he was sitting in the living room on the couch, sipping tea and listening to classical music on the stereo, I would do my best attempt at crossing the room and in front of him doing ballet leaps. I would bound through the air as if I was jumping a hurdle on the track – one hand over my heart and the other outstretched towards the sky as I bellowed loudly, trying to mimic the way an opera singer would sing. Not only would he get pissed that I was disturbing him because he couldn't hear his music, but he was also beside himself with frustration that I was pretending to sing opera when he was quite obviously listening to a Mozart concerto! (*Everyone* knows that!)

The other thing that got to him more than anything was when he was cooking something in the kitchen and I would walk in and pick at it. He wanted to be a chef and took his work (even in our home kitchen) very seriously.

This made it all the more exciting, rewarding, and fun when I snuck little pinches and bites off of whatever he was preparing. Whenever he saw me do it, he would chase me down and shake me upside down from my ankles if he caught me.

As little, bratty kids, my friends and I had a favorite term used to describe everything we didn't think was cool, and no matter what it was, we would refer to that un-cool thing as "gay." I cringe at the thought of this now, because it is *so* not cool to use the word "gay" to describe anything in a negative way. I can't stomach the thought of people being bullied for being gay, and have absolutely no tolerance for this type of prejudice in *Girls With Sole* or in my life in general.

I often tell the kids I work with that using the word "gay" in a negative connotation is wrong, and that I don't want to hear them do it. I don't hear them do it very often, but now and then I hear them use an expression that is completely new to me, and I have had to tell them not to use it anymore. When the girls tell each other that they think they are pretty, or they like something about each other or their looks, they will either preface or finish the compliment with the expression "No homo." For instance, "No homo, but you have nice eyes." The girls I work with learn very quickly not to say anything negative about each other at all, but especially in reference to anyone's color, religion, or sexual orientation. They are always really respectful of this after it is pointed out to them, and it makes me happy that *Girls With Sole* can help teach acceptance and tolerance of others.

Clearly, now that I am an adult, I know there is nothing wrong with being gay, and I feel horrible that I must have called my brother gay at least 500 times per day. My only excuse or defense is that I was a goofy kid who even snickered every time I heard *The Flintstones* theme song when, at the end of the song, they exclaimed, "We'll have a gay old time!"

My friends and I even called inanimate objects gay, which shows how much we knew! If we didn't like a movie or a hairstyle or a couch, we called it gay. I'm sure it was exactly this type of behavior that made it to the top of the list of the reasons that my brother Paul and I didn't get along as kids or during our teen years. I didn't know it at the time, and maybe Paul wasn't quite sure himself, but unlike my bedroom furniture, the couch, the dog across the street, and my math homework assignments, Paul *was* and *is* gay.

I was always very "sheltered" from things that went on in my home because I was the youngest, but mostly because my parents were deathly afraid of my big mouth and my propensity to share anything that I heard with anyone who would listen. I have often been told that I lack the filter most people possess, which is conveniently located in between their brain and their mouth. Apparently I was born without such a filter, and I wear my heart out there on my blood-red sleeve for all to see. (This wasn't a good thing for a kid who still hadn't learned that everyone she meets does not always wish her well.) I lived by the motto: "What you see (and hear) is what you get," but not everyone agrees that this is a good thing, so my parents told me *nothing*!

This is not to say that "intel" couldn't be collected by a nosy girl. Conversations by parents in hushed tones were a direct invitation for me to eavesdrop. (If they had kept the volume at a normal level, I probably would have ignored them.) There were also times I answered the phone when Paul or Dave would call home from college or their new home, and when I was asked to hang up the extension

I was on, I would hold the button down and then let it back up as carefully as possible. Then, with the ear end of the receiver pressed hard against my head, I would hold it so that the mouthpiece end was pointing up over my head to ensure my breathing wouldn't be detected.

I was always a big fan of those puzzles that were called mystery pictures (especially when used in game shows, or with my parents) where you had to guess what the mystery picture was but it was only revealed one piece at a time. Over the years I had honed my investigative and discovery skills to the point that I may have missed my calling to be an FBI agent or a forensic scientist. When I collected enough bits and pieces, it wasn't hard for me to see the big picture, but sometimes comprehending it was another story. I was the only kid left at home, and it required a lot of "recon" on my part to figure out the puzzling hints I picked up about my brothers.

By happenstance, both of my brothers were living in Washington, D.C., at the same time. Dave was working as a campaign aide to Senator Simon, and Paul had completed his schooling at the Culinary Institute of America and had secured a position in a downtown hotel as some type of chef. From some of the other "overheard" conversations of my parents, I found out my dad was giving Paul some money to use as a down payment on a brownstone he said he wanted to buy in the amount of $10,000. (I guess back then that amount went a lot further than it does today.) I also picked up that my mom was upset and that my parents were trying to find "help" for Paul. There were a few areas of the picture uncovered, but I couldn't make out what the mystery picture was at first. Slowly but surely I figured it out. They never told me he was gay, but I deduced as much when my mom said he would never be happy living like that, without marriage and children, that he would "grow out of it," and that he should talk to a priest to help him. I finally put it all together and realized my mom wanted to "help" my brother because he was gay.

The next round of eavesdropping revealed that Paul was in fact missing. He seemingly vanished without a trace, a note, a goodbye, or a forwarding address. He was just gone.

Dave was travelling with the Senator on the campaign trail and had asked Paul to collect his mail and keep an eye on his apartment while he was away. When Dave returned, the mail was piled up and it was clear that no one had been in to water the plants or keep an eye on the place. Paul's boss called my parents at our house in Rochester, asking if they knew where he was. He wasn't showing up at work, but he never called in sick. My parents were extremely alarmed and confused. This wasn't like him at all, and they feared the worst.

Thanksgiving Day arrived and there was still no word from him, although over a month had passed since the last time anyone had spoken to him. From that point on, especially on holidays, whenever the phone rang my mom jumped from her seat and flew to the phone hoping and praying it was Paul. It never was. Time went on and still no word from him. We had no idea if he was dead, in a Turkish prison, or had joined a cult, and it drove my parents insane with worry. My father went as far as to hire a private investigator to help find him. Over a period of two years, the investigator was able to track him down to various cities such as San Francisco and Los Angeles, but was never able to pinpoint his location or make contact with him. Accepting that Paul was indeed alive, and had simply chosen not to be located or contacted, was not easy for my parents, and although heartbroken, they called off the search for my brother. There was no point in continuing to pay someone to look for a person who clearly did not want to be found.

As a parent, I can't imagine the heartache and pain my mom and dad endured, never mind the anger and feelings of betrayal. They had adopted him and raised him. They loved him very much and supported him financially as well as emotionally. Although our parents could be extremely controlling and prying when it came to our lives, and although they had handled the initial disclosure of his homosexuality extremely poorly, was that reason enough for Paul to never speak to them again? I don't think it is for me to judge or to decide. I'm not exactly the best person to pass judgment on other people's behavior or choices.

I wouldn't say I condone what Paul did, and I *do* find it to be harsh and mean, but part of me understands it to a certain degree and I don't hold it against him. I have done some very harsh and mean things in my life as well, and many of them were also directed towards my parents. These are the same parents who brought me into their home, loved me, raised me, educated me, and gave me experiences that anyone would be grateful to have.

People make mistakes and it isn't my place to judge them. I know what it's like to be judged, especially by people who don't really know the basis of my actions and emotions. People may have deeply rooted reasons for why they do the things they do; things may not be as simple as we think they are. There are certainly a few people in the world I can look at and earnestly say that I think their actions are wrong, and that I believe them to be bad people in their hearts. I have come across some of those people in my life. Nevertheless, the majority of the people I have encountered in the 40-plus years I have been on this Earth can't be placed into clear-cut, black and white categories so simply. There is much gray area that surrounds most people, and I feel we need to make allowances and to keep an open mind when we do our silent, internal, and mental surveys of those individuals.

I know my parents were devastated by Paul's "leaving," and it cut my mother to the core of her being. Most likely to avoid the pain, they eventually stopped talking about him altogether, and it was as if he was never there in the first place. Ironically it was as if Paul had taken a page out of my mom's very own playbook. It was as if the playbook had been stolen and the opposing team was using what it had learned against her. You can't just pretend someone doesn't exist when he still does. You can't pretend someone isn't gay when he is. You can't pretend someone wasn't sexually abused when she was. And I know the pain must be horrible and very real when a son pretends he doesn't have any parents when he does.

Almost ten years after Paul's name was swept beneath the bulging proverbial carpet with the rest of the unpleasantness my mom wished to ignore, I was in a relationship with someone who I thought I might actually marry. His name was Mark and he was the last boyfriend I had, just before I met my first husband, Joel, and flew off to Vegas to marry him. Mark and I were living together and loved each other, but when he told his family that he wanted to marry me, they made it clear they didn't approve. His family (particularly his sisters) didn't like me, thought I was crazy, and did not want me to marry their baby brother.

At 24 years old, Mark was the youngest of 13 kids and the only one not married. His family's opinion meant a great deal to him, so he informed me he couldn't marry anyone without his family's approval. I told him I couldn't marry anyone who didn't have a backbone, so it would all work out very nicely for everyone. As I recall, the bed we were sharing was his, but the mattress was mine, which he made a big production about – so I left the bed on the lawn for him to pick up.

Before all of this nonsense occurred, however, during the much-happier early stages of our relationship, I had told him about my brother Paul and the circumstances surrounding my not having seen him in about ten years. It may have taken less than a week after telling him about Paul that Mark had produced his name and phone number from a people search on the internet. I was positive it would be Paul, because there are not that many guys in the world who share my brother's name, and probably even fewer of them specifically in the Los Angeles area. I would need a plan before calling him, in the event that he tried to deny who he was and hung up on me (which I fully anticipated) if I just blurted out who I was. I decided the best approach would be to get him to admit who he was to me before I admitted who I was to him, and then go from there.

I dialed the number and Paul answered the phone! I would know his voice anywhere. It was him! I said, "Hi! I'm from the Culinary Institute of America. Paul Vidmar was in my graduating class, and I am trying to locate him."

He said, "This is he."

I said, "Paul, it's Liz."

Still under the impression that I had graduated with him, he replied excitedly, "Liz Russo?"

"No, it's your sister."

There was only a second of silence and then a stretched-out, lilted

"E-*liz*-a-beth."

I didn't expect what came next. I thought for sure he would hang up. But he didn't, and we talked for quite a while. I asked him why he left and he explained that it was mostly the intrusiveness my mom and dad would often exhibit and that he couldn't take it anymore, coupled with his being gay which they didn't take well. He said he had also been involved back then with a very smooth-talking, con-artist type who talked him into leaving without telling anyone about it. Paul was young and impressionable and (much like me) was used to having my dad take care of everything for him. When this guy told him that my parents would never understand, and then they reacted exactly as he predicted, it was easy to convince Paul that they didn't deserve to know where he was. He said the longer he was away without talking to them, the easier it was to continue that way. The passing of time made it more and more difficult to turn back, to call, to apologize, and to face whatever lecture or tirade might ensue.

I told him I did understand to a degree, but that the approach he used was harsh. I let him know I wanted to stay in touch with him and that I could separate one thing from the other – much as a child separates an Oreo cookie but only eats the cream filling, leaving behind the chocolate cookies. It may seem as if the cookie needs to stay intact, but once it is separated you can enjoy the part you like and discard the part you don't. I told him he is my brother; we are the adopted ones; and I want to have a relationship with him. I felt as though we should stick together even if the rest of our family didn't think so (and I had a feeling they wouldn't). He felt the same way, so we have kept in touch ever since.

My brother Dave was plenty mad when he found out I had located Paul and that he and I would remain in contact. He asked me, "How can you talk to that asshole after what he did to Mom and Dad?"

I explained to Dave that I had chosen to separate what Paul did from who he is and I would not judge him. Dave doesn't hold it against me that I have a relationship with Paul, and for that I am very glad.

My mom was blown away that I had not only found Paul, but I had spoken to him as well. She wanted to know if he was okay and if he was in good health. I told her everything was fine with him and that he was healthy. She asked me for his address and phone number. Paul had said I could give her the address but not the phone number. I don't know how many letters went back and forth, but I do know my brother Paul sent Christmas presents for our family to my parents' house every year for a few years in a row. My mom refused to open the presents from him because he didn't apologize to her. I said that by sending presents he was "reaching out," and maybe that was his way of saying he was sorry. I tried to explain that it may not have been the way she wanted him to apologize but it was what he was able to do at that point. She didn't accept this line of thinking and said she didn't want his presents. She said that unless he called her on the phone and apologized to her, then it wasn't an apology.

I continue to keep in touch with my brother, but I am the only one in the family who still does, and no one talks to me about him anymore either.

I went out to visit Paul and his partner towards the tail end of my marriage with Joel. Joel hadn't moved out of the house yet, but we were in the process of getting divorced, and I had already begun dating the hot mail room guy at work. No wonder no one could keep up with my relationships with men; there were too many and they were too fast and furious. Speedy Gonzales himself would have been exhausted. Even though it was no secret that my marriage was over, my relationship with the mail room guy was a secret at work and I kept it a secret from Joel as well.

While I was out visiting my brother for a week, my boyfriend also happened to be on a trip to Las Vegas. I rented a car and drove to Vegas from L.A. to see him. It was exciting driving through the desert just as they do in the movies, just to see my "forbidden love" for one night. That was a ton of fun – but I really did go out there to see my brother, and I had a blast with him, his partner, and his partner's daughter and her sons. The whole motley crew of us went to Tijuana, Mexico, and had so much fun touring the shops and the bars and then crashing out in a hotel room for the night.

The rest of the time I was in Los Angeles was spent doing the usual touristy things, as well as getting to know my brother for what felt like the first time. I knew he was into antiques as a kid, and he still is. He also still cooks a little bit but doesn't do it as a profession anymore. When I was out there to visit he was working as a handyman and helped manage Section 8 apartments where he and Brent (his long-time partner of 15-plus years) lived. Brent also worked at night in a hotel behind the front desk. Their bosses thought they were brothers so they went along with that, letting them think what they wanted. I learned they were also officers in their local chapter of a national leather club called Trident, for which my brother was the president at that time, and Brent was the treasurer. From what my brother has told me recently, the Cleveland chapter has folded, but the Toledo and Chicago chapters are still going strong.

Of course I had no idea that these clubs have national meetings where all the chapters come together in a designated city, but Paul and Brent informed me that sometimes they would have cause to fly to places such as

Columbus, Ohio, to take part in the big meetings. As luck would have it, on the night of my engagement to Frank (my second and final husband, who was living in Columbus when we met), there was just such a meeting there that my brother and his partner were attending. It was perfect! I told Frank all about it, and we decided to drive to Columbus from Cleveland so Frank could meet my brother, and I could meet some of Frank's friends. It was the perfect plan to announce and celebrate our engagement and introduce my fiancé and my brother.

We got there in the late afternoon and met Brent and Paul in a downtown gay bar in Columbus. Frank is extremely open-minded and not at all homophobic. We had drinks with them while Brent showed a bunch of pictures to Frank that he had taken in some of the bars the night before. The pictures were of various guys they had met in Columbus who had agreed to pose for Brent in leather or handcuffs. Frank looked at the pictures just as he would if they were shots from Paul and Brent's latest vacation to the Grand Canyon. He did say that a few of the positions looked painful, but Brent assured him that the people in the picture enjoyed it. This is how everyone celebrates the engagement night, right?

I know this lifestyle would freak out a lot of people, but it didn't bother me and I actually found it all fairly humorous to a degree. I don't like pain of any sort, especially when it comes to sex, but live and let live, and all of that. They are good people and they aren't hurting anyone who doesn't want to be "hurt so good."

Another time, after my daughter was born, there was another meeting which was in Toledo, so my brother and Brent came to stay with us for a night in Cleveland. Morgan was only a few months old at the time, and Jake was just approaching 3 years old. During the afternoon while Brent and Paul were in town I had to think of activities that we could all do together, because I didn't have anyone to watch the kids. They wanted to spend time with all of us, so I planned a fun day that would keep us all occupied and also show them different parts of Cleveland (on a budget). We went to antique shops and out to lunch, but by later in the afternoon we had run out of things to do. They suggested we go to a gay bar for a drink. It was the middle of the day, but why not?

What a bizarre sight we must have been! There was me; a toddler; a baby fast asleep in a car seat; and two guys with long beards like ZZ Top, wearing jeans with chains hanging from their pockets that connected to their wallets – all together hanging out in a gay bar in the middle of the day. After going to one bar with them, the seal was broken, so we just kept on going. I was only drinking Cokes and became the official designated driver for our impromptu gay pub crawl, with the kids in tow. One of the bars we visited is known for its music and dancing at night. During the middle of the day with all the lights on, and barely any people inside, it looked huge, and the big black box-like stages showed empty reflections in the silvery smoky mirrors. The dancing platforms served as the perfect playground for Jake while Morgan continued to sleep in her little car seat carrier. The owner of the bar walked over to me and I thought for sure he would ask me to leave and to be sure I took the kids with me. Instead, he handed me some crayons and a coloring book for Jake to work on when he was done doing the *YMCA* on center stage.

Have patience with all things, but chiefly have patience with yourself. Do not lose courage in considering your own imperfections but instantly set about remedying them – every day begin the task anew.

—Saint Francis de Sales

XVII

ALMOST INTUITIVELY I was drawn to the sport of running. Running to something or running away from it didn't matter as long as I was moving. This was true literally and figuratively. When I was a kid, my mom was constantly trying to keep me from doing cartwheels to the car in busy parking lots. I hated to walk, so I would run everywhere I went instead.

For most of my life, lacing up for a run has been as much a part of my day as taking a shower. Actually, taking a shower after a great run becomes more like a luxurious reward than a way to get clean. Just like many avid runners, I have found running to be the ultimate therapy. Running alone helps me sort through the churning thoughts or worries that can often plague me. Running with friends is like a moving group therapy during which all of the world's problems can be solved in one hour – just like on TV! (Or at least it feels that way.) I have walked into many workouts feeling really bad, with the weight of the world on my shoulders and self-hate looming overhead. I can honestly say that I have never walked away from a workout with those same dark feelings.

The sweat or pool water seems to wash away all the heaviness in my heart and on my mind, and replaces it with a joyful and light-hearted feeling which I can't wait to feel again after it fades. Maybe this is why people get hooked on heroin? I will never know because the empowerment that I receive from running and crossing the finish line is the best high in the world to me. It keeps me coming back for more so I can feel it again and again.

No matter what you need from your run, it will grant it. A runner and athlete cannot stay motivated for over 30 years unless there is a true love and passion for her sport. If the real reasons for running or racing are derived from something other than the empowerment and joy that it brings to your mind, body, and soul, there is no way to stay so highly motivated for such a long period of time. It can't be solely about losing weight, or trying to look good, or impressing others in some way. It has to be about you and your own personal goals and accomplishments for it to remain a way of life.

I have always found bliss in movement. Pulling my body through water, pumping my legs on a bike, or running anywhere and everywhere all make me very happy. As a kid, doing cartwheels and round-offs were almost as good as ice cream. Movement equaled pleasure, and seeing how far I could go was a thrill.

As an adult athlete, especially as a triathlete and distance runner, you tend to meet a lot of other Type A, highly driven, and successful people. The common ground and love for racing form a bond and a camaraderie like nothing else in the world. You respect the talent and effort that comes with balancing a home life, job, and friends as well as training and racing.

There is a flow of positive energy that washes over me when I meet a friend to run or when I'm training in groups. The physical exercise kick-starts my brain, waking it up and causing synapses to rapid-fire, bringing about some of the wittiest banter, and the best (and funniest) bonding I have ever experienced. My closest adult friends are all people I have met through running, swimming, or triathlon. We have trained and raced together, and our friendships seem to grow stronger with every mile.

Until a couple of years ago when life and schedules got in the way, I ran at least six days a week with a group of women friends at 5:45 in the morning. None of us wanted to miss the workouts because it was our time to talk and to be there for each other no matter what any of us might be going through. We were like "sole sisters" who understood the importance of running and female friendship and how combining the two creates an unstoppable force and an unbreakable bond. In that group of women we helped each other through divorce, sickness, death, issues with our children and our families, and basically just saw each other through tough times and tough miles. At the end of each run we were ready for anything the day could bring. We might not be able to run together as often as we used to, but from that group, Mo L. and Tricia K., in particular, hold a special place in my heart as my "sole sisters" and best friends. Those two women are like a second family to me and I love them dearly.

When my training buddies and I get together, we cover serious topics, but we also love our fair share of buffoonery! For me, being silly out there is a major reason I run in the first place. Laughing, joking, and having a blast during a long workout keeps me going and makes getting up at such ungodly hours to do it worthwhile. All is fair in love, war, and running...I always say! No topics are taboo, and once the creative juices begin to flow you never know what will happen.

"New Mommy Clubs" aside, I don't think there are too many places where discussing poop is as common and as socially acceptable as it is with people who run. It is completely normal to spend lengthy periods of time talking about poop if you are a runner. Favorite topics under this umbrella include: Pooping Too Much, known as the Runner's Trots; Not Pooping Enough (ouch...need more fiber); and the biggest and most important one of all: Taking a Dump Before the Start of a Race. My buddy Larry (a.k.a. Dawg) and I like to refer to this immensely important act as "Signing the Constitution." Every runner knows that if you don't Sign the Constitution before a race, you will not only be very uncomfortable, but you also run the risk of needing to sign it *during* the race. This is never a good thing, because you might not be able to find an appropriate place to sign it – or worse, there will be no paper! Because early morning race starts dictate very early wake-up calls, this can wreak havoc on your body's "poop clock." Every race I have ever done with my pal Larry (and there have been hundreds of them since we have been running together for about 13 years) starts with the same serious question: "Did you Sign the Constitution?" We are always genuinely happy for each other when the answer is yes – and it's an added bonus if you signed it *and* had time for an amendment or the beginning of the Bill of Rights.

Other fun and popular topics amongst any of my various training buddies and myself include, but are not limited to: children, husbands, dogs, the ebb and flow of certain friendships, gas (the prices of, and in fart form), sex, bunny rabbits doing cartwheels and deer wearing scarves playing leapfrog with a bear (okay...when you run at five in the morning, in the dark, and you are in your 40s and probably need glasses, the shadows of a plastic bag blowing in the wind or a tree stump and some bushes can take on very realistic and strange forms when seen from a distance as you run up on them), piercings on genitals, poison ivy on genitals, music, movies, people you know and the famous people they resemble, and the list goes on. Now, I'm not saying that *anything* on this list directly pertains to me, or anyone I know specifically, but I *will* tell you that piercings on your genitalia and bicycle riding do *not* mix, and wiping yourself with a leaf when you pee in the bushes is *highly* inadvisable. Scoff at our chosen topics if you will, or feign some semblance of indignation, but at mile 23 of a marathon I bet you would line up Pied Piper-style with the rest, letting the entertainment and the storytelling carry you through.

Thinking back, the first training buddy I ever had was actually my dad. This would come as a surprise to people who knew my dad, because he wasn't really the type you would picture as an athlete. He was a serious sports fan and even coached my brother's baseball teams, but would probably be more aptly described as a fan or spectator. In the 1970s the latest fitness craze, "jogging," inspired Americans everywhere to don short shorts, sneakers, and sweatbands and hit the streets and high school tracks. My dad fancied himself a "jogger" and had the coffee mug to prove it. I remember the cream-colored mug, which was often filled with coffee of almost the same color inside and sported drips that trickled in blood-like streams down the sides that he sipped on. On the mug the word "Jogger" was printed in big navy blue and red letters. I loved that mug because in my eyes it meant my dad was an athlete. If the mug said so, it must be true!

The only thing more telling and accurate than a T-shirt, coffee mug, or bumper sticker was my brother's Magic 8 Ball. All of these were law in my book. That mug was also a daily reminder that I might be able to spend time with my dad doing something I loved to do. When my dad said he was going jogging at the high school I couldn't wait to go with him and run around while he jogged! There was nothing better than getting in the big blue station wagon with him and setting goals for myself as we drove the two miles to the high school track. (Wouldn't a real runner actually run to the track?) I would ask my dad if he thought I could make it two times around, three times around, four times – and he would always say yes. I wanted so badly to please him, and to be able to go farther every time. So, no matter what goal we set on the way there, I made sure that we always celebrated the achievement of it on the way home. Riding home with the windows down, sweaty and smiling, I was on to something. My dad was just happy to tire me out and channel my energy someplace positive. He was on to something, too!

Those days didn't last long…but I cherished them while they did. My father always took time to be with all three of the kids, but his job was stressful and busy, and often took over his Jogger mug status, to be replaced by another prominent coffee mug in our house. On it was a quote by Shakespeare that read: "The first thing we do; Let's kill all the Lawyers." I wish my dad had done more jogging and less lawyering, bologna eating, and TV watching. His health problems could have been avoided at the onset with proper diet and exercise, but we lost him to Type II diabetes and kidney and heart troubles in July of 2000.

He never met my daughter, and only briefly met my (at the time) soon-to-be second husband, Frank, only two short months before he died. It was in the ICU that I introduced Frank to my dad. We weren't engaged yet, but we knew we were in love and would be engaged soon. My dad kept fading in and out of consciousness, but he was lucid when he took Frank's hand and told him he was happy that Frank was going to be part of the family. (We had never mentioned to anyone that we were going to be engaged; my dad just knew.) Then he told Frank, "I'm just sorry you're gonna miss the show."

I thought for sure his medication was making him say goofy things, so I said to Frank, "He doesn't know what he is saying."

I turned to my dad and said, "Dad, there is no show."

He shook his head at me in frustration, looked directly at Frank, and clearly stated, "*I'm* the show."

When I was a kid my dad left work during the afternoon and put his career's responsibilities on hold so he could attend every swim meet and every track meet I ever had. He always encouraged me to pursue athletics and reveled in my strengths and abilities. He saw I had talent and that sports benefited me in ways nothing else could. He had no idea I was being abused by my next-door neighbor, to whom he waved from our driveway and chatted with every day. He just knew that his daughter was difficult at times and needed to burn off "bad energy."

It was my dad who signed me up for my very first 5K race when I was in 8th grade. My friends Lisa and Mara ran it too. It was July, and the course started and ended in front of the Town Hall. Although my memories of that dead-of-summer race are blurred with salty sweat and the sting of fatigue, something deep inside of me responded positively to my mind and body's demand to push myself. I actually knew, for the first time, what it was like to truly come out of my comfort zone. At the finish line, my friends and I draped our arms around each other and I felt utterly triumphant!

It is not a coincidence that athletics has played such an enormous part in my life and how I live it. Bringing this realization and reality to young girls today through *Girls*

With Sole is indeed a gift that I have been given and one that I am blessed to be able to share.

Too often we underestimate the power of a touch, a smile, a kind word, a listening ear, an honest compliment, or the smallest act of caring, all of which have the potential to turn a life around.

—Leo Buscaglia

XVIII

OVER THE YEARS I have seen my share of really bad therapists. A bad therapist, in my opinion, is much more detrimental to a person's mental health than not seeing one at all. In the sea of horrible therapists I have had, there was one I saw for a little while who was actually really great and helped me immensely. Unlike the others, she didn't judge me or try to pin the newest and hippest diagnosis on me. She really seemed to understand my issues and why I had them, instead of somehow using them against me. Dr. K didn't encourage me to keep a "tell all" type of journal which most of the others had asked me to keep.

Instead she wanted me to keep a "Happy Journal."

Every day I was to write down three things that made me happy on that day. Until Dr. K and her brilliant Happy Journal, I had been afraid to ever again keep a journal. The last time I kept a journal, the things I wrote in it were used against me, and the pain I experienced from that was as though someone punched a hole in my heart. I felt as if I was violated, as well as punished, for my own honesty. I was in a tempestuous relationship with Danny at the time, and the therapist I was seeing was the one I was ordered to see in order for me to be released from the hospital after the overdose. It was a bad situation all around, especially when my therapist also took on my abusive fiancé as a patient and disclosed to him what I said during my sessions! Together they discussed all the things that were wrong with me. Together they decided that I was bipolar.

Danny stole my journal and took all of my thoughts and fears (which I had thought getting down on paper would help to sort out and heal), and used them against me. He told people what I wrote, which caused friends of mine to look at me in a negative light. By taking the information he read in my journal and telling people (even showing some of them), he began to win them over to his side and had proof that I was as crazy as he said I was. He was able to take the information and control me with it by making me feel like a horrible person for writing down what I thought and how I felt. It was horribly similar to when my mom confronted me with the things I wrote about my next-door neighbor, and accused me of finding what he did to me so "important" that I felt compelled to write it down.

Although I had vowed never to keep a journal again, I decided it couldn't hurt to write down the things that made me happy. This was something that could only bring good, and couldn't be used against me unless the things that made me happy were in fact against the law, which was not so.

I was spurred to take the new journal leap one day as a direct result of the happiness brought to me by my daughter, Morgan. I was having a bit of a rough day, one in which I was down on myself for no real reason but it felt as though I was carrying the weight of the world. Morgan lifted the heaviness away from my heart and made me cry tears of joy as I laid her in her crib for the night. I felt so blessed and fortunate to have such a beautiful and wonderful family – the family I had always hoped and wished that I would have someday, but never thought I would. For so long I was convinced that a life like that was for other people, but not for me.

I often imagined myself as an old lady, alone and destitute. I actually saw myself in a bathrobe and slippers, shuffling through Discount Drug Mart on Christmas Eve – the crazy old lady getting her Ripple, and fiddling with the blood pressure machine, because she has no place else to be. This was a very real fear I had. I was fairly sure it would be a reality for me in my future.

That night after I laid Morgan in her crib I wrote the first three entries of the things that made me happy that day in my new Happy Journal. They went like this:

1. I decided to cancel my plans to go out with friends, and instead rent a couple of movies, eat some Taco Bell tacos, and stay home with Morgan.

2. I watched a sappy love story called *Sweet November* that made me cry. Instead of *wishing* I could find a love like that, I happily knew that I had actually found that deep and beautiful "only-in-the-movies" type of love – with my very own husband!

3. Hugging and kissing Morgan, and seeing her full-gums smile as she looked up at me! Giving her a bath and watching her roll over on her tummy to play with her rattle, listening with bliss to her funny little laugh, and knowing that I made her with Frank. Being alone in the house tonight with the baby, and knowing that I am not alone.

I love Jacob, Morgan, and Frank with everything that I am. I hope that is enough for me to remember the next time I am feeling sorry for myself for no good reason. My family makes me rich with love, and these rewards are greater than any others.

I didn't keep up with the journal every day, but was often inspired to write in it because of my children and the joy that they brought to my heart.

When Jake was 3, he went to a Montessori preschool in the suburbs even though Frank and I still lived in my "doll house" in Cleveland. I was so proud of him. Every day my heart would simply overflow with happiness when he came around the corner by the water fountain where all the moms stood waiting at pick-up time. Jake would round the corner with big, wide, searching eyes, and a look of expectation in them. He knew I would be there waiting for him, but there was always a tiny bit of question in his eyes as he came around that corner. I loved that he never had to be disappointed. I was always there.

The kids marched down the hall in a line, sometimes with their hands behind their backs in a "proper" fashion and other times holding onto a rope. Once they hit that infamous corner and they caught a glimpse of their moms, any semblance of order was lost. Jake's face lit up and my heart returned the sentiment. He would yell out "Mommy!" as he rushed to me with open arms and bright smiling eyes. It made everything right in the world for that moment, and I was thankful that I could be there to experience it.

Sometimes after school, if Frank could be home with Morgan, I took Jake to the park or the nature center. I felt it was important for Jake and me to have some one-on-one time. I didn't want him to feel forgotten, or as if the baby got all the attention, so I did my best to show that I loved them both so much. It was hard to believe that not too long ago I was a single mom and thought it would always be just Jake and me.

Now we had Frank and Morgan in our lives, and we were all a family. Morgan looked up at Jacob and her face lit up when she saw him. You could see all of her gums, she smiled so big at her brother!

There are no "halves" in our house. We are all whole people – and they are whole brother and sister. We are Mom and Dad. The only steps we have lead to the bedrooms or the basement. "Step" is not a word we use to describe a parent or a child in our home.

One day Morgan was taking a nap in her crib and Jake was on the couch watching *Stuart Little* in his pj's with his sippy cup, cookies, and some stuffed animals. He asked me to sit with him and if I wanted to "watch the mouse." Of course I said "I would love to," and snuggled in!

This is a far cry from how I felt at his age.

I loved sitting there with him, with his little bare feet and his big brown eyes. I watched him as he was watching TV and was overwhelmed with how happy it made me to see how truly secure he felt in his home and in his mother's love. I loved knowing Morgan was cozy in her crib and that my family was everything to me, and I was everything to them. I have never yearned to find my biological parents, but having children of my own has really strengthened my appreciation of the importance of the bond between mother and child, and the warmth and security it brings.

I know that having my children safe and healthy in my home with Frank makes me feel secure, and I am happy in the knowledge that I am no longer alone, or living only for myself. Living for others means much more to me than being completely self-centered and focused on me and only me. There is too much love in my heart for me not to share it. For many years I was afraid to give it away – until I found the right person to help me feel confident and unafraid enough to let down the walls that surrounded my love and guarded my heart. It is now a deep ocean which invites people in, instead of the fenced-in swimming pool – with a sign that says "closed for the season" – that it used to be.

Morgan is yet another sterling example of all the things in my life that have most definitely happened for a reason, and that were unequivocally meant to be. She is a shining star that twinkles in a midnight sky and she has brought a great joy to both Frank and me, and her big brother, Jake, and our family wouldn't be complete without her. We were thrilled to have the family that each of us had always wanted, and decided that we both wanted to have one more child. Frank and I began trying to conceive our third child when Morgan was almost 2 years old.

I experienced a crazy and heavy menstrual period that continued a lot longer than usual, so I made an appointment to see my gynecologist. That appointment was a giant shiny balloon filled with air one moment and stuck with a pin the next. In the same sentence I was told that I was pregnant, but that I was also losing the baby. To find out all at once that there was a picture of a baby, a snapshot of our future child, but that it was quickly fading away like the opposite of a Polaroid developing before my eyes was a crazy roller coaster ride that no one should have to take. My hormone levels were dropping rapidly. By the next day I had lost the baby. A combination of confusion and sadness was imposed upon my life, uninvited. For quite a while after that, things just looked different and my daily routine was a little bit heavier and more routine than usual. The sun was shining, but I always felt cloudy.

Eventually I was able to pull myself out of the drab gray that surrounded me and was happy to be back in the land of living color. Of course Frank and I wondered what it would have been like to have another little person in the family, and we liked to venture guesses whether it would have been a boy or a girl. We tried to have another baby over the next couple of years, but it never "took." Neither of us wanted to look into the use of fertility drugs or to force it in any way. The approach we both wanted to take was that if it happened it happened, and if it didn't it wasn't meant to be.

As it turns out, it wasn't meant to be, but we are no longer sad about it.

The two incredible children who already complete our improbably perfect family were most definitely meant to be, and I consider them both gifts given to me by God and the Universe. I am so grateful for what I have been given and for what I have created.

Enjoy when you can, endure when you must.

—Goethe

XIX

THE SECOND Iron-distance triathlon I did was on the very same race course in Florida as the first one, but it was *ten years later in 2005*, and had a *whole different* type of drama and excitement surrounding it than the first. By then I had already married and divorced Joel; given birth to Jake; married Frank; and given birth to Morgan. We were living our lives happily and I was stronger in mind, body, and spirit than I had ever been in my life. It is truly amazing what you can accomplish when you have love for yourself; and you have a partner in your life you love and respect; and that person loves you, respects you, and is your best friend. Because I was in such a good place and was free of the stresses which surrounded the last one, that meant it was time to do another Ironman, or so I thought.

A strong and bossy lady named Wilma had a different agenda, and decided she was going to match wits with me and about 1,200 other athletes that year by surprising Florida with the most intense hurricane on record in the Atlantic.

In athletics and in life, having a plan is the key to succeeding, but having flexibility is a necessary and crucial part of any plan. Without flexibility, the best-laid plans can instantly blow up in your face, or, perhaps, blow away your intended course of action with no chance of recovery. As many endurance athletes know, when we commit to a race in our hearts and our minds, the first thing we do to solidify that commitment is to register for the race. Once you are registered, it is official – and turning back is difficult to do, not to mention embarrassing as well. (I don't know too many athletes who do not have an enormous amount of pride as well as a healthy competitive spirit, so backing out of a race is not an option.)

The second thing to do, after registering for the race, is to find out who else you might know who was "crazy" enough to sign up for the same race, so you have someone to train with during as many of the long workouts as possible. For the Great Floridian in 2005, that person was Ross, one of my friends and training buddies and a very fun travelling companion. Ross is from England, so he sports a very smooth, James Bond-like accent that is hard to miss.

(Recently, Ross and I went with two other awesome friends to do a Half Iron Tri in Muncie, Indiana, called the Muncie Endurathon. The four of us had so much fun on the road trip down to Indiana laughing our heads off in the car and overindulging on chocolate cookies and other snacks. We had so many inside jokes after that trip and so much fun together, I hope that isn't the last time I go to a race with Ross, King Fu Panda, and I See No Movies. Just sayin'. Anyway, the night before the Endurathon we went to a BW-3 and sat outside to get some dinner and a beer or two. A woman enjoying her cigarette outside near our table heard Ross talking and came over to ask him where he was from. Ross said in the thickest accent possible, simply dripping with all that is sarcastic and British: "Cleveland, Ohio." She was a little drunk anyway and just walked away confused. We all laughed our butts off that he said "Cleveland" when he knew damn well that the woman was digging his accent. I love the dry British humor and I love making Ross laugh.)

Having good friends to train with, and to go to the races with, makes the whole experience so much more enjoyable! It's not only a great way to bond, but being silly with your buddies, or even complaining to them about the race the night before you do it, is a great way to blow off nervous energy. It always makes me feel better to do some halfhearted bitching the night before the race about the mileage, or why the hell we are even doing this, we must be crazy…that type of stuff. It's like a bunch of kids before the big exam saying things like: "I didn't study;" "I'm probably going to flunk;" "I haven't even bought the book for this class;" but after you get in the exam room and sit down for the test, all the talk is just that – talk, and then you get down to business.

Our schedules didn't allow us to train together much for the Great Floridian, but Ross and I did manage to fit in a couple of long bike rides and a few bricks the summer before the October race. In preparation for the big day, Ross and I planned out the logistics of our trips down to Florida, and decided that because Frank and I and the kids were planning to drive down, we would take Ross's bike for him so he wouldn't have to ship it on the plane. It would save him a lot of money and effort, and we didn't mind doing it as we had the room. Ross took a flight down to Florida about a week prior to the race to acclimate himself to the Florida heat, and the plan was for my family and me to see him when we got there with his bike and a built-in Ironman cheering crew. We didn't know it at the time, but Wilma had other plans.

By October 19, 2005, Wilma had reached a Category 5 status and its winds neared 175 mph in the southern parts of Florida. My family and I were still in

Ohio watching the official race website as it was virtually set ablaze with thousands of athletes blogging and deliberating on the status of the race. The new "logo" of the race website was a creative cartoon of Wilma Flintstone with a big black line drawn through it. Competitors all over the world were glued to their computers, waiting with bated breath to see if all of their training was for naught. Decisions needed to be made regarding travel plans, assuming the race wasn't called off, but nobody liked the available options. The choices boiled down to: staying home and forfeiting all the training and mental and physical preparation altogether; versus knowingly going into a hurricane with prospects looming that included getting hurt, stranded, or killed.

The Governor of Florida had been brought in to make the call on whether or not to cancel the race. We anxiously awaited the Governor's and the Race Director's decisions – while Marco Island, Fort Myers, and Naples were being evacuated.

Frank and I had to make decisions of our own whether or not we should get on the road and make our way to the race or stay put. We didn't have the luxury of time and should have been on the road already, but with everything so up in the air we didn't know what to do. Our decision to stay or go would not only affect our family, but because we had Ross's bike, if the race wasn't cancelled, it affected him directly as well because he was kind of going to need his ride.

Frank nervously packed the car and I kept checking the latest updates on the race website. The officials still weren't sure whether they would have to cancel the race, because the forecasters were predicting that Wilma would strike Clermont (and the race site) sometime on Saturday night, which, for most of the athletes, would be smack in the middle of the marathon portion of their race. Waiting for the final decision was an emotionally taxing exercise of pins and needles proportion. Finally the report came in: the forecast indicated that the storm wouldn't hit land before late on Sunday – and the race was *on*! So, now we knew there would be a race, but the question still stood whether or not we wanted to drive our children into a potentially extremely dangerous situation. The answer to that question was no and Frank and I decided last-minute to have the family stay home, and I would fly down to Florida on my own.

At that point it was the only viable option, but it posed one very big problem: Ross and I would both be down there without a bike! I immediately called Ross and asked him if he would rather have me come down by plane without the bikes and we could rent some from a local shop, or, I wouldn't make it at all and he would bring his British butt back to Ohio. He opted for me to fly down there and we would look for some rentals. The next morning I was on my way to Florida without a bike and less than 24 hours before the start of the race.

Locating rental bikes proved to be much more difficult than Ross and I could have anticipated. We scoured the city and only found one bike shop that would rent us bikes. If we were looking for the type of bike to leisurely cruise the boardwalk, this would have been great news. Unfortunately we were looking for the type of bike that could withstand a 112-mile road race with some monster hills, and preferably one with some semblance of comfort and speed. Surprisingly the bike shop had only one type of bike to offer us, which if we wanted to rent would cost $250 each. In terms of weight, speed, and aerodynamics, these bikes were nowhere near ideal at any price. To add insult to injury, if we wanted aerobars or clipless pedals we would have to purchase them separately and have them put onto the bikes temporarily (of course, paying for the labor as well.)

I was doing everything I could to hold it together, remain positive, and keep Ross off the ledge that both of us would have loved to swan dive from at that point to simply put an end to the madness. We told the shopkeeper we needed to think about it for a minute, and as I massaged my low-grade migraine, we stepped outside to weigh our limited options in private, and felt the 98-degree heat and the imminence of the race weigh upon us like a lead blanket.

Out of earshot of anyone standing in the cool air conditioning of the bike shop, we both voiced our deeply colorful opinions of the dude who ran the store (wanker) as well as his rental offerings (thanks for nothing). Neither of us was happy about our choices, and Ross declared that he was out of the race.

Ironman, like any endurance event, is over 90 percent mental, and to have this much trepidation before a race is complete lunacy. We should have been hydrating all day with our feet up by now, but we were walking around in the heat trying to figure out if we even had bikes to ride. I did not want to rent the crappy bike any more than Ross did, but I also didn't want to let Wilma cost me my race. These are very personal choices, however, and mine was to go back into the store, rent the crappy-ass bike, and try to make the best of it. Ross was completely fine with his choice to watch the race this time around and give it a go at another Ironman in the future. I could feel my inner strength slowly deflating and I needed to pump myself back up – right along with the tires on the rental bike.

It was getting very late in the afternoon and we still needed to head over to the Expo where all the athletes had to check in and rack their bikes. I had been on my feet all day, when I should have been resting and mentally preparing. I hadn't had anything to eat or drink since my flight into Orlando, when I really should have been hydrating and fueling. It had already felt like the ultimate emotional and physical roller coaster ride and the actual race hadn't even started yet.

I kept reminding myself that I could not give up on my goal after everything I had been through to get there. I had been through much worse than this in my life, and I wasn't about to let a few obstacles stand in the way of what I wanted to achieve. My rational and logical side was nagging at me because I was about to attempt a 112-mile ride on a "Huffy," and that I actually paid an additional $250 – which I couldn't afford to spend – in order to do it! I promptly told my rational and logical side to piss off; I had an Expo to get to!

We poured our sweat-slicked bodies back into Ross's rental car and drove to the Expo. I was determined to find a better bike option, so I proceeded to chat it up with every volunteer and fellow athlete who crossed my path. All of the athletes had the most amazing racing bikes, but they probably seemed even more amazing to me than usual, as I didn't have one too. I tried not to burst into tears as I laid my eyes on their beautiful, shiny, and sleek riding machines that they probably took for granted. During my various conversations, I came across an angel of mercy! She was the head pastor at a church in Clermont who just happened to be one of the race's biggest sponsors, and she and her husband were also both seasoned triathletes. This was no ordinary angel. Upon hearing our story she immediately offered to let Ross and me borrow two of her racing bikes. She had one for me, and her husband had one that Ross could use. This was incredible news, and upon hearing it – quicker than you can say "Bob's Your Uncle" –

my buddy was back in the race and we were both back in his rental car to return the bike I just rented, and then to follow our new friend to her home to pick up the bikes. Pastors must make more money than God because our new friend and her husband had a gorgeous home on Lake Minneola and a garage full of "old" tri bikes. I couldn't believe how kind and generous they were to go out of their way and let two strangers take their bikes. But really, it shouldn't have been all that surprising because triathletes and runners are probably the nicest, most giving people on the planet! (All those endorphins and dopamine make the brain go soft, I guess, but still…this was huge.)

Even though I was so stoked that we actually found racing bikes to use, it didn't stop me from suddenly noticing that there was the slight matter of our 5-inch height difference. Her frame was perfect for her 5-foot-10-inch stature, and I am about 5-foot-5-inches. I thought better of pointing this out for fear I would seem ungrateful, and simply thanked her for her generosity and kindness. We all said our thank yous and wished each other luck in the race. We talked about the logistics of returning the bikes, and then Ross and I had to get moving if we wanted to make it back before the athlete and bike check-in at the Expo closed. By that point I was sweltering and running on pure adrenaline, which actually turned out to be quite helpful, as there was only room enough for one bike in Ross's rental car.

I watched my friend drive off in the air-conditioned car and tried to tell myself that riding back to the Expo in my street clothes wouldn't be that bad. I tried to convince myself that it wasn't a big deal that the temperature was almost 100 degrees; that my back was dripping like Niagara Falls; or that the front of my shirt was plastered to my chest before I even pushed off to begin pedaling. I wasn't going to let this get me down; I had a bike and I was going to do this thing! I was sweating worse than a hooker in church when I pulled up on a pastor's bike at the race Expo. It was the second time we had been there that day, I was soaked and thirsty, and it was 8:30 p.m. We still needed to get the bikes on the racks, find some dinner, organize our crap for the race, and then try to get a few winks of sleep. I kept my mantra going in my mind: "This ain't shit. This ain't shit."

Waking up at the butt-crack of Dawn isn't my favorite way to start the day (no offense to Dawn, of course). Morning just arrived much too soon and before I knew it Ross and I were waiting in the dark outside the transition area with the rest of the nervous and sleep-deprived-looking athletes so we could have our bodies marked. Body marking is when volunteers use a fat black permanent marker to write your race number on your shoulders and usually your calf as well. Everyone must be marked so officials know who you are in the water and out on the race course.

As I was waiting in line, my body gave me just barely enough advance notification that the time had arrived to Sign the Constitution. I asked Ross to save my spot in line so I could do some Spring Cleanin', threw down all the gear I had in my hands, and took off for the bathroom. When I got back to the body-marking line I felt ten pounds lighter, but the trade-off wasn't worth it when I noticed that in my haste to get to the bathroom, I had broken my goggles beyond repair by throwing them on the ground. I was horrified! What else could possibly go wrong? It was an hour before the start of the race and I had no goggles for the 2.4-mile swim, and would then have to ride a bike for 112 miles that I had never been on before and that didn't fit me.

Although in a slight state of panic, I tried to appear as if I was calm as I went from person to person and asked if anyone had a spare set of goggles I could use. Almost everyone said no, and I thought I would be doomed to doing the swim without any, until I found the one kind soul who offered a pair of dark, smoky-gray goggles which would have been perfect if it was sunny outside, and around noon, and if the water wasn't the color of Cherry Coke. But, beggars can't be choosers, so I accepted them with a big smile and an even bigger thank you! I couldn't understand why the water was so scary-looking; it was as if we were swimming in Camp Crystal Lake and Jason left behind more blood than water.

After asking a few of the locals, I discovered that the trees around Lake Minneola will sometimes seep a certain type of sap into the water which makes it an eerie brownish-red color. A couple of people also offered extra information, which I could have done without, confirming my fears that the lake was indeed home to a few 10-foot alligators. The gun hadn't even gone off yet, and I was drained and exhausted!

As usual, however, after I was out on the course I was able to relax and have some fun. Although the dark water and goggles made it seem as though I was swimming with my eyes closed, the swim went (dare I say) swimmingly! I finished strong and felt pretty good, with no gator run-ins to be had, and had a decent time of about an hour or so for the 2.4 miles.

The bike ride was going fine for the first 60 miles as well, until I spotted my buddy Ross up ahead, on the side of the road with his bike. He was sitting down on the street but holding the bike up in front of him. I yelled out to him to see what was up, and he yelled back that he was dropping out of the race. Once I was upon him I decided to stop and see if he was hurt, and, if he wasn't, I would try to talk him into continuing on to the finish. (It turned out he wasn't injured, but the bike's cable had snapped so he couldn't ride it without some serious maintenance and repair.) As I was about to pass him, however, I didn't know any of that yet, and I squeezed the brakes with the amount of pressure that I was used to on my own very old bike. The amount of squeezing I had applied to the brakes proved to be way too much, causing a surprisingly and alarmingly abrupt stop that sent me head over heels with the bike still attached to my bike shoes.

So, try to imagine a person and a bicycle somersaulting in a complete, and quite ungraceful, choreographed flip. I broke my fall with one hand, my shoulder, and also the aerobars of the bike that didn't belong to me. I had 50 miles to go with cockeyed handlebars and a bleeding hand. I was really upset and worried about having to bring the bike back to the pastor after I broke it; and I guess, technically, Ross broke her husband's bike as well! It wasn't how I imagined it would turn out, and I hoped they wouldn't be too mad at us for messing up their bikes, but I had to keep my mind on the task at hand, which was getting to the finish line.

Ross was forced to back out of the race and although it seemed that the forces of nature were against us both, I still wouldn't let myself quit. This was now a personal affront to my ability to persevere. It was as if my will and my tenacity were being tested to the fullest extent, and I was *not* about to fail that test. I told Ross that I would see him at the finish. He said that was cool, and he would keep Frank posted by phone, and he would be at the finish line when I got there. I got back up on the bike and gutted out the remaining miles with a searing pain that shot up from my hamstring and bit into my butt muscle. The improper bike fit was now speaking up and making its presence known. I told it to shut up.

I got back to the last transition and psyched myself up for the marathon by changing slowly in the tent and gulping a couple of GU packets with water for the road. Leaving the changing tent was tough, but after I was back out on the race course the miles weren't that bad, and I was having some fun again. It's crazy, but I actually felt really good for the first half of the marathon. As I ran around the lake I enjoyed taking in the scenery, and I noticed a lot of the same people I had seen earlier in the day going about their lives like normal people. Okay, I won't lie; I did silently curse them (in the nicest way possible) because the same families I had seen reading the paper and sipping coffee on their porches that morning were now getting pizzas delivered for their dinners, and I was still out there running.

By the time I reached mile 15, "happy time" had come to an end because my stomach blew up and I was in some serious pain. The nausea I was experiencing rivaled both of my pregnancies put together, and I was bloated to the point of looking as if I was currently carrying twins. It felt as if my head was in a vice and the guy from the *SAW* movies had given me no alternative way to get out of it. The temperature was almost 100 degrees, and a light rain began to fall as I ran alone and disoriented in the dark. I had an overwhelming and irrational feeling of loneliness and the green glow sticks of the other runners seemed to be very few and farther between as I began to cry but continued to move forward. I had never felt that bad during a race before, and I had no idea what was happening to me. I figured I was dehydrated and tried to take in more water at each aid station.

It wasn't until I got home and was able to Google my severe and unprecedented symptoms that I discovered what I was experiencing was hyponatremia, or water intoxication. Inadvertently I had tipped the delicate balance of blood-sodium concentration from the long hours of sweating sodium out, but replacing it with water instead of sports drinks or salt tablets that add back proper amounts of sodium. This explained the headache and feelings of disorientation, as well as the major bloating and nausea that I felt out on that Florida race course. As I read about hyponatremia I also discovered that this condition can potentially cause stroke or death. While I was out on the dark lonely road of the run course I had no idea about any of this. All I knew was that I was a survivor and a fighter and I was going to keep moving forward. Like a traveler on a long and tiresome journey, the finish line beckons you with the rewards and riches that come from achieving your goal. The warm beauty of the finish line after a race gives you the feeling of home, and makes all the efforts of getting there worthwhile.

My one and only goal was to reach that finish line and call Frank to tell him and the kids that I made it and I loved them; and nothing would stop me from getting there, including Wilma, bike troubles, or my fear of alligators. I wouldn't allow the thought of not finishing inside my head and refused to think about anything but the road ahead of me, leaving what had already happened in the past behind me. Out on the run course, just as in life, you can't worry about what has already been. You have to concentrate only on moving forward, one step at a time. All that mattered to me that night was getting to the finish line.

I thought about my husband and kids, and how they were pulling for me at home. I thought about all that other people (like my dad) had done for me and that finishing this race was something that only I could do for myself. My dad was no longer alive, and no longer supporting or helping me both emotionally and financially, but I thought of him while I was out there and he brought me strength. I thought about his illnesses, and his amputated leg, and I reminded myself I was happy and lucky to be physically able to do this race.

I thought about people who had put me down or didn't believe in me, and knowing that they were wrong about me made me happy and motivated me to focus on the finish line. I thought about the love and support from my true friends and my husband and the bright shiny faces of my children. And I was able to continue. I did the "Marathon Shuffle" – which is part walking and part dragging-your-feet jogging – for the next few hours and finished the race in my slowest Iron-distance time to date: 14 hours and 37 minutes. When I crossed the finish line, Ross was there, and he and Frank were both worried that I was out there for much longer than anyone anticipated. My first Iron-distance finishing time was an hour faster than this one, and they wondered where on Earth I was and if I was okay! The minute I crossed the finish line Ross walked over to me wearing a warm smile and handed me his cell phone, instinctively knowing that I would want to talk to my husband. He even dialed the number for me. I took the phone and told Frank right away that I was okay, but I couldn't talk. I told him I loved him and told him to tell the kids I loved them when they got up in the morning. I hung up the phone and burst into tears. It was over, and I didn't feel good at all, but I didn't feel as if I needed to go to the medical tent. It was nothing that the Wendy's drive-through, a hot shower, and sleep wouldn't cure. I finished, and no matter what happened on the way there, it is still an accomplishment that no one can take from me.

The next morning I got up, and although tired, I felt wonderful and happy. Ross and I packed up and headed to the airport to catch our flights home. The area where we had just been was walloped by Hurricane Wilma the following day, October 24th, 2005. By the time it ended, Wilma's unexpected force had demolished buildings; destroyed a portion of the state's major north-south highway; severed power to more than three million dwellings and business establishments, resulting in hardship to six million-plus Floridians; and caused 25 deaths.

Accomplishing a goal like an Ironman triathlon is an incredible accomplishment to be proud of, but for me to feel even more empowered and to give my miles more meaning and purpose, the two most recent races I have completed were dedicated to *Girls With Sole*. Although I trained for the second two ultra-distance triathlons with all my usual suspects, including Ross, they were fueled by a completely different set of motivations. Both of them were to raise money and awareness for *Girls With Sole*, but also to set an example for the girls I work with that nothing is impossible and that we can all "Lace Up for a Lifetime of Achievement." If I expect my girls to come out of their comfort zones, I can't ask them to do anything I am not willing to do myself. I need to push myself and show them that the finish line feeling is worth pursuing.

As of today, the two ultra races I have done for *Girls With Sole* were the Rev3 Full in September of 2010 and Ironman Zurich, Switzerland, in July of 2011. I did both of these races as part of TEAM LULA (*Girls With Sole*'s endurance racing and fundraising team; LULA stands for Lacing Up for a Lifetime of Achievement), and even though I trained for them the same way that I had trained for the first two, the feel of these races was completely different. I felt energized and empowered knowing I was out there for the girls. I had a true mission and every mile completed was with true intent. It was awesome to have a dream and a direction connected to all the hours of training and racing. Each of these races was an amazing journey and simply knowing that I was out there in support of young girls who need our programs gave me strength and carried me through the tough stuff. Because I was racing for the girls, I had an extra dose of courage, power, and strength which helped me overcome obstacles, believe in my abilities, and achieve my goal. And ironically, that is exactly what *Girls With Sole* programming does for our girls. Each of the two races I did for *Girls With Sole* posed its own set of challenges and obstacles, but I finished each feeling extremely strong and extremely happy, one in a 12:08 and the other in a 12:27. I couldn't fail with my girls on my side.

I really wish I was a profound-enough writer to describe the elation, joy, and pride I felt in Sandusky, Ohio, *and* Zurich, Switzerland, when I came across the finish lines of each race to hear the emcee announce to the whole crowd that I had completed the race for *Girls With Sole*! At the Rev3 race, Frank and the kids were there for me at the finish as well as some of my training buddies, and to see the pride on their faces was enough to make my heart overflow with gratitude for what I did that day and for our *Girls with Sole*! Many times the hardest part of the race is getting to the starting line. It is always scariest at the start of the race, but once you are out there you just do what needs to be done, and it is always so worth it in the end. There is nothing I love more than helping girls in need feel what it is like to cross that finish line! With *Girls With Sole*, they are truly learning what it is like to "Lace Up for a Lifetime of Achievement" (LULA).

I often wonder how many more Ironman races I will do, and what adventures they will bring. I wonder if someday any of my *Girls With Sole* girls will do one as well; and it is my hope that at least one of them will. I hope that crossing the finish line at a race like an Ironman will be one of the many gifts they will receive during their lives, for to do so is truly life-changing and empowering beyond their dreams.

For a tree to become tall it must grow tough roots among the rocks.

—Friedrich Nietzsche

XX

MY SON JAKE recently brought home a permission slip for a program at his school called Challenge Day, and the slip had a spot that requested parent volunteers. I was familiar with Challenge Day because it is a quite powerful national and international program that has been around for about 20 years. It focuses on changing the way students view each other, with the goal of ending oppression and bullying of any kind in school. I learned about Challenge Day when I first started *Girls With Sole*, as many people had told me that our missions are very similar and there is an alignment in our efforts to stop abuse or ridicule of kids by conducting fun games and exercises that build self-esteem and leadership skills. During Challenge Day, however, facilitators delve deeply into specific highly emotional situations and circumstances of each student by having each person disclose information that completes the sentence: "If you really knew me…"

Other exercises during Challenge Day require students to cross the line when a certain topic applies to them. The topics include everything from being bullied for being small, big, gay, or having skin of color; to alcoholism or abuse at home; and much more. It is quite eye-opening and emotional for the kids to see that their friends and peers might be going through situations similar to what they too are experiencing, but had thought they were alone.

Jake actually asked me to volunteer for Challenge Day, and I couldn't have been happier even though I knew it would be a rough roller coaster ride of a day! I was happy he actually wanted me to be there and had no feeling of embarrassment that his mom would be interacting with him and his classmates all day.

When we broke up into our small groups to do the "If you really knew me" exercise, I could hear Jacob crying in his group and it hurt me but I was proud of him. I knew he was opening up about his dad, and later I found out that the only thing he was able to get out before he was unable to speak through his tears was that his biological dad was an alcoholic who couldn't hold down a job or a residence. I think it was a cleansing day for him and he wanted me there to experience it. I was glad I was able to be there and I felt that our already strong bond had reached titanium strength that day, which truly warmed my heart.

At the end of the program the facilitators handed out special Challenge Day note cards and asked all in the room to write to someone who means a lot to them, or to whom they wanted to apologize, just to let them know how they feel about them, and why that person is important to them.

We had a short two minutes to write our notes, and then some participants were given a chance to read their cards out loud. I raised my hand to read mine to Jake. The facilitator had Jake come up and stand before me so I could read it to him, and afterwards Jake hugged me and wept into my neck while the whole room clapped. My note card said:

Jake – Having you was so important to me. You are everything to me in my life and my world, and you saved my life. You made my heart grow and I became a better person, and wanted to better my life, *because* of you and *for* you. I know that having Joel in our lives can be hard and sad and difficult — but I should thank him. Because without him, I wouldn't have you, and I wouldn't be whole. I love you and hope that you know I am always here for you (no matter what) and that you can tell me anything. I love you, Jake. You are special and you saved me.

Love, Mom

I didn't know it until Jake got home and gave me his Challenge Day note card, but he had written his to me as well. It said:

Dear Mom,

You're the most amazing person in the world. You have always been there for me when I needed you. You stay strong when things get tough. You are my hero. We stick with each other until the end. Just as we have always. I love you.

Love, Your Son,

Jake

When Jake was 10 years old and Morgan was almost 8, I was in the early stages of starting *Girls With Sole* and told them both what I was planning to do, why I wanted to do it, and what I wanted *Girls With Sole* to be about for the girls who need it.

I told both of my kids that I needed to create a logo which would evoke the feeling and the meaning behind *Girls With Sole*. (I also explained to them what the heck a logo was and why it was important to the organization.) I wanted my own children to have a big part in *Girls With Sole* and its development. I thought if they came up with the logo, it would be exceptional and fantastic. If it didn't work out that way, at least Morgan and Jake would have the satisfaction and joy of knowing that they were involved, and that I valued their input.

Jake and Morgan both sat down at our kitchen table and were excited to begin imagining and creating different logo art. They were excited about the organization that their mom was about to start, and they were proud of me for wanting to help other kids by doing something cool.

Jake immediately drew, on his very first attempt, the logo which is not only the one that *Girls With Sole* uses today, but which is also now a Nationally Registered Trademark with the United States Patent and Trademark Office. He spontaneously and flawlessly designed it in its entirety as if he looked into my heart and drew exactly what he saw there.

For so many reasons, I can see that much of what has happened in my life, and many of the things that I have done, have been for a very specific purpose that no one could have ever prophesied. Both of my children have beautiful hearts and a glow that shines so brightly from within them. You can see it in their eyes, their smiles, and their actions. I am constantly in awe of the incredible person Jake has already become, and I know as he grows and matures, he will only get better with age – just like his mom.

Go confidently in the direction of your dreams. Live the life you've imagined.

—Henry David Thoreau

XXI

DREAMING AT NIGHT is one of my favorite things to do. I love the crazy movies my subconscious mind reels out while I am reenergizing for the next day. I don't watch much, if any, TV during the day, but I get to sleep and be entertained by my dreams at the same time, without all the mindless snacking! That is multi-tasking at its best.

Some people try to avoid things that will give them "scary" dreams, but I embrace all types of dreams. I love the scary ones; the emotional ones; the sexy ones that allow me to be with people I'm not married to with no repercussions; and I especially love the crazy ones that make absolutely no sense in the real world. The darker and crazier the dream is, the better, in my opinion. What the heck, you want them to be worth the price of admission, right? I mean, if you are in the middle of a boring dream, you can't get up and leave the theatre unless your bladder, your husband, the kids, or the dog is nudging you hard enough, so ya might as well make it good! Most of my dreams blend into one another, and although they are enjoyable at the time of viewing, I can't remember much about them when I am awake. There are only two dreams I have had which I would say go beyond just being memorable – one of which, I am not convinced was a dream at all.

The first dream I will never forget is from when I was a child. I had this dream only once, and although it probably wouldn't faze anyone else, I will never forget how realistic and horrifying it *felt* to me, deep inside my heart.

In the dream I was lost in the mountains in Germany. It felt as though I was really there, and the fear of never finding my family again took over my body like an illness. I kept hiking higher and higher, taking note of the villages and the unfriendly peasant-looking people that inhabited them as I searched each stranger's face for my mom. The day was beautiful and full of crisp mountain air, warm sun, and the bluest of skies, yet somehow the villagers still looked drab and gray.

Near the top of the mountain, I reached a meadow with tall green grass and beautiful little yellow flowers growing in clusters everywhere. There were women in German dirndls scattered about, but their heads were all facing down as they picked the yellow flowers and placed them in their aprons, skirts, or baskets.

Each one of them looked glorious and beautiful in the sunshine as they gathered up their skirts to hold the freshly picked wildflowers. It looked like an ad for Ivory Soap or maybe a Swiss-made chocolate bar. The women remained bent over, precluding me from seeing any of their faces, yet somehow among them I could clearly see my mom.

I spotted her among all of the women and I was positive that it was her! I had been living with her for over ten years by then. She was my mother, and I would know her anywhere! I was overcome with happiness to have found her, and I ran toward her screaming, "Mom! Mom!"

When I reached her she wouldn't look up at me, so I placed my hand on her shoulder and said, "Mom?"

She snapped her neck in my direction in a gross, bird-like manner, and I could see that it was her, but she was monstrous-looking, extremely dark and frightening. She growled at me in an inhuman voice that chilled me to the bone as she spit, "I'm not your mother."

I don't scare easily, but this dream scared the crap out of me, and I will never forget it. I know you don't have to be a professional dream analyst or a psychotherapist to recognize the myriad meanings behind it. It is fairly blatant what the dream means, but it was the way it made me feel even after I was awake that bothered me the most about it. It was a frightening chill that overcame me like a sudden gust from the unknown, and lingered like the breath of a ghost.

The second dream I will absolutely never forget is the one that I am not sure is even a dream. I will need to preface this: although I was raised Catholic, I am not at all someone who would be considered a devoutly religious person. I have a faith of my own, and I am extremely open to any and all beliefs held by other people. What other people believe is fine with me, but I do prefer not to be preached at or to have others' beliefs *forced* upon me. In news headlines, the super-extreme zealot types are often those who have the most to hide. Sometimes, but not always, when people are squawking the loudest about the wrongdoings of others, they themselves are probably not the best people on the inside (for instance, Ted Haggard, George Rekers, and Tony Alamo).

I wouldn't place my mother and father in the "squawking" category by any stretch, but I would have to say that they were a bit above average when it came to being active in their faith. They went to church every Sunday, and my mom went to 7:00 a.m. Mass almost every day during the week when I was little. We were all expected to go to church, and on many occasions my father took me there literally "kicking and screaming" as he liked to phrase it. Both my parents were Eucharistic Ministers who gave Communion at Mass, and they read Scripture to each other every morning at our house. My mom read her Bible in what was known to everyone in our house as her "Prayer Chair." (This is the part where people who know me make jokes about how I must have caused her to wear it out, and if I were ever to have sat in it, the chair would have spontaneously combusted into flames.)

When I was growing up, it was not strange to have a priest sitting at our dinner table, or a nun dancing an Irish jig or a polka in our living room at one of my parents' house parties. When my dad travelled to Japan for his work, he often went for a month at a time, leaving my mom at home to contend with my two brothers and me. Since my brother Paul and I were like oil and water as kids, we would torture each other, which in turn tortured my mother. I once bit him so hard that I drew blood, and some of our fights included overturned furniture as well as some type of bodily harm to one or both of us. There was a time I recall that was so bad, and my mom was so close to the end of her rope with us, that she actually called a priest to come over to the house to help her. Maybe she was looking for a friend to talk to, or for him to perform an Exorcism. I'm not really sure which.

I went to a Catholic school from kindergarten through 7th grade, but I *still* had to attend the religion classes that my mom taught after school to the public school kids in addition to the classes I took at my own school. She wouldn't dare leave me alone at home, or with

Paul, so I went with her to religion class and sat in the back where I could cause trouble with some of the boys.

My parochial education did not end there. My first two years of college at Niagara University required that I take many religion classes as well, because it is a Catholic school inspired by the work of St. Vincent de Paul. Of course I could continue describing the type of Catholics my parents were, but I think everyone gets the picture. What I probably also do not have to explain is why the minute I had the chance to never go back to church once left to my own devices, I ran and never looked back. You can only force-feed someone for so long before she can't take another bite.

I felt that I was either missing something, or maybe I really was just a horrible person, because whatever I was supposed to get out of all the Masses and Scripture and homilies, I simply wasn't getting. Whatever joyfulness in my heart, spiritual growth, or peaceful strength religion was supposed to invoke was completely lost on me, because I wasn't feeling any of it.

But when I go for a long run, to me, *that* is quite spiritual in nature. Running is meditative, brings joy to my heart, and makes me feel like a better person. These are the things that I think you are supposed to feel in church, but I never have. Going for a run, for me, is more religious than going into a building on a designated day and time to stand, kneel, sit, check out the person's butt in front of you, listen to how you will go to Hell if you are bad, and then eat doughnuts and drink Kool-Aid punch in the church hall. I'm not saying that church is wrong or bad. I think it is great for people to practice their individual beliefs if they are truly getting something positive out of it, no matter what religion they practice. I'm just saying that *for me personally*, attending church has never moved me or lifted me up the way I felt it should have.

That being said, I truly believe that Mary (the Mother of God, the one in the blue robes) came into my room one night and paid me a visit.

This is something that I have only told two other people on this Earth. I knew that the rest of the world would think I was nuts, and it took me a long time to get to the point where people didn't think that way about me anymore, so I wasn't about to blow it by telling them that Mary presented herself to me in my bedroom. Besides, why would she visit someone obviously not very religious who would probably laugh her head off at anyone else who claimed he or she had a visit from her? One of my best friends told me that those are *exactly* the type of people before which she will appear. My friend and my husband are the only two people I have told about Mary, until now. The morning after it happened, Frank and I were standing in the kitchen and he was making coffee. I casually said to him, "Mary was in our room last night."

He obviously had the wrong impression, and with a sly smile and an excitable look he eagerly asked me, "Mary, who?"

I said, "Mary, Mary! Like the Virgin Mary?"

I lost him there, and we never talked about it again.

My best friend, on the other hand, is a very faith-based person who strongly believes in appearances by the Virgin Mary. We have had many conversations over the years about the miracles of Lourdes and Medjugorje, as well as Padre Pio. I knew I could tell her and she not only wouldn't think I was nuts...she would believe me.

As I have said already, my dreams never scare me, especially not to the point where I am startled out of sleep. I really do embrace them as if I were watching a movie with a trough full of popcorn and a large soda.

On the night that Mary was in my room, I remember that I wasn't dreaming anything at all. It was a peaceful and dreamless sleep until I was suddenly startled out of it. It was the type of thing where you wake up with wide eyes as big as saucers, and an awful (and loud) snort reverberates through your nose and throat.

I was fully awake and when my eyes opened, I saw Mary standing next to my bed, holding one arm outstretched before her, pointing in a forward direction. She was so beautiful, with a luminous face and soft, long, brown hair. Her blue- and cream-colored robes hung all around her and I could see that she was telling me to go forward, and then she was gone.

At that time I had been worried about starting *Girls With Sole*. There were a lot of people who doubted that the organization, or my attempts to start it, would be successful. Negativity regarding the entire organization, including its structure, mission, and approach, was cast upon me by people I knew very well, as well as those I didn't know and hadn't ask for their opinions in the first place.

I kept telling myself that if *Girls With Sole* didn't work out, it couldn't hurt to at least help a few kids along the way, and then I would let it fizzle out on its own. There was no harm in trying, and inside my heart, I wanted to follow my plan and my dream – but I was letting the negative voices creep in, causing me to question if I was doing the right thing.

Mary, being the smart and strong woman that she is, came to me to tell me that I must move forward. I don't think she cared what religion I did or did not practice, if I went to church, if I prayed the Rosary, or if I had a specific chair in my home in which to do it. I think she came to me as a woman who had to believe in herself, and who had to know she was right even when everyone said she was wrong. She wanted me to know that I was going in the right direction and that I should keep moving forward.

In our short two years of existence, *Girls With Sole* has succeeded faster and helped more girls than anyone could have believed. Quite often, events and circumstances that have contributed to its success seemingly fell into place as if it were on a path or course of its own, which no one could impede upon even if they tried. I am often reminded by my dear friend, with whom I had shared the story after it happened, that Mary is pointing the way.

"It's impossible," said pride. "It's risky," said experience. "It's pointless," said reason. "Give it a try," whispered the heart."

—Unknown

XXII

I AM ASKED all the time why I started *Girls With Sole*. People want to know the exact defining moment of its inception. This is not an easy answer to give, at least not in a 30-second sound byte. *Girls With Sole* grew and evolved organically from my own life experiences and from my desire to help girls who may also experience similar circumstances in their own lives. If you have ever completed a race (of any distance or type), and put your heart and soul into training and achieving your goal, then you know the feeling of electrifying empowering excitement at the finish line. All at once you feel as if you are coming home and the whole crowd is there to welcome you. It feels as if you won the lottery or cured cancer. At the moment you cross that finish line, you are the most extraordinary person you can be and you feel as if you can do *anything*!

I wanted to bottle that feeling and give it to girls who needed it most. *Girls With Sole* is for any girl who feels that she is not good enough, worthless, alone, bullied, ugly, stupid, put down, neglected, abused, or simply in need of a boost to her self-esteem. I founded *Girls With Sole* for girls who need someone to believe in them so that they can believe in themselves. I wanted at-risk girls and those who have experienced abuse of any kind to be given a sporting chance in their lives, and to experience the finish line feeling. It's a feeling of empowerment and achievement that no one can ever take away from them. The closest I could get to bottling it and giving it to them was to start *Girls With Sole*.

The mission is to use free fitness and wellness programs to empower the minds, bodies, and souls of girls ages 9 to 18, who are at-risk or have experienced abuse of any kind. *Girls With Sole* programs include traditional team sports, running programs, yoga, dance, and self-esteem building exercises. The programs encourage girls to make healthy choices in every part of their lives and build their self-esteem.

Because I did not receive any help or support when I was abused as a child, I had to find an outlet and a healing strength. I found it in sports. As an adult I began volunteering and also working for various nonprofits in Cleveland and realized there was a huge need that wasn't being met for kids who have experienced abuse of any kind. The at-risk communities and kids in the system (foster or juvenile justice) have very little, if any, access to fitness programs of any kind, and therefore might never make the mind/body/soul connection that I made as a child. Someone needed to show them that there is a way out of the darkness, and each of them can find her way out without drugs, alcohol, or self-harm.

I knew the sedentary lifestyle and the type 2 diabetes epidemic in today's youth could also be addressed by starting an organization that serves girls ages 9 to 18 who have been abused or are at-risk. It was clear to me that if I put my passion for athletics and fitness together with my passion for helping kids, the combination couldn't lose.

It was a winner for me – and now it was time to help others with the same formula that worked for me.

I don't judge people when they don't "get" what it is that *Girls With Sole* actually does for the kids. (It happens a lot more than I could have imagined.) The only thing that matters to me is the happiness I see in the girls as a result of the programs, and the way they embrace and respond to the programs in such a positive manner.

All of the girls with whom I work are truly amazing and wonderful people. I love having the chance to get to know them and to see the confidence and strength they develop throughout *Girls With Sole* programming. The girls bring me so much joy and fulfillment, and I often think they give more to me than I could ever give to them.

Many of the girls we serve are in foster care and/or residential treatment of some kind, and some of the girls are in juvenile detention centers. It is amazingly gratifying and exciting to see how *Girls With Sole* programs can turn their behavior and attitudes around in such short periods of time. They begin to take on leadership roles and help to ensure that the newer girls in the group participate and behave respectfully. When girls first begin programming, most of them are shy and quiet, and because fitness is a new concept to them, they aren't thrilled about participating and they don't have proper workout attire. This is why we supply every girl with brand-new jog bras and brand-new running shoes, as well as water bottles. It not only motivates them and makes them giddy with excitement, but also ensures that they are comfortable and properly outfitted to avoid injury.

In some situations, to ensure the girls don't forget to bring their shoes to the sessions, we arrange with the facility for the shoes to be left and stored there, and taken out each time they are needed for a session. This way the kids can't say that they forgot their shoes and therefore can't participate. If their shoes are always left on the premises, that excuse isn't ever going to cut it.

At one of these particular facilities, on the day I gave out the shoes, one young lady approached me and asked if she could please wear her shoes home. I said she shouldn't because she might forget to bring them back next time. To this she said, "Miss Liz...I can't forget to bring them. They are my only pair of shoes."

In this same group of girls there was also a pair of sisters, ages 15 and 17. They were brought to *Girls With Sole* sessions on a weekly basis by a couple of counselors from their facility, and had responded very positively to the programming. Neither of them had ever worked out before, and I was proud of them because they kept putting in the effort, they kept showing up, and they even completed their first-ever 5K race put on by *Girls With Sole,* called the LULA race. (LULA stands for Lacing Up for a Lifetime of Achievement.)

After the workout one day, all the girls were busy painting posters of things that "moved their souls" and the session began to run a little longer than the usual one-hour time frame. All the girls were really engrossed in their art projects, but I noticed that the two sisters were getting really antsy and I was surprised by their outward display of worry. I asked one of the counselors what was wrong. She explained to me that the two girls lived together in a homeless shelter, and if they were not in the building by 5:00 p.m. they would not get anything to eat for dinner. Any problem that I thought I had that day evaporated.

I will also never forget the 15-year-old who told me on the very first day of programming at her facility that she hated physical activity and she would not take part in anything that I may have planned on doing. She was very dark and moody and had issues with various types of self-harm, including cutting and ingesting objects. Within a month she brightened up and loved taking part in *Girls With Sole* so much that she told everyone who listened that she was part of the coolest program around, called *Girls With Sole*. In her free time she began creating posters with motivational quotes and sayings that promoted healthy living. She told her counselors that Miss Liz was her role model. The counselors couldn't believe it and wanted to know what on Earth *Girls With Sole* could have done to change her so dramatically. She went from never smiling and not wanting to participate to actually getting up on stage at the beginning of the LULA 5K race to recite the *Girls With Sole* Creed for over 400 people – by heart.

The *Girls With Sole* Creed is said at the beginning of every session and it goes like this:

We're *Girls With Sole* and we're on the move

We're strong and proud you can't stop our groove

We know who we are and who we want to be

We sail through life with resiliency

At *Girls With Sole* we set goals and believe

If we keep lacing up we will always achieve

This young lady has become the leader when new girls join her *Girls With Sole* group, and the one who encourages others who don't want to participate. She encourages them to keep going and keep trying when they feel as if they can't do something or if they want to quit. She also told me recently that she might have a potential placement – which means her behavior has improved so much that she can leave residential treatment and live in a foster home. But she was worried that she would "sabotage it" before it could happen.

So often I see (and hear) myself in my *Girls With Sole* girls and can empathize with their fears and worries because I felt the same at their ages. In the same way that I did, they see themselves on the perimeter of the "real world" and fear the way they are perceived by others, as well as how their behavior will affect the outcome of their lives. I am so proud of all of my girls for their resiliency and their good hearts.

There were many moments in my life when I almost gave up and gave into these same fears. I almost quit college. But I didn't. I almost committed suicide. But I didn't. I was a single mom with no child support and a job I wasn't happy with, while working a second job at night. I can honestly say that being an athlete – and feeling the confidence that comes with it, as well as the emotional strength that builds with every run or workout – is what kept me going.

Being an athlete taught me that I was a survivor even in the face of adversity and pain. I could keep going no matter what, and I would succeed as long as I didn't quit. Additionally, after having my first child, I knew I had something greater than myself to work for. When you are a *Girl With Sole* you keep on going no matter what. *Girls With Sole* is doing some great things for a lot of girls. But as an organization it is still in its infancy. We regularly experience the highs and lows and growing pains that many established nonprofits have worked through over the period of many, many years, which we still have to face. As an organization, we are constantly growing, changing, and evolving – much like the girls in our programs.

Some of the low points in the beginning were when people told me that what we were trying to do would never work, that our approach was all wrong, and that it would most definitely prove unsuccessful. Many people came to me and said that I needed to change the entire mission.

Others questioned our business model as well as my business and marketing experience. I had to rely on what I knew in my heart was the true mission of *Girls With Sole* and resolve not to divert from that mission even when people told me I should. I stuck to what I knew in my heart would work, and, so far, it has.

We are only two years old and have gone from helping four girls to almost 400, and we have requests from all over the nation to make *Girls With Sole* a national organization. Girls in our programs are doing better in school and in counseling. Many of them contact me when they are released from the detention center or the residential treatment center, because they want to continue on with the programs. We work with many different schools and charter schools, and the girls thrive in our programming as they learn to respect themselves and others, and gain confidence and leadership skills. Their teachers are thrilled with the programs, and with the positive impact they have on the girls.

Girls With Sole has been featured in many local magazines, as well as on the news here in Cleveland. We have also been in *Ohio Magazine*, *Runner's World Magazine*, and *Traditional Home Magazine*.

The *Traditional Home Magazine* article featured an honor I never thought I would personally receive, although the Classic Woman Award was something I had always admired when flipping through the magazine I have subscribed to for many years. *Traditional Home* has been awarding the Classic Woman Award on a yearly basis to five women across the country who represent incredible organizations that give back to their communities. The past seven years or so that the magazine has been honoring these amazing women, I wouldn't have guessed in a million years that I would not only be nominated among thousands of others, but that I would be picked as an honoree for 2011, to be featured in the November/December 2011 issue. The honor and the experience were emotional and intense, and I was beyond thrilled that *Girls With Sole* would receive such unbelievable recognition.

In the summer of 2011, after Meredith Corporation informed me that I was chosen to be a Classic Woman, I was flown to its corporate office in Des Moines, Iowa, for a photo shoot, a YouTube video shoot, and a dinner with the other honorees. It was incredibly surreal and wonderful to be recognized in the company of these amazing women whose work included: providing comforting toys and items to homeless children; helping poor women in Latin America get business loans in order to support their families; providing brand-new musical instruments to children in need; and extending financial and emotional support to people who are undergoing bone marrow transplants.

Their organizations were all extremely well-established, they were helping (or employing) thousands of people and had tens of thousands of volunteers helping them, and they had disbursed billions of dollars to help those they serve. I was in some great company, indeed.

In early November the magazine flew my husband and me to New York City where we were treated as absolute royalty for two days. The night we arrived we had a fabulous dinner with the executives of the magazine and the other honorees at the Gramercy Tavern. The following day was the awards luncheon at the Mandarin Oriental Hotel with over 250 industry bigwigs in attendance. I walked into the lobby of the ballroom and there were life-size cardboard posters of each of the honorees displayed on giant easels. We were ushered into a room off the dining area to be interviewed by a television show that Meredith also owns, and to meet Natalie Morales (news anchor for NBC's *Today*), who would be introducing us and giving us our awards at the luncheon. She was so beautiful and nice, and told me that my organization really speaks to her as a runner and a triathlete.

After we were seated and the luncheon began, Natalie introduced me and then played the YouTube video that described *Girls With Sole* and what we do. There weren't too many dry eyes in the room after the video, and I was approached by many people at the end of the luncheon who wanted to donate, get involved, or tell me that they commended what I was doing. Of course, there were also some awesome athletes who came up to me to tell me that they were also Ironman athletes and they did triathlon to maintain their sanity.

All of the honorees were given $2,500 for our organizations, two Oscar de la Renta chairs (donated by Century Furniture) that we can auction off to raise money, and an amazingly beautiful silver cuff bracelet donated by

Savor Silver and the SilverMark. If there was ever a time I felt like Cinderella, it was at the Classic Woman Awards!

Back home in Cleveland, during the very same month, the honors continued to come pouring in.

On November 14, 2011, I was awarded the American Red Cross of Greater Cleveland Hero Award at the InterContinental Hotel. There were various Hero categories, and I was recognized along with two other Innovation Heroes, which defined us as a company, organization, or individual that performs a service or produces a product that uniquely contributes to the betterment of our community. Again, I was in the company of extraordinary and well-established individuals, including an MD and PhD who has raised millions of dollars to help students in at-risk neighborhoods pursue medical careers. The award luncheon was attended by the higher echelon of Cleveland's medical, government and civil service, and corporate arenas. I was introduced by Denise Dufala of 19 Action News Cleveland, and given the award by the CEO of the American Red Cross of Greater Cleveland and an executive from the event's main sponsor, Majestic Steel USA. This local honor means so much to me and is a testament to what we are doing for girls in need all over Cleveland and Canton, Ohio.

A week later, *Girls With Sole* was the cover story in *CBC Magazine*, which is a business-to-business magazine featuring business trends and networking. It's distributed to over 20,000 businesses in Northeast Ohio.

It seems silly and trivial to label these momentous happenings as our organization's "high points" – it doesn't do it justice or reflect the intensity of these honors. Since we are a grass-roots organization that is still growing, we still have a lot of challenges to work through. Ongoing challenges for *Girls With Sole* include a lack of staff, and as part of that, a lack of people to conduct the programs with me. (We call these people "coaches.") Because we don't have the funds to pay the coaches, it's tough to find people who can volunteer all over the city and conduct programs in the middle of the day or late afternoon when they are not being paid to do so. We could serve more kids, and continue with our much-needed program growth and outreach, if we had the funding to hire a small staff. At this time, however, I am running the organization basically on my own, working 80 to 90 hours per week, and I do not receive a salary. I am fortunate that I can work early in the morning, late at night, on the weekends, and during the day while my own kids are at school, so that I can still spend time with them and be actively involved in their lives.

I am confident that we will reach our financial goals very soon, and we'll find a corporate sponsor, foundation, or an "angel" to help us develop *Girls With Sole* so it can reach a national level within the next five years.

My goals are to continue to work with the girls here in Cleveland, but also to work across the country in order to find the best people in each city and teach them to run a *Girls With Sole* chapter and change the lives of girls in need across the nation. *Girls With Sole* is all about collaboration. There is strength in numbers, and teaming up with other organizations is smart, practical, and can serve more people than when you try to stand alone. That is why we should be able to easily replicate what we are doing here anywhere in the nation. *Girls With Sole* can team up with any school, residential treatment center, or juvenile detention center, among others, and bring our programs directly to the girls where they live and spend time.

Because my background is very diverse but doesn't include a license in social work or a previous development director's title, my experience – as well as the mission of *Girls With Sole* – has often been questioned. I was a fitness instructor for over 18 years and worked full-time jobs at the same time which included sales, recruiting, and a brief stint as a nonprofit executive director. I can honestly say I *never* thought I would be doing what I do today if you had asked me even five years ago! (Not to mention that when I was young and in my 20s, I struggled to help myself, let alone anyone else...but I always wanted to.)

But we have proven that teaming up with agencies and schools which already provide the counseling for girls in need, but do not have our programs, is the perfect combination of strengths and expertise. The result is healthy, strong, well-rounded girls who are ready to overcome obstacles and "LULA," or "Lace Up for a Lifetime of Achievement."

The greatest degree of inner tranquillity comes from the development of love and compassion. The more we care for the happiness of others, the greater is our own sense of well-being.

—Tenzin Gyatso, the 14th Dalai Lama

XXIII

MOST RUNNERS LOVE to share their sport. We don't like to hog all the fun for ourselves, and we take great pleasure in spreading the wealth of positivity that comes from running and its culture. This is why there are so many adult running clubs, and also why my dad was my first running buddy. My latest and greatest running partner is an incredible athlete, a very fast runner, and he is also quite handsome and funny. He is great company on long runs and is actually a wonderful listener. His name is Rico, and I can tell him anything. No matter what, he stays by my side and he looks up to me. Okay, fine, he looks up to me because he is only about a foot tall. Rico is my rescue dog and he is *the* great love of our entire family.

He really is a great sport to even humor me that we are "running" together, as he is *actually* only walking fast or trotting. I love the way his big ears fold back onto his head and bounce to the rhythm as he happily trots along. Much like me, Rico doesn't have a family history to speak of, even if he could speak. He was a homeless dog eating garbage off the street, which resulted in a horrible case of "garbage belly." (This occurs when dogs can't keep anything down because their digestive system is messed up from eating too much garbage or spoiled food.)

A few different times, Rico was taken in by families who decided they didn't want to keep him. (Rico and I have so much in common, it is almost uncanny.) He had his name changed by one of his previous owners from Samson to Rico, just as I went from Tammy Ann to Elizabeth. Rico's adoption fee was around $150. I recently came across the legal paperwork for my adoption in a box tucked away in our basement. My adoption fee was $600.

Luckily for me, Rico was then taken in by a local organization that a good friend of mine volunteers for as a foster mom. The organization is called Public Animal Welfare Society (PAWS) and is considered one of Ohio's most reputable longstanding cat and dog humane rescue groups. It is dedicated to the rescue of pets in Northeastern Ohio and its mission is to rescue stray and/or abused cats and dogs and place them in good homes.

It was meant to be that two misunderstood, high-energy, and good-hearted "pound puppies" would find each other. Rico and I know what it is like to be displaced and to wonder how it could be that people failed to see the good in us. My friend Susan was fostering Rico and posted his picture on Facebook, letting her friends know that he needed a good home. She gave fair warning that he is obsessed with playing fetch and needs lots of exercise! I took one look at his picture and knew he was my dog. His ears are something to behold. They are about the size of a kangaroo's ears, yet he is only a little bigger than a Jack Russell Terrier. We think that he is a mix of Jack Russell and Basenji. Rico is both regal and sweet, and we can't go anywhere without being asked a million questions about what type of dog he is and how we trained him so well. We got him when he was almost 2 years old (the same age that I was adopted), and he was instantly a part of our family and our hearts. We don't know what he is for sure, but we do know he is a "Ferro Hound" as my friend Susan likes to call him. He brings energy and liveliness to our home that I didn't realize was missing until he arrived, as we already had a plenty lively home.

Because *Girls With Sole* is a true "family affair," Rico has attended programs with me on a few occasions and loves to run with the girls and play chase and fetch with them as well. They get such a kick out of him and although he is not a certified therapy dog, he brings a certain comfort and healing energy to any program session that he attends. Running with that little guy lights up and warms my heart much like the way the sun reflects warmly off his rusty brown scruff that matches the autumn leaves. He runs so proudly and happily with his head held high, and it makes me laugh when he looks back at me every now and then to make sure I am still there. Rico and I get each other. We both know what it is like to finally trust someone with your whole heart, and, after feeling displaced and discarded, to be in the happiest place you could ever imagine.

In three words I can sum up everything I've learned about life. It goes on.

—Robert Frost

XIV

ULTIMATELY I KNOW my brothers both love me; my mother loves me; and my dad had loved me more than life itself when he was alive. I don't hold anyone to blame for anything that has happened to me, and I have grown to realize that even when people wrong you (as will happen to *everyone* somehow and sometime in his or her life), you need to (as my buddy Larry loves to say) "Build a bridge and get over it."

Truly, if anything, I am grateful for every one of my life experiences, both good and bad, for without them I wouldn't be the tough but kind-hearted person that I am today.

For a good portion of my life, *no one* would have been able to convince me that I would ever be happy or proud of myself and of the way I was living my life. No matter what was said, I wouldn't have believed it back in those past chapters of my life.

It isn't an exact science, and there may be relapses, but when you are a *Girl With Sole*, you learn to put your head down, to keep moving forward, and to persevere. A *Girl With Sole* lives (and she forgives), and she never gives up. She may have to endure the equivalent of running into a hurricane, with the fear of being swept away whirling all around her, but she can rely on her strength and resiliency to reward her with the gift of the Finish Line Feeling.

Life is ten percent what happens to you and ninety percent how you respond to it.

—Lou Holtz

XXV

THERE IS A CONFIDENCE and a positive light that radiates from an athletic person. It is easily recognized by others and attracts them to you like a moth to a porch light on a summer's night. Quite often, someone I don't know will ask me if I am a runner or a triathlete, and my affirmative response creates a great leaping point in the conversation that almost always leads to great things. I have also been told many times that I have inspired people simply as a result of the events that I compete in, or by my energy and enthusiasm for fitness, as well as my work with *Girls With Sole*.

I have always loved helping others with their fitness goals, and found it empowering to give them training programs to follow, or to go out and train with them when they needed me. If you live from your heart with true passion (and you do the things you love for yourself or to help others, and not to impress others), you inevitably end up touching other people's lives in a positive way – oftentimes without even realizing it.

During almost every single job interview I have ever had post-college, the interviewer wanted to discuss the Ironman races I have done more than anything else, because they demonstrated a goal-oriented tenacious person able to overcome obstacles, make sacrifices when necessary, and achieve great things. I know that I have been hired for various positions in the past because I am an athlete. This is certainly not my reason for becoming an athlete, but it is often the byproduct of being one.

As a child I had no idea that athletics would connect me with some of my best friends, business contacts, and even my husband, Frank! I ran to lose myself and find myself at the same time. I ran to savor the sweat and the pounding of my heart. I ran to clear out the anger and replace it with joy. Without swimming, biking, and running, as a youngster on the playground I would have been causing trouble and starting fights. In high school I would have been wrapped up in dieting, smoking, and drugs like the girls in school who didn't play sports. There was a lot of trouble I was able to find in high school, but it would have been a lot worse if I wasn't involved in sports.

College was a lot harder on me than I expected, especially considering how much I longed to get away from my hometown and be on my own. Once again, being involved in sports saved me. While I was in college, I overdosed and "took up" bulimia to punish myself. I transferred schools and I almost dropped out. I don't know what I would have done without my workouts to keep my head on as straight as possible.

Pablo Picasso said, "Art washes away from the soul the dust of everyday life."

This is exactly what I believe running (or any sport) does as well! Even if the road is long and dusty, it is worth taking, and can bring you to destinations you never dreamed you could reach.

Having been sexually abused as a child and in several bad relationships, I have been in dark places in my life where feeling sorry for myself and giving up could have been my course of action. Instead, I kept running, biking, and swimming, and I used the strength gained from training to become empowered and to feel stronger emotionally. When I reflect on those times, I am happy in the knowledge that "I am not what happened to me – I am what I choose to become" (Carl Gustav Jung). People can draw from difficult experiences in their lives, and they can use those experiences when things get tough on a race course or training run. I often think of things that have happened to me (or to some of the girls I work with) while I am struggling on a training run or bonking on a race course, and I think: Compared to *that* – this ain't shit!

During a *Girls With Sole* program with a group of high school-aged girls who are in residential treatment, I was asked, "Miss Liz…what do you tell yourself when you are running and you need help to keep going?"

I was honest with the girls…and they loved my answer. I said:

"I just tell myself… this ain't shit!"

After they all laughed their butts off, they said "I love it Miss Liz! I am going to use that!"

"This ain't shit!"

It's raw, and pretty basic, but sometimes that's just what it takes to get you through.

Just as you can draw strength from difficult life experiences while you are running, you can most definitely use the strength and empowerment gained from being a runner and an athlete to get through tough times in other areas of your life. The beauty is that it works both ways.

Setting goals is the key to getting where you want to be in running and in life. Some of the goals I set for myself came out of a constant pursuit to push myself and my body to go farther. Some came from the concern that without a goal I felt as if I was running aimlessly. Having a plan gave me control and purpose and made my runs become *training*. I liked that. Once you are "in training," you feel as if you have just earned super-hero status. Whenever someone asks you what's new, you can immediately take that super-hero stance, feet shoulder-width apart, hands placed squarely on the hips, red cape rustling in the wind behind you, and in your best Captain America voice you can proclaim, "I'm in training." Trumpets will begin to sound and confetti will fall from the sky as you make this proclamation and explain what it is you are training for, and the person you are speaking to will stand in awe, mouth agape. Okay, I made that last part up, but it feels that way in your head, and that's all that really counts.

I began setting long-term and short-term goals for myself a long time ago, and I still do. I don't take my racing as seriously as I did when I was new to triathlon and road racing (when I was young and without kids). I still set goals for myself, but I am a lot more easygoing and relaxed in how I go about reaching them. I truly run, bike, and swim for the pure joy they bring me, as well as for the mental housecleaning. I take it one workout at a time, and I don't get too bent out of shape if I miss a few here or there. I know that if I keep going in the right direction each day as best I can, I will reach any goal that I set.

All the years of being an athlete have taught me that I can believe in myself and my abilities. It all comes down to our choices in life, and we can all choose to move forward and move on. If, metaphorically, a lighthouse is a beacon that we look to for guidance when our boat is lost at sea, it is still necessary for us to act as *Captain* of that boat.

Without the Captain making the right decisions and choices that will steer the boat towards safety, the lighthouse is just a light in the dark, no different from the moon or the stars. It isn't able to get you where you want to be of its own accord.

We must *choose* whether we want to take action and navigate – or just float. We can choose to wallow in unfair circumstances, or we can get stronger by choosing to get back up and keep moving forward.

In *Girls With Sole* programs, the girls learn that sports and fitness make them stronger, more confident, and ready to face life with a healthy mind and body. They also learn that to be successful they must sometimes be willing to come out of their comfort zones. Breaking out of our comfort zone can cause some people to give up in life as well as in athletic endeavors. All top athletes have learned this lesson well, but athletes are leaders and leaders don't give up when things get tough. There is no better way to learn to be a leader *and* a team player than through athletics. You might be on a run by yourself – but you are never alone.

Over the years I have learned that being an athlete affects everything I do. It brings me rewarding joyfulness by carrying me through tough times, and has taught me how to deal with negative emotions in a healthy way. If you ask anyone you know who has taken up running after a bitter divorce, a break-up, or a loss of some kind – or to ease the stress at home or work – I am sure he or she will concur. Athletes find strength from deep inside that spurs them on – no matter what. Athletes know they will reach the finish line by taking the course one step at a time, moving forward, and *never giving up*!

One of the girls with whom I have worked in *Girls With Sole* programming wrote a very moving and profound testimonial to her experiences with running and with *Girls With Sole*. She is someone I have trained to run in 5Ks as well as her first half-marathon. I will never forget the look on her face as she crossed that finish line. Her name is Abbey and she was 17 years old when she wrote:

My life is like a race.

I'm always running toward the goal but never looking back...because the things that lurk behind shouldn't slow you down or keep you back.

Your mind might tell you can't go on but your heart will always beat and believe; so move on.

For life is just the beginning of a long race!

I'm glad I never let people stop me from believing; I'm glad I pushed myself to greater things.

I'm a runner with a lot of guts; I'll never stop, never ever.